I thank you for being a channel of the Bro... channeled lines and a phenomenal amount of ... instantly. I meditate regularly, and this is the ...

I am clairaudient, have been for twenty years, and work closely with the archangels and ascended masters. I am an artist working in England in order to spread peace through the energy of plants — to the art world and beyond.

Thank you for opening up a direct link to the Brotherhood of Light. I feel healed and ready for action!

—Endellion Lycett Green, September 2011

Thank you for the wonderful gift you sent me! I certainly did not expect anything other than my much-needed refund. And the most amazing thing has happened using your gift.

I had cataract surgery last week and ended up with a scratched cornea. It was very painful, and I have had two trips back to the surgeon to attempt to cover the scratched area. It has gone from being painful to varying levels of discomfort to pain once again.

Fortunately, I arrived home yesterday to find the package you sent. I did a healing session last night as I went to sleep and another this morning. I truly feel that the scratch is completely gone! Thank you very, very much!

I wish you and yours the very best of this wondrous Christmas Season!

—Margaret, December 2010

Just wanted to tell you I received the book and was so very honored that you signed it for me. It makes it very special. I am very excited to read and learn more with it.

It was really nice to talk with you on the phone; you answered a lot of things that I needed clarification on. It will be nice to move forward with what I have learned, and it will open more doors to move through to help others heal.

I know it is a freewill planet, but it always feels good to help others smile. Thank you for bringing the Brotherhood of Light into the hearts of all of us on the path. I smile every time I think of them.

I thank God for bringing you into this world to help the rest of us who want to move on. Take care, and I will write you again as I read The Circle of Grace.

—John Greenwood, June 2010

I just wanted to say thank you for putting all of your published articles on your website for free. I read one of yours on Spiritlibrary.com and wanted to see more, and then I found your webpage. What a fantastic source of knowledge! In only a week or so, it's made a huge difference in how I feel and how I am able to help others in the energy healings I offer. I have already sent thanks to the Brotherhood, and now I just wanted to let you know you are appreciated!

—Vanessa Jarvis, March 2009

It's kind of a long story to tell you how I was introduced to the Brotherhood, but your channelings on Spiritlibrary.com were instrumental in helping me understand what I was going through in terms of extreme head pressure, fatigue, and so on.

I got your book and read the Circle of Grace, and I'm sure you can understand when I say thank you. They're helping me. It's awesome that any question I've had in my head or belief I've felt in my heart is echoed in the book. I've been doing the Circle of Grace for a few months before I got the book, and now I have the information on exactly how to ask for their spiritual help.

My goal is to move into 5D. That's what I desire to do and be. And I know that once I do this, I will help others do the same. I have a friend who is on the same path as me and is going to read the book as well. I feel he and I are like brothers — like coworkers in the spirit realm. Anyway, your channelings are invaluable, so thank you again!

—Scott Wells, July 2009

Oh, how wonderful to find you! I feel such a lovely golden glow of spiritual unity. I would look so much forward to hearing from you. I am a long-time reader of A Course in Miracles, looking for that perfect way of expression to heal and bless in Miracle Life. Thank you.

—Penny Gordon, February 2012

I have been meditating, or really just talking to, the Brotherhood of Light since 2004. I call them in nine nights out of ten when I get into bed. I say the simple prayer, and the wonderful energy begins to flow through my body. I have had a total of three surgeries on my left knee during 2002 and 2003, and my knee never healed properly. I suffer from chronic pain.

My life is very difficult. Calling in the energies from the Brothers and Sisters when I go to bed has kept me in relatively good health. Being able to call in this loving energy whenever we want is truly a wonderful blessing from the spiritual realm. I pray to the Brother's in my waking hours as well, and they help me with gentle intuition. I love them.

—Daniel McTeigue, July 2012

I wanted to send along a note of gratitude for your work with the Brotherhood of Light and the publishing of The Circle of Grace. I have been working with the earth as an organic farmer for the past twenty years and now have shifted my intentions to the healing of our Mother. I have found your book to be most helpful in my own spiritual development, as so much of its content rings clear with my own frequency at this time. As I seek to become a clear and open channel for Earth's energy, the Circle of Grace is a positive tool for reaching this goal.

I am new to this practice of this meditation, although I have been working with the MAP technique for a few years now. Every day I feel a new level of energy and awareness; it is truly a blessing. We all need guidance during this time of positive change, and your work helps to fulfill this need. I hope I will have the opportunity to study with you in the future.

—Jeff Dawson, January 2009

— Second Edition • Updated • Practitioner's Manual —

THE Circle OF Grace

FREQUENCY AND PHYSICALITY

OW TO CLEAR PAIN & STRESS • THE WAY TO REGAIN & MAINTAIN HEALTH

THE BROTHERHOOD OF LIGHT THROUGH EDNA G. FRANKEL

Publications by
Edna G. Frankel

Le Cercle de Grâce, fréquence et physicalité, 2005

Contributions to: *Le Retour de la Lumière,* 2007

Au-delà du voile, 2008

The Circle of Grace, Frequency and Physicality, 1st Edition, 2008

THE Circle OF Grace

FREQUENCY AND PHYSICALITY

HOW TO CLEAR PAIN & STRESS • THE WAY TO REGAIN & MAINTAIN HEALTH

The Brotherhood of Light through **Edna G. Frankel**

3ॐLIGHT Technology PUBLISHING

Some of the information in this book was previously published in different forms by the international monthly magazine *Sedona Journal of Emergence!* Also, parts were previously published in 2003, *The Circle of Grace*, ISBN # 0-9746-415-0-2 (out of print). Text channeled 2001 through 2012.

MEDICAL DISCLAIMER

Information in this book is meant to supplement and support current medical practices. It is not intended to diagnose or treat any medical condition, nor replace the services of a physician. The material in this book is provided for informational purposes only and is not a substitute for professional medical advice. You should consult a physician in all matters relating to your health, and particularly in respect to any symptoms that may require diagnosis or medical attention. The author is not liable for any claim, loss, or damage resulting from use of the information in this book.

ISBN-10: 1-891824-18-X
ISBN-13: 978-1-891824-18-0

Published and printed in the United States of America by:

ॐ LIGHT
Technology
PUBLISHING

PO Box 3540
Flagstaff, AZ 86003
800-450-0985
www.lighttechnology.com

Dedication

I dedicate this book to Spirit,
For I am just their human scribe.
I dedicate my life to Spirit,
To keep their flow of words alive.

No matter how dark the day may be,
I give thanks for all my blessings.
For my happy, healthy family,
For shelter, food, and yes, our lessons.

It is not enough to just survive,
For all you souls seeking completion.
When I look into your eyes,
I see you too are on a mission.

Join me on this journey through life,
Make each day an easy glide!
Release all sorrow and claim your joy,
For Spirit will always guide and provide.

SARA
September 30, 2003

Mission Statement

The human consciousness is rising very quickly into awareness, and the energetic changes on planet Earth within the next decade will be overwhelming for many people. In addition to helping people to help themselves, the Brotherhood's Circle of Grace is a process that will help bring holistic modalities together to work in synchrony. Learning to release pain and stress from the meridians of our nervous systems is key to clearing and balancing our lives at all levels. In my private practice, seminars and other gatherings, I have discovered that all hands-on modalities can be applied to this clearing process we all have within our bodies.

No matter what brings lightworkers together, it is essential to merge our talents, for we each hold a piece of the healing puzzle. By working in groups, hands-on practitioners can apply their knowledge to clear and heal all types of physical, emotional, mental, and spiritual imbalances. By using the Circle of Grace with other modalities, we can and will work miracles.

The true goal of the Brotherhood of Light is to facilitate the ascension of humanity. They offer their knowledge of healing and of higher concepts to further our integration of science and spirituality, physics and metaphysics, alternative healing and allopathic medicine. The Brothers focus on teaching us how to heal our entire Be-ings, beginning with the physical body. This will empower each person to reach self-mastery, and consciously connect us all back to Spirit.

—SARA

Acknowledgments

The Circle of Grace: Frequency and Physicality has been ten long years in the making. I hope that this book will help people around the world for many years to come. I would like to thank all the people who supported my efforts to create this work. To my dear family, who put up with a lot! To Julie, who believed in my connection to Spirit. To Rich, the man of many talents, who helped make my dream take form. To Melody and Monica, my mentors at Light Technology Publishing, my heartfelt thanks for getting the Brothers' messages out to the world. To my dear Reiki friends and students. To Lisa, who contributed her knowledge and intuition when most needed. To Hazel, who was midwife to my first book. To Martine, who launched the French version and gave me wings to fly. To Kezia and Donna, who read and read and read. To my dear Reiki friends and students, from whom I learned so much over the years. To all my dear readers, whose emails, letters, and phone calls kept me going through the most difficult times. And love to my dear Brothers, without whose whispered words of encouragement I would never had made it this far.

The energy and wisdom of many, many souls are in this work.
To All, I give thanks.

—*SARA*

Author's Note: The "Brotherhood of Light" was the title Spirit chose to call its voice when I entered into active meditation with them back in 1990. The Brothers' original name is the Order of Melchizedek. In our history, we have also called them the White Brotherhood and the Great White Brotherhood. I just call them the "Bros." I had a ton of questions and found that they have infinite patience.

At first, they called me "little Brother." When I pointed out that I was female in this life [dualistic chuckle], they gave me the gift of my Spirit name, Sara, formed from the first two and last two letters of my Higher Self's name, Sanat Kumara. I work alone with the Brothers, and I see myself as their scribe and voice for information on healing at all levels. I hold no affiliation with any person, group, or organization currently representing the Melchizedek or (Great) White Brotherhood names.

Table of Contents

Section One: The Circle of Grace Clearing Process

Section Two: The Laws and the Keys

Section Three: Frequency and Physicality

Section Four: Advance Techniques

List of Illustrations

Foreword

Welcome to 2012 and Beyond!

Greetings, dear ones, and welcome to the most exciting, most fabulous times in your recorded history. We are so delighted to be back, working on the Circle of Grace with you. Over the past twelve years, we have written many times on the subjects of self-clearing, self-help, and self-health. It may seem to others watching that your journey is a very solitary, often lonely one. But those of you with the eyes to see and the ears to hear know the true story: We are always with you, supporting you and cheering you on, every step of the way — no matter what your direction may be. That, dear ones, is simply unconditional love. One day, we will meet, and you will finally understand the depths of our love for you.

By now, those of you who have long been on the path should be well into constructing your future foundation. Most awakened and aware ones have either moved or decided to stay put. You have been taking care of your physical vehicles with exercise, rest, and pure food and water. You have been loyal to a daily practice, clearing your energetic layers of old 3D density. You know to take vitamin supplements, avoid stress, and listen to your body's instructions. So with only months left to go before the Great Shift of the Ages, why do things seem to be deteriorating? Ah, dear ones, it is the emerging face of an old friend you call chaos. Any cook will tell you that soup needs stirring occasionally and that certain chemical reactions must occur between the ingredients, the stove, and your intent before the food is ready.

We speak of transformation in seemingly simple terms, yes [chuckles]. Chaos is simply part of the cooking process. Politics must be pushed to a tipping point before change can happen. All of the "dark" institutions that were run without spiritual integrity have come into the light of awareness and change — from Enron to Wall Street, from the global banking industry to the mortgage house of cards that inevitably had to tumble down. The worldwide financial downturn that followed is a clear lesson that you are all interconnected, that what you each do affects all of you. The weather has also increased in severity, causing misery and devastation with earthquakes, volcanic eruptions, floods, and drought on every continent. All of these seemingly disparate things going on contribute to the general feeling of chaos all around you.

When you factor in the speeding up of time, no wonder you feel stressed! To quote Alice's white rabbit, "So much to do, so little time!" The best antidote for chaos is to slow down, take it easy, and take the time to take care of yourself. The Circle of Grace is but one example of a meditative practice that can be more healing than you can imagine. The need for daily cleansing is becoming vital, children, truly vital. Whether you are a runner, a sunbather, or a yoga enthusiast, do *something*. Feeling better is within your reach, and a daily practice is just as vital as clean water, good food, and plenty of rest. You will find that the same rules apply after the shift as well. Once there, your healing will be much easier to complete and faster done. Oh, the miracles awaiting you.

All That You Can Imagine, You Can Create

You have a saying, "It is always darkest before the dawn." As of this moment, April 2012, you stand nine months away from the fulcrum point of the Millennium Shift of December 21, 2012. You could look around at the global level and mutter to yourself, "It can't get much worse than this." Or you could hike up your perspective a bit and see what we see:

nine months until the birthing of a whole new human, a whole new Earth history, a whole new game, dear ones, with you standing next to us and rejoicing at all the lovely chaos that needs to swirl up, break down, and clear the playing field of the dysfunctional social systems that have ruled your lives. Why try to fix something that does not — and never has — served you? That is what your politicians are doing while trying to convince you that all is well and will always be as it is. Do you agree?

Do you see clearly yet? Do you realize the many ways in which you have, up until now, lived in someone else's version of reality? Do you realize your own power — inherent in every sacred, blessed human being — to create a better version of reality? We are describing the upcoming shift, dear ones, and your role in it. As we have said before, every person is vital to the final outcome. Every thought, every emotion, every action, every choice made or ignored weaves the fabric of your future. You all weave it together!

As there were different levels of awareness in your reality before, so will there be differing levels of awareness after the shift. Ah, but with a major difference: The levels will stretch way beyond your current imaginings, offering you choices you never dreamed possible. And this is the crux of our message: All that you can imagine, you can create. Indeed, manifestation time is quickly speeding up, so be careful what you wish for. Work with and within the Universal Laws, and all will be well.

Frequency Defines Form

You are in the last stages of your transformation, your energetic expansion into a greater realm of human potentials. In its simplest essence, the shift represents a refinement in the human form at the energetic level — yes, like an upgrade from regular TV to cable TV! Why do you think we have been saying all along to clear and cleanse your vehicles [bodies]? Because, dear ones, frequency defines form.

Ten years ago, we began teaching you the Circle of Grace through this channel. Our goal has been to help you increase your light quotient capacity through your understanding of how your internal cleansing system works. Now, in the short months left before 12-21-2012, you are in the "crunch time" of the shifting process. As we describe in the chapter called "Pre-Ascensionitis," the new energy vibrations are shorter, faster, and carry more complex information than the energies you were accustomed to in 3D. Your bodies have been sorely taxed since all the energetic changes that occurred after 1987 at the Harmonic Convergence. That was when, dear hearts, your courageous choice, made by the human awareness, put you on to the high road to ascension.

We commend you, dear lightworkers, for all the beautiful light you have generated for your planet; you have no idea how proud we are of you, for there are no words to express the magnitude of your accomplishments. From our place in the nonphysical realms, we cheer you on and we pour grace around you and within you. For those who feel lonely and helpless, please know that you are never alone. We work in groups of five Brothers for every person on the planet. If you thought that the nonphysical realms were huge and spacious, think again. In one sense, of course, the Void of Eternity is quite vast. All dimensions reside in the same space, buffered one from the other by octaves of frequency. The shift from 3D to 4D in the year following the new millennium [2001] was very subtle, and it went largely unnoticed. But the jump from 4D to 5D is happening through a thicker barrier, a null zone (we used to call it a ring-pass-not, for you older lightworkers) that keeps the physical and nonphysical realms from clashing together.

Once you pass through that frequency "speed bump," dear light warriors, you will graduate to multidimensional reality. Remember, all roads lead Home, and no soul ever dies — it is always transformed, or recycled, if you will [chuckles]. No matter what the form of your return, the same reunion and party await you. Death is not a negative issue for us; it is a graduation! Soon, we hope you will feel the same way. This and other perspectives will become clearer to you and easier to embrace as you process the energetic changes from 4D to 5D. But keep in mind that there are many layered reasons for the events that occur, not just the obvious circumstances.

Why have we counseled you to get energetically clear? To ease you into 5D with grace rather than a confusing experience that many people will dismiss as a nightmare or a "vivid dream." If you know that this evolutionary event is about to occur, you can grab hold with both hands and become the transition rather than retreating in fear from the unknown. Your soul is seeking not only to graduate from life after life but also has lessons programmed into your current journey. So if you see an old lesson pop up in the middle of the chaos, don't get discouraged! It is Spirit's way of saying, "Here, let's make sure you can do this one last time, from your new higher perspective."

For those of you who keep asking, "But where will we end up?" we counter gently that this is an impossible question to answer before the shift. Why? Because that is a question whose time has not yet come to answer. That question can only be answered by you, *after* the shift. Once you go through the process of sensory expansion, you will have vast new quantities of information available. Consider the shift as a physical, emotional, mental, and spiritual evolution of the human form, yes, a transformation of *you* at all levels.

Do you follow? We so hope you will!

New, Better Social Mores Will Evolve

Once the new energies reach their crescendo in December of 2012, the changes will be incredible to behold. Imagine, dear ones, being totally immersed in the unconditional love of God, the Creator, or whatever image your religious precepts hold. Being at-one-ment with the entire universe, feeling nature in your body like a second heartbeat, seeing divinity in every face you behold — even in your pets and plants — knowing that you are a part of All That Is, and feeling God's vibration within your bodies, that's what will end war, hunger, poverty, disease, and despair. That is the bliss of the shift! Once you have felt the Divine frequencies, your whole world will change. Why? Because your perspective of the world and your place in it will be greatly elevated. It may take years to assimilate all of these changes, but group cooperation and human ingenuity will combine to smooth the process.

New, better social mores will evolve, built around the tenet of treating others as you wish to be treated. Working with and within the Universal Laws will guarantee your success. Earth and all living things will be cleansed and energized simultaneously. Your DNA will receive a great boost, which will bring in all manners of new information and experiences. New health will clothe you; new abilities will emerge. The power of prayer will be greatly augmented also, since it is a form of materialization. Yes, you will see miracles — and learn to cocreate your own!

Our love for you, dear lightbearers, is beyond words. Your search for meaning, for answers, is what motivates the human awareness to expand. No matter if you just stumbled across this book or have been studying metaphysics for years, every seeker contributes to the ascension of all. We so look forward to your graduation and your return to the multidimensionality of the True Reality of Spirit.

— Until then and beyond, we remain, in all joy,
the Brotherhood of Light, April 2012

Introduction

Thoughts from the Brothers About Time and Dimensionality

Greetings, dear ones, from the Brotherhood of Light. We are your ancient guardians, the Order of Melchizedek, the spiritual caretakers of humanity. We work in many ways, at many levels, to help humanity evolve to the next octave of consciousness, to the next dimension of potential reality. We come before the Veil of Forgetfulness in your time now to offer you a new, yet very old way of maintaining health in the human body. We await you in full force to bring you gracefully through the window of "energetic opportunity" in this pivotal span of human history. We say to you, simply:

> Let us help you to evolve
> To the higher levels of Love.
> Let us teach you how to heal,
> And in healing, Be-come real.

We will begin by explaining the basic energetic parameters of your life on Earth, and then explain the terms we use to show the step-by-step evolution of your dense 3D form to your potential light-bodied 5D form. For those of you who have been on the path for years, this work will be a concise review and explanation of metaphysics. For readers new to the genre, this work may take many readings to fully assimilate. The text encompasses many levels, from simple physical energetics to the higher concepts of metaphysics. You may note that the very narrative tone of this work changes as the material becomes more complex. Then, as in all of life, it will come back to the beginning again as you learn not only to heal yourself but to heal your entire life and all the lives that came before it.

Dear ones, we await you, each in his or her own time, to reach inward and upward for healing. There you will find us patiently waiting to work with you, in the Circle of Grace. Then you will have your proof that God exists within you. Once you feel us down to your bones and know that we are with you, you will rise into the I Am energy. Your faith will be boundless, as will your compassion and your understanding.

What Is the Millennium Shift?

We feel that Earth fully ascended to the fourth dimension (4D) as of the month of May in your year 2000. At that time, a "heavenly arrangement" occurred of all the planets in your solar system into one long line. This gravitational pull created your "slingshot" from the third to the fourth dimension (3D to 4D). Most of humanity is still unaware of the higher realms and lives in 3D. To those of you reading this page, we say you are now in 4D, and have been since May 2000. Your goal in the ascension process is to access the fifth dimension (5D) and above, where we work and reside. So when we speak of your world in general and of your history, we will refer to your existence as 3D. When we speak of the population's current transition, we will call it 3-4D. Since Earth has raised her vibratory rate to 4D, we will call your current now time 4D. Please understand that these gradual steps are designed to help you evolve without risking any harm to you.

For those of you awakened and aware, working with us in the Circle of Grace raises you into the 4-5D level of transition. Mastering each dimensional frequency shift automatically makes you a student of the next dimension, so your transition from 4D to 5D and 5D to 6D. Your final shift from 6D to 7D is beyond the scope of this text, but we'll give you a hint: Choosing to go beyond that point will depend on whether or not you choose to keep your current body.

Confused yet? We're not done!

We will remind you in this text, time and again, that all dimensions reside in the same space, separated only by levels of vibratory frequency. Since your physical sensory input has always been plugged into 3D, that is all you have known. What you are used to calling a "higher conscious-ness" is actually an energetic expansion of your awareness to include sen-sory input from those outer levels of existence. Once you finish shifting with Earth, your new "comfort zone" will probably be 4-5D. Though we endeavor to keep this information within your linear framework of refer-ence, once you reach 5D and beyond you cannot keep counting the higher dimensions in numerical order. Why? Because the rules of linearity no longer apply!

While you see each dimension as having specific physical parameters, we see the dimensions as being different states of consciousness that we access by meshing with those specific vibratory parameters. What defines each dimension? The variables that affect the total vibrational range of existence in that space, such as 3D has three variables: height, width, and depth. These parameters have formed and limited your awareness of physi-cal reality for thousands of years. Once you become aware that there are other variables at play around you, it will become easier to understand that there are other dimensions, and therefore realities, around you as well.

When you move into 4D, what change do you add? The variable add-ed is time.

"What?" you exclaim. "Time is constant! It never changes. It defines our past, present, and future. It is beyond our control. It controls us. To think that we can affect time, or change it in any way, is crazy."

Dear ones, in his time, Columbus was called crazy for daring to think that the world was not flat. If he had succumbed to societal pressures, then human history would have been very different. Indeed, there are many cas-es recorded in your history of events that ultimately expanded the human consciousness, but that came at great cost to those humans brave enough to transcend the limitations of their time. Now you have reached a point in your evolution where we can say, yes, time is one of your perceptual limitations!

Time exists as rigid in 3D to give structure to your duality. As you expand into new dimensions, you will leave linear time behind you. Time is only constant in 3-4D, a line on which you stand that defines your past, present, and future. In 4D, you will begin to notice that time is not rigid; it speeds up and slows down, depending on your awareness of it and the depth of your focus. From our 5-6D perspective, time is a circle with no beginning and no end. Time is one of many variables that define our existence in the higher realms. We call it "now" time, and will speak often about "living in the now." Now time is all time during which all is happening at once; therefore, time is open to us to enter and exit as we will.

At first, this concept will be difficult for you to understand. Since we are dealing with difficult concepts, we offer you a similar paradigm to study: All dimensions reside in the same space, separated only by levels of energetic frequency. As all time is now, so are all the dimensions together as one. You will come to understand this as your current reality expands into the full bloom of 4-5D, and you still must deal with many people who are in 3D. Each dimension expands to include the next. Indeed, they already exist in eternal space, waiting for you to expand your sensory range to match the frequencies of the next level — and the next. In this text, we will often repeat that 3D and 4D are included in 5D, and so on up the scale. Though of course, [chuckles], there really is no scale.

You already know the parameters of 3D quite well. Since Earth's expansion to 4D in the year 2000, many of you have begun to sense an expansion of energy around you and within you. In truth, you are becoming sensitive to refined levels of stimuli and will inevitably realize that you are becoming psychic, telepathic, and empathic. The fourth dimension is the psychic expansion corridor between 3D and 5D. In 4D, the Veil of Forgetfulness begins to thin, letting in glimpses of other dimensions you have never seen before.

By now, you may be wondering if all of this is true and all dimensions reside in the same space, then what keeps them separate from each other? What keeps them from bleeding into each other and causing chaos? Ah, good questions! [Chuckles.] Imagine each dimension as a different musical chord. In between each chord there is a null zone, what early metaphysicians called a "ring-pass-not." These null zones are aptly named because they carry no frequency at all. The mechanics of how the zones are calibrated and how they act as buffers are beyond the scope of this text. Simply put, the dimensions of physicality in which you reside have thinner null zones. That is why you may not have felt the shift from 3D to 4D in the year 2000. Your entire duality-reality is fixed in place, and held in place, by the null zone between 4D and 5D. That is the big one! Why? So glad you asked!

The 4-5D null zone separates the physical realms from the nonphysical realms.

The ancient Maya were quite correct when they predicted that December 2012 would be the "end of time." However, the true meaning of the Mayan Calendar has been eroded by time, as were their magnificent edifices. The "end of time" meant the end of time as you know it: linear time. Yes, to be replaced with a new kind of time — circular time — the beginning of a new time for humanity! [Chuckles, we are inveterate punsters.]

Dear ones, please do not be afraid of the upcoming Millennium Shift, for it is being divinely orchestrated. Your arm of the Milky Way galaxy is entering a new region of space, one filled with much heightened energies. December 2012 is when Earth will pass through the 4-5D null zone and fully expand into the fifth dimension. You are riding the crest of a dimensional shift that is affecting much more than just your solar system. It will take another eight years — until 2020, at least — for all of these changes to settle into balance. What an exciting ride! What a great time to be alive!

What happens when you reach 5D? The separation of duality will be gone, linear time will be gone, the Veil will be gone, and you will reach wholeness. Wholeness is oneness with Spirit. You will intimately know your Higher Selves, and still have much time left to play on this beautiful planet Earth. What a wondrous journey lies ahead for you! We are here, directions at the ready, to facilitate your transition from the limited humans that you thought you were to the Eternal Beings that you truly are. This book you hold in your hands is your road map Home.

Do you follow? We hope you will!

—We are, in All love, the Brotherhood of Light.

"Blessed are the flexible, for they shall never be bent out of shape."

—*The Bros*

The Circle of Grace
Clearing Process

① The Physical Body

The Circle of Grace is a simple meditative exercise that helps you heal all levels of your total being: physical, emotional, mental, and spiritual (PEMS). At the same time that it releases stress and pain, the Circle of Grace replenishes your body with new energy. This process occurs naturally in your nervous system while you sleep. It is how the human body is designed to clear, replenish, and repair itself.

Healing your body will heal all of your lives. Heal all the layers of your total Be-ing, and rejoin us in the True Reality of Spirit. It is time to remember who You are. We invite you to join us in the Circle of Grace. With your focused awareness and our guidance, you can master this internal process and learn to heal yourself.

The Brotherhood Healing Prayer

If you wish, light a candle or incense to help focus your senses. Adapt the first two lines of this generic prayer to reflect your personal belief system. Please use the eternal divinity of your beliefs in place of Father/Mother God. Add any religious figures you hold dear, along with, or in place of, the ascended masters, guides, and angels. Speak aloud your desire to have a healing session with us in this four-part prayer:

"Dear Father/Mother God, Creator of All that is, was, and ever
will be, please join me in this healing session.

Dear Ascended Masters, guides, and angels, please join me in
this healing session.

Dear Brothers, the Brotherhood of Light, please join me in this
healing session.

Dear Higher Self, please join me to guide and lead this healing
session."

Say this prayer aloud. Say the words, say how you feel, and say what
you choose to manifest and what you desire to release. [A simple example:
I choose total health in my hands; I release my arthritis.] The vibration of
your voice brings your ideas, your sentiments, and desires into the fruition
of your third and fourth dimensions — the dimensions of material and
materialization. Due to the parameters of your freewill zone, we await your
spoken intent before we can begin. Why? Saying the Healing Prayer out
loud creates a vibrational bridge between dimensions, giving us your energetic permission to join with you, to merge our 5-6D energies with your
4D space in order to work with you at your physical level.

Do you follow? We hope you will.

The Circle of Grace clears the meridians of the aura via the meridians
of the body. Both come into play when you do the work of clearing your
energetic system. Once you get accustomed to doing the Circle of Grace,
you will gain mastery over your own healing. You will learn to tap into the
Circle of Grace whenever you need energy, and learn to release stress as it
comes in so that it does not accumulate and clog your meridians.

The Circle of Grace is your natural birthright, the physical link to
your inner divine power. We offer to work with you to bring you into full
self-mastery. What is full self-mastery? Having control over the health of
your total Be-ing and the use of your energy, at all levels. Then you will
begin to create your own future at a level where dreams, indeed, can and
do come true.

Expand Your Frame of Reference

Successful healing must occur in three domains: physical (medical), emotional/mental (psychological), and spiritual (auric/energetic). When science and spirituality finally meet and merge, healing will become a simple process.

Your biggest obstacle to healing is thinking that your physical body is your entire being. It is less than half of you! The rest of you — your auric or energetic self — is entwined with the physical core. Modern medicine does not honor the energetic half of each patient, because it is invisible. But your aura is invisible only to your senses that are anchored in the third dimension. Think of the concept of a dog whistle, which is an octave above man's range of hearing. Blow on that whistle and you hear nothing, yet your dog comes running because he has heard your call. In the same way, your auric or energetic self has been beyond the range of your 3D senses, but that does not mean your aura does not exist. It only means that you have not been able to see, feel, hear, or interact with your auric self in the same way you do with your physical self.

Once you begin to flower into the 4-5D sensory range, all of that will change!

When your medical community understands and accepts that it only focuses on part of a human being, people will begin to create instruments capable of tuning into the interdimensional layers of a person, measuring the aura and the level of health or disease carried in that electromagnetic field. Indeed, you have begun: electroencephalograms, or EEGs, measure brain waves or energetic brain activity. Your electrocardiograms, or EKG tests, measure the energetic pulse of your hearts. These are both auric functions that are now essential to proper diagnosis.

Once you begin exploring the aura's form and functions, you will finally understand the full workings of the total human being. This will move your medical knowledge forward greatly and eradicate many current illnesses, especially in the areas of mental, hormonal, and immune imbalances. These physical imbalances often arise from too much pressure within the nervous system, caused by etheric and/or physical blockages that prevent the proper flow of energy through the body's many layers.

You keep looking in the body for ways to fix these systems. Look instead for etheric pressure imbalances in the auric field. There you will find the system controls, and there you will find the source of what needs to be fixed!

You already have Kirlian photographic equipment, which shows the energetic field of any living subject. When you develop similar equipment in the form of movie cameras, you will be able to track the movement of etheric energy and truly show the effects of lightworkers on the human energetic system. This new "auric x-ray" equipment will ultimately provide invaluable diagnostic information for the medical community. You will learn to find and clear auric blockages, or "pressure pockets," that are magnetized to the body's electromagnetic field. Once you release the spiritual dis—ease, it will not manifest as a disease in the body's physical core.

Doctors now agree that most illness is a result of stress in your lives. By the time they are presented with an illness, they can only track it back to where it appeared in the body and then label it according to which area, system, or organ has been affected. Without alleviating the circumstances in your life that caused the stress in the first place, you will have either a failed or incomplete healing, or a temporary remission. Release that "stress pocket" by fixing the situation in your life that caused it, and the physical symptoms will withdraw from your body.

There are many hands-on modalities that release stress from the aura before it causes physical symptoms. Since Reiki is the most well-known foundational modality that uses universal energy to clear and balance the aura, we use it as a familiar reference. There are many other wonderful energetic modalities available now. Plus, let us not forget older modalities such as acupuncture, shiatsu, and reflexology, which work directly on the physical meridians to clear blockages. These are all tools, dear ones, energetic healing tools to apply to the Circle of Grace clearing process.

Once an illness has manifested in the body, it is more difficult to clear. Heal the damaged aura and you will not get sick.

The Veil of Forgetfulness

Your body is an incredible conglomeration of organs and systems that forms a symphony of life essence: earth matter married to energetic matter. Once you have a clearer understanding of how the aura interacts with its physical core, you will realize that the aura is as complex and as miraculous as the body within it. How could it not be?

The biggest challenge to healing is that you cannot yet see or interact with your energetic self. Since it is not part of your everyday awareness, you cannot feel your aura, much less heal it. Why not? Your left brain connects you to and directs your physical body. Your right brain connects you to and directs the etheric layers of your aura.

Why do you feel your body but not your aura? Because of the Veil of Forgetfulness. Your right brain houses your slumbering connection to Spirit. We say "slumbering" because the Veil is a spiritual mechanism anchored in your right brain that shields you from knowledge of other dimensions, of your life before birth and after death. The Veil is designed to block out the higher levels of your awareness in order to keep you focused on each current life in the third dimension, and thus ensure reincarnation.

Because of the Veil, you do not remember that you are Eternal.

Due to the Veil of Forgetfulness, you have had little conscious knowledge of anything other than your 3D world. Through your left brain, you are in constant, concrete communication with your physical body. Your right brain connection to your aura is "muted" by the Veil so that you are barely in touch with your energetic self; that is, your emotional, mental, and spiritual layers. If you do manage to connect with your aura, what you receive is a flow of emotions — feeling good, bad, or indifferent about a situation, place, person, or thing. This is your aura communicating with you.

You call this your "intuition." Learn to use it! Assess every emotion that arises as guidance for your current now moment. Realize that your aura, by virtue of being in higher-dimensional frequencies, sees and knows more than your physical senses that are keyed only into 3D. As you flower into the broader sensory range of 4-5D, you will understand that the Veil is thinning! Once you shift fully from 4D into 5D, you will outgrow the need for separation from Spirit, and outgrow the limitations of the Veil of Forgetfulness altogether.

When you are awake, the Veil is down. When you are asleep, the Veil rises and you are free to link with Spirit. You already know that while the body needs a certain amount of sleep each day, your mind never rests. In dreams, the mind continues to function, whether you remember your dreams or not. Some of you (older souls) do astral work while asleep, meaning that the spirit aspect of your being does nonphysical tasks in the higher realms while your body rests. Why does the body need rest? To clear itself of daily stress, physical strain, and emotional baggage, both old and new.

How does your body accomplish this layered process of self-healing? By clearing and replenishing the energy in your nervous system while you sleep. By the activation of what we call the Circle of Grace, which clears your auric layers through your physical core. Forgive the long introduction, but the framework of reference is much more intricate than the actual work. Once you understand in your mind and body how this clearing takes place, you will be able to activate it at any time you wish, to regain and maintain your health and stamina. What we are teaching you is simply this: care and maintenance of your aura.

You have the power to heal yourself. You have a clearing mechanism already present in your body! If you will, let us teach you how to use it.

Why People Get Sick

People get sick in one of two ways: either a disease establishes itself in a region of etheric blockage, or too much stress overloads the body, which breaks down at the site of the genetic predisposition to illness. We are all in favor of using the modern technology available today — doctors perform an invaluable service to humanity. **If you are ill, we urge you to first seek medical attention!** Once you know what is going on at the physical level, you can choose which medical therapies and holistic practices will best support your healing process. Use your common sense, dear ones; a broken bone requires casting, pneumonia must be treated with antibiotics, and so on.

But what if you were to go to the doctor and say, "I have pain in this region of my body, which is invisible to you. Please help me!" That is the situation faced by most modern healers, scientific or holistic. The scientific mindset discounts what it cannot see or measure. The holistic mindset focuses on wherever the pain may be and tracks it back to its true source, such as areas of blockage in the auric field, which you call stress, strain, and pain. Many holistic practitioners get diagnostic impressions in their hands and can feel their way to righting the damage they find. This is, in a true physical sense, reading the aura. Some rely on inner sight for guidance, another gift that will grow with your expansion into the new human 4-5D sensory range!

Here is a concept important to assimilate: stress and pain have physical properties of mass and density that exist in the higher dimensions of your body — in your aura. Because your energetic meridians are intricately tied into your physical nervous system pathways, stress and pain also exist inside you as physical objects. While your body must deal with them as causing painful pressure, your senses cannot track what is happening to you from the third dimension. Since you cannot yet see these stress, or pain, pockets of dense etheric blockage, just as you do not yet see your own auras, you discount their existence.

Even though you cannot see your pain, did you ever wonder why you feel it so clearly? Because pain is as real and concrete as is your body, and its presence inside you causes painful pressure. Once you realize that stress and pain are solid objects in your auric layers — as real as your skin, muscles, and bones are in your body — you will reach a new perspective on how to get clear and stay balanced. In regards to explaining the phenomenon of pain, your language is limited. You have over fifty names for bread and cakes, but only one word for pain! It must be qualified in different ways to express what type of pain you are feeling, as in a sharp pain, a throbbing pain, or a dull pain. Stress is actually a form of low-level pain that causes a constant, unrelenting build-up of pressure in your meridians. The accumulation of too much auric pressure is eventually transferred to your nervous system, result-ing in etheric blockages that prevent your body from receiving the cleansing flow of new, universal energy that keeps your total Be-ing healthy.

In this work, we shall use your language to help explain the Circle of Grace. Think about the expression, "You're getting on my last nerve!" What does this mean in energetic terms? Your clearing mechanism, your nervous system, is so clogged with old, tainted energy that there is no room left in it to absorb any more stress. What happens when the system gets overloaded? Again, pain is a physical object in your body; it has to go somewhere. Where does it go? Where do you stuff your pain away? What are the chronic weak spots in your body that rear up and hurt when you are "stressed out"? Those are the areas where your energetic meridians are blocked, causing the overflow of pain to settle in your tissues, muscles, and bones. Since it does not belong there, the overflow causes physical pressure that you recognize as chronic pain.

That is how blockages are formed, dear ones, and these blockages stop the Circle of Grace flow. The body switches to smaller alternate meridians in order to keep releasing pressure in the entire system. The more alternate routes it is forced to take, the weaker the flow becomes in that region of the body. If you have chronic pain that eludes a diagnosis and your doctor can find nothing wrong, you may well find relief from doing the Circle of Grace in healing sessions with us. We offer to teach you how to clear your etheric blockages and carry more "life force" in your body.

You already know that illness strikes in one of two ways — either in the area of the etheric blockages or through weak spots in your genetic make-up, such as the inherited tendencies of illness in families, like cancer or heart disease. We offer you this clearing exercise in hopes of expanding your awareness of how your body works, and how to stay healthy. You can carry etheric damage for a long, long time before it manifests in your physical core. If you regularly clear your auric self of pressure, you can prevent etheric dis-ease from physically manifesting as a disease in your body.

You do not need to succumb to illness. With the Circle of Grace, you can clear yourself, keep your body healthy, live longer, and have a better quality of life.

Do you follow? We hope you will.

The Circle of Grace is an active meditation. Through the quieting of the mind and the inward focus of attention, you can feel this miracle of self-clearing happen naturally in your body. We ask that you focus on the energy moving inside you and track aloud for us whatever you are feeling. If you argue here that you do not meditate and have no intent to do so, please know that this is a meditation focused on augmenting body awareness, not just trying to relax and not think. If you don't want to meditate, see it as an active relaxation session! You can also activate the Circle of Grace to clear yourself as you are falling asleep, resting, reading, or watching television.

You have an old saying, "In prayer you speak to God, in meditation you listen to God." By saying the Healing Prayer aloud to connect with us, you are speaking to God. As you slide into the Circle of Grace, you switch to feeling our presence and gentle ministrations. Thus, this process works in perfect balance — giving and receiving. Give us your time and your faith, and you will receive God's Grace.

Our goal is to teach all human beings how to heal themselves. In energetic terms, a "healed state" is one in which all four PEMS layers of your dense etheric body (physical, emotional, mental, and spiritual) are cleared and balanced to work as an integrated whole. Please understand that learning and using the Circle of Grace will greatly facilitate your imminent evolution. How? By clearing out the old 3D density from your body, and recharging you with new clean energy of a higher frequency.

Since we work at all levels, know that our session time together goes way beyond the simple physical clearing process that we offer here. The real, deep-down work we do with you can help release old emotional wounds, mental loops, and faulty belief systems that rule your biology. In other words, yes, do the Circle of Grace whenever you feel the need for physical clearing, replenishing, and rebalancing, but please do not forget to schedule time to work with us at the conceptual level, as well.

Why the Circle of Grace Works

The Circle of Grace clears excess internal pressure from your nervous system. Your nervous system is embedded in your body, but it also exists throughout your aura, or electromagnetic field, in a holographic pattern (as are all of your "physical" systems). Your internal nervous system has a reflected pattern in the aura that you call the body's "energetic meridians." Yes, both are really one and the same system! Your auric layers are energetically woven through your physical core. Stimulating any level of this system, physical or auric, will cause all PEMS levels to release. This is how your body clears itself automatically at night while you sleep. For some who wake up each day with pain in the same spots — those are chronic blockages that interfere with your energy flows. In our healing sessions together, we can help you clear those aches and pains, and release cumulative stress as well.

To heighten your understanding, know that the energy meridians traced by the Chinese over three thousand years ago for acupuncture are, in reality, an overlay of your nervous system. Acupuncture works well to accelerate healing because it clears both the energy meridians and nerve pathways appropriate to the damage. This allows the Circle of Grace to flow, which aids the body to clear itself of excess internal pressure. For those with a fear of needles, there are many other hands-on modalities that help quicken meridian release. Explore shiatsu, jin shin jyutsu, foot reflexology, acupressure, and the many forms of therapeutic massage that stimulate blockages to clear.

The aura sustains the total body's life flow by circulating universal energy through its physical core and all of its etheric layers. The nervous system is to the aura what the (blood) circulatory system is to the body. While blood is meant to flow in only one direction, the nervous system is much more versatile. Your nervous system also has an internal flow — a constant intake and output of universal energy — that can go in any direction it needs to clear itself. The purpose of this flow is to collect stress and pain in your total being, both physical and auric, and release it so that it does not accumulate.

This process also energizes the body as it is clearing. How? Universal energy is food for all of the PEMS layers of your body. No matter where the Circle of Grace begins, as it releases pressure, it also takes in new, clean energy at the same time. Why? Your nervous system is a closed-pressure system. When one end releases, the other end automatically rebalances its internal pressure by taking in an equal amount of new, clean energy.

Whenever you do this exercise, you clear and replenish the energy in your body at the same time. There is never a drain without a gain!

Your nervous system is much more than just a communications network between your brain and body parts. It has many different functions. Your nerve pathways within the body are connected to your energetic meridians through the skin. Yes, this is how your aura is energetically woven through your physical core. Stress and pain are the waste products of your body's energetic and physical functions. Your nervous system is designed to flush away this waste from all the layers of your total PEMS Be-ing.

The universal energy running through your nervous system absorbs your energetic waste in a magnetic way. The stress and pain literally melt into the golden flow, which becomes dark and tainted as it progresses through your body. Imagine this energetic flow akin to oil in your car. The oil keeps everything running smoothly but gets dirty with the byproducts of released energy. You have determined how long your car can run efficiently before the oil gets so dirty that it needs to be changed. We say to you here: Your body requires "oil changes" much more frequently than your automobile!

Dominant and Nondominant: the Right and the Left

A moment is needed here to explain dominant and nondominant sides of the body. Most people are right dominant and write with their right hand. If you are ambidextrous, try to remember which hand you used as a small child when first introduced to writing. If you were left-handed but were forced to write with your right hand, your body is still left-side dominant. When you are clear of blockages and your meridians are free flowing, you will feel more movement and release down your nondominant side, which may feel cold and flat. Your dominant side, which absorbs new energy in an upward direction, may start to feel warm and puffy.

This dominance aspect of the body also defines which hand is positive in hands-on healing and which hand is negative. A note to the holistic healer: your dominant hand is the positive flow of energy and your non-dominant hand is the negative flow. Together, they form a closed circuit by which energy is channeled through the body of the receiver.

For left-side dominant people: Please understand that your approach is simply the reverse, or mirror image, of right dominant people. In the balanced Circle of Grace pattern, your receiving foot is the left, and you will feel energy rise up your left side. Your releasing foot is the right, and you will feel more clearing occur down the right side. For those who are unsure, you may sense during the Circle of Grace which foot is receiving (it will feel like it is being pushed back and upright) and which foot is releasing (it will feel pulled forward and down).

Please remember that while we focus on teaching you the physical level of release, all of your energetic levels are also being cleared as you do this work. Is it not remarkable, dear human being, how elegantly you are designed? Yes, God is truly in the perfection of life's every detail!

The Circle of Grace Meridian Flows

When first beginning this exercise, most people find themselves clearing from the head on down the body on both sides, with pressure draining down both arms, the torso, and the legs. To keep this process simple, we are — on purpose — not naming each meridian, nor drawing every little zig and zag each takes. We are instead showing you numbered "flow lines" that your body uses to expel pressure and refuel itself. Indeed, you could say this is a course in "energetic plumbing!" [Chuckles.]

We will start with two very important facts about your internal clearing mechanism: blockages above the armpits usually exit down the arms; blocks below the armpits usually clear down the torso and legs. Figure 1.1 shows the twelve flow lines that you will learn to feel as you gain aptitude with this process. To avoid confusion, we are describing only one side of your body, and have numbered only flows one through six. Please keep in mind that these flows are bilateral; they run through both sides of your body at the same time. Don't worry about memorizing all of the flow lines and their numbers. You will learn to recognize them as the different patterns your body chooses for releasing and re-energizing.

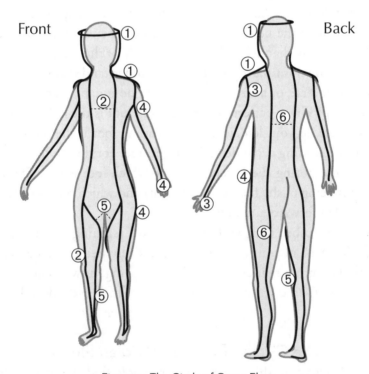

Figure 1.1: The Circle of Grace Flows

When internal pressure is high in the body, the release begins from the temples ①, travels down through your open jaw joints, down your neck, and across your shoulders. Your body naturally splits this releasing flow to other meridians to decrease the pressure in each individual meridian. The first split occurs at the base of your neck, with flow ② going down the front of your body and flow ⑥ branching off down your back.

From the neck, flow ② goes straight down the front of your torso, through the nipple, the hip joint, and down the front of your leg to the top side of your foot chakra. At the hip, flow ② splits inward to create flow ⑤, which courses down the inside of your thigh, knee, and ankle. Flow ⑤ exits at the bottom of the sole chakra in the foot. At the base of the neck, flow ① also splits off to flow ⑥, going over your shoulder blade, down your back, behind your hip, behind the knee and ankle, then exiting down the heel and out the sole chakra.

The releasing flow from the head ① also continues to spread across your shoulders. At the top of the shoulder, flow ① ends by splitting into the two arm meridians, ③ and ④. Flow ③ runs down the back of your arm, through your elbow, and exits at the hand chakra or continues out the fourth and fifth fingers of your hand. Flow ④ goes down the inner arm to release through your hand chakra, or continues out your thumb and index finger. The middle finger can carry either flow, depending on the needs of your body.

Flow ④ also splits under your armpit, going down the side of your torso and down the outside of your leg. Your legs each have four clearing meridians: two parallel on the inside ⑤ and outside ④ of your thigh, and two centered in front of ② and behind your knee ⑥. The meridian behind your knee is an extension of the sciatic nerve trunk, a major path of release running straight down the back of your leg from the lower back to the heel.

When in cleansing mode, the meridians of your arms and legs always move in the same direction. In other words, you may feel your dominant arm releasing pressure down both ③ and ④ together. When your dominant side takes in energy, the flow reverses in that same arm and the meridians will flow up, ③ and ④ together. Similarly, the four leg meridians all work together in the same direction, ruled by the instructions of your nervous system. Please note that these six meridians are on both sides of the body, totaling twelve in all.

Yes, there are thousands of meridians and chakras throughout the body, all of which are interconnected and serve multiple purposes. Even the twelve meridians we describe herein have other flows and functions. We are, indeed, keeping the information simple and direct to facilitate your learning how to use the clearing mechanism already within you. Your nervous system releases pressure in pulsing, peristaltic waves, which you will learn to control through focused breathing. This can be a fascinating process for those who seek inner knowledge or deeper levels of meditation.

Once you become adept at doing the Circle of Grace and have cleared your major blockages, you will eventually release down the front and/or back of your body in waves of pressure that exit at the hands and feet. You will learn how to release lower-back pain down the back of both legs, through the sciatic nerve trunks (flow ⑥) and out the feet. You will be able to drain a headache down both arms and out your hands. Yes, you will gain mastery over your health and your energy. Come cocreate with us a better quality of life, using the divine power already inside you!

Doing the Circle of Grace Exercise

Since we are dealing with the mechanics of pressure flows in and around the body, we offer first a few tips to remember:

- It is important to wear loose, comfortable clothing (preferably natural fibers) and remove your shoes.
- Loosen whatever you can: tie, belt, bra, shoes. Any constriction to the physical body causes restriction of your energetic meridians.
- In addition to loose clothing, we advise you to have a blanket handy in case you get chilled and a glass of water within reach if your mouth gets too dry.
- If possible, breathe in and out through your nose.
- There is no need to keep your tongue up against your palate; this forces your tongue, throat, and neck muscles to clench, and then you cannot fully relax your jaw.

A note for people who have physical damage in and around the jaw: The jaw joints, or temporal-mandibular joints (TMJ), are the only joints in the body that work in tandem, as a pair. All of your other joints, both fixed and moving, are single joints that work alone. Your lower jaw is suspended like a seesaw. If one jaw joint is damaged, the other joint eventually suffers damage by force of misaligned pressure. Even if only one side hurts, always clear both sides! For TMJ sufferers, use a high pillow beneath your head so that your jaw naturally points down, then drop your jaw open to let the pressure flow through. If you lie too flat and your lower jaw slides back instead of forward, this position will cause more pain rather than relieving what is there.

When beginning the Circle of Grace, lie face up with the head and spine aligned straight, the legs slightly apart, and the arms at your sides. You can progress to sitting, but it is easier to begin practicing on your back. Place pillows beneath your head and knees to prevent lower-back strain. Do not cross your arms or legs, since physical pressure short-circuits the meridians and the flow may cease. If you cannot lie flat, lie on your side with three pillows, one beneath your head, one between your knees (to prevent lower back strain), and one to hug to your chest (to prevent upper-back strain).

You must open your jaw to activate the Circle of Grace. Your jaw is your on-off switch that starts and stops the Circle of Grace. When your jaw is tense, your whole body is tense. When you relax your jaw, the body follows suit. When your jaw is clenched, the meridians will not release. When the jaw joints are relaxed, the meridians open to flow. After opening your jaw, tip your head left, then right (small motions will do) to activate the meridian flows. Then bring your head back to center, making sure that your head and spine are in alignment.

If your mind wanders away from the exercise, merely open your jaw and tip your head again to either side to reactivate the release. If the flow slows down, another good way to activate the meridians is by flexing your hand (or foot) back up against the wrist (or ankle) joint, as if making a stopping motion. That will tug on the meridians from the exit points (joints and chakras of the hands and feet) to stimulate release.

Being focused on your breathing helps to keep the process moving, and it also gives your left brain busy work to do. We offer here an elementary version of yogic breathing, which you can modify to suit your lung capacity. It matters not if you can only count to two before exhaling; the key is to breathe slowly and deliberately so as not to hyperventilate. Breathe in slowly to a comfortable count between 1 and 7, pause for a count between 1 and 3, breathe out to a count between 1 and 7, and then pause for a count between 1 and 3. If you have trouble counting or cannot sustain long breaths with two pauses, focus on breathing evenly in and out, and pause just once after the exhale. Each pause presses down on your meridians and creates a wave of release down your body.

Dear ones, we are re-creating here the cadence of your breathing during sleep, which actually pushes the meridians to release pressure in slow, pulsing waves. By consciously controlling your breathing, you will learn to direct your body's internal cleansing mechanism. Between this focused breathing and your speaking aloud to us what you feel during our sessions, do you see why we call the Circle of Grace an active meditation? Your left brain has plenty to do while we are working with you. Through this process you will develop the ability to control your thinking, your breathing, your clearing, your energy levels, and your healing.

Now, how does the Circle of Grace feel? It varies with each individual, yet the sensations always follow the same energetic patterns and pathways. Someone who is relatively healthy and balanced will not get the same intensity of sensations as someone who is ill. You may feel a "flow" descending or slight sensations of fullness in the nondominant hand and/or foot as pressure leaves your system. Some people report feeling a cool liquid sliding down inside their nondominant arm and/or leg while others feel a more "bubbly" release. You may feel an electric "spark" at the blockage site, then another "spark" in the hand or foot as that pressure pocket reaches the exit. Some people only experience a tingling in their fingers and toes when beginning the exercise. Some will feel nothing at all, yet find that they have much more energy to get them through the day. If you have no time to meditate during the day, know that you can begin the Circle of Grace as you're going to sleep, and we will gently augment your clearing process during the night.

When working alone with Spirit [chuckles], know that we begin by opening your system from the bottom up: first the feet, then the hands, and lastly the crown. Once the feet and hand chakras are open, the clearing can truly begin. Some of you may only feel areas of warmth and cold, others may feel each "lumpy bump" come down and out the entire length of your meridians. These sensations are transient; do not be afraid of feeling discomfort in this process. What you are feeling is the passage of each blockage, an echo of its progress that tells you of its path. Just remember to do your deep breathing, for it will help to push those pressure pockets down and out.

For those who do not notice any sensations, focus on the energizing aspect of the Circle of Grace. A half-hour of this exercise in the morning will give you much energy for the day, making you feel younger and stronger. Once you become adept at this process, you can actively participate in your own self-healing clearing stress, releasing meridian blocks, clearing headaches and back pain, or eliminating any pain anywhere.

Many lightworkers are accustomed to closing a session after working with Spirit, having been taught that their energy will drain away if they do not. Here we will explain why we do not ask you to formally close a healing session. We bring you into 4-5D when we work together, which is where the earth is now vibrating. Leaving the session open in our way allows your body to gently oscillate back down to the current vibration around you. Dear ones, do not be afraid of having your personal energy drain away if you don't close a session. Saying thank you to Spirit is enough closure for us! Have we not shown that you are a self-contained, self-maintaining, electromagnetic life form?

The Circle of Grace Clearing Patterns

Please remember that the Circle of Grace can run in any pattern that your body needs at any given moment. No one pattern is better or healthier than another. Your body needs them all, at different times. Start with the Fully Blocked Pattern and allow your aura to shift into the other patterns as it needs in order to clear all of your PEMS layers.

Fully Blocked Pattern: For those who are highly pressurized, the direction of the Circle release will begin from the head on down, using both sides of the body to flush out stress and pain. Pressure will exit from the hand and foot chakras simultaneously. If you require a visualization to help you along, imagine a golden cloud or shower of universal energy above your head. See it descending around your body and into the top of your head, going through your open jaw joints and down both sides of your neck, then flowing down both arms and legs at the same time. This full-body release will occur at your direction once you gain familiarity with the Circle of Grace exercise.

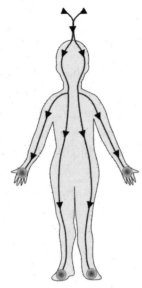

Figure 1.2: Fully Blocked
Pattern

Using our car analogy, we point out that the engine goes through many gear changes to get you to your destination, depending on the traffic flows and which roads you travel. In the same way, your nervous system is designed to switch between patterns, depending on the needs of the body at that time and the amount of pressure built up in your internal environment. If you are fully blocked and there is no energetic movement in your meridians, you may need the intervention of human hands. A Reiki practitioner, massage therapist, energetic lightworker, acupuncturist, and so on, can help break up those blockages, release pressure, and channel new universal energy to refuel your body.

Alternating Blocked Pattern: Once your system has been partially cleared, your upper and lower meridians will begin taking turns. You will feel your arms releasing pressure, then that will cease and your legs will release for a while. This alternating pattern will continue until enough pressure has been relieved inside the nervous system for your body to assume the Balanced Circle of Grace Pattern.

An example of the Alternating Blocked Pattern: to clear headaches, you can run the Circle of Grace down both arms at the same time. Open your jaw to open the head/neck meridians, and tip your head left (a tiny motion will do). This activates the left meridian flow. Then tip your head to the right to activate that side, and

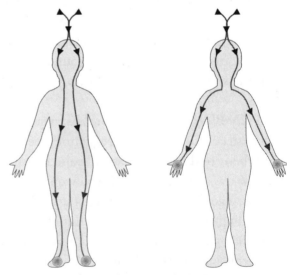

Figure 1.3: Alternating Blocked Pattern

go back to center. Keeping your jaw joints open, you will feel the headache actually coursing down your neck on both sides, and then down your arms in waves of pressure. If it is a very deep headache, you may feel waves flowing down your whole body as the headache exits through the arms and the nausea flows down the legs, taking turns to release.

Balanced Pattern: For a person with clear-flowing, unblocked meridians, the Circle of Grace begins and ends at the feet in an inverted U shape. Your aura absorbs universal energy through the dominant foot and hand chakras, draws it up the dominant side of the body, then circles around the head and releases excess pressure down the nondominant side. As fresh energy enters your system, it pushes ahead of it old, spent energy laced with debris from your PEMS functions. That is why by the time the Circle crests around your head and comes back down the nondominant side in the balanced pattern, you may feel the energy change into a sensation of pressure or an achy feeling, sometimes even a sharp line as it slides down and out.

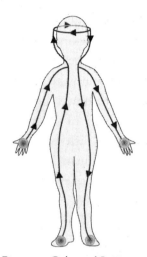

Figure 1.4: Balanced Pattern

Once you become sensitive to the energy flows as your body switches to the balanced pattern, you may feel as if your dominant foot is being pressed up and back, while your nondominant foot may feel as if it is being pulled forward and down. You will have this sensation even if both feet are in exactly the same position. What you are feeling is the tug and direction of the energy circling through your body.

You may also feel an expansive warmth permeating your dominant side as new energy enters your system, and a flat, cold sensation down your nondominant side as old, spent energy is released. Many receivers of Reiki, which provides an energetic push of universal energy for the Circle of Grace to begin, have described this sensation as a feeling of champagne bubbles going up the dominant leg, and some feel a dominant-sided heaviness as universal energy enters their systems.

This new, clean energy is pushing waves of spent energy before it that are released from the nondominant hand and foot chakras. You may feel achy waves of pressure flowing down your nondominant arm/side/leg. You may feel a tiny hot line within your muscles as a blocked meridian is cleared. If the flow gets stuck in a spot, tell us aloud and we will move it down and out. You can also rub the spot in a downward motion. Even the focus of your mental intent without any external help can clear your meridians if you understand how this is possible.

We will teach you how to do this in our healing sessions together! For those of you who prefer to meditate with visualization, you can add this refinement once you feel your body in the Balanced Circle of Grace Pattern: Breathe up the dominant side, pause as it circles around your head, then breathe down the nondominant side, and pause again. See each inhalation as a wave of clean, golden energy flowing in and up your dominant side, and see each exhalation as a gray, cloudy wave flowing down and out your nondominant side. In this way, you will learn to use this exercise efficiently and effectively as part of your routine body maintenance.

Multiple Blockages: When clearing multiple blockages, please know that the one nearest the hand or foot exit must clear first. The very nature of a blockage does not allow any energy to pass through that meridian, so nothing can get around it. Yes, like a single-lane road with no passing allowed! For example, if you have a sprained wrist and a shoulder injury on the same side, the wrist blockage must be released first or the shoulder damage will stay lodged behind it, unable to move down the arm and out the hand. For hands-on practitioners: You can pull directly from a pressure pocket to reduce its size, and what is left will flow down and out the meridians much more easily.

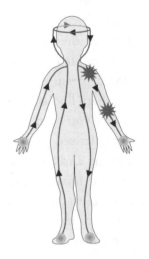

Figure 1.5: Multiple Blockage Pattern

Reverse Blockages: If you are ill or have an injury, know that you can direct the cleansing flow to release pain from the nearest hand or foot exit. For example, if you injured your dominant elbow, you can reverse the flow to release through your dominant hand instead of going up, circling around the head, and releasing down and out the nondominant side. Merely ask us in session to clear the injury through the closest exit, and we will do so.

For energetic practitioners: know that you can attune the exit chakra and the site of blockage to open them energetically. Then add energy to the blockage and move it down and out with a gentle stroking motion. If you do not know how to do energetic attunements, simply make six to nine counterclockwise circles with your dominant hand above the exit chakra (palm the hand or foot chakra for a minute or two), and then repeat above the area of blockage. Your intent to open and clear that pressure pocket will work just as well.

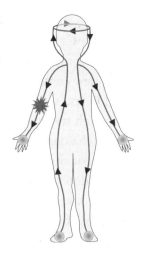

Figure 1.6: Reverse Blockage Pattern

Working in Session with the Brotherhood

You need only give verbal intent to do the Circle of Grace with the Healing Prayer, and call in the higher help as we described. Then lie down and speak to us aloud. Tell us what you want, what you are tired of, what you wish to heal. Tell us aloud if you feel a blockage and we will work on releasing it. Some of you will feel us working, some will not. Do not worry about missing the session if you fall asleep; we sometimes work best when you are asleep. You have not missed the session! Some Brothers work at the physical level, some at the etheric level, while other Brothers work with your higher mind at the conceptual level. Remember, healing must occur on all levels, not just the physical. Simply tell us at the beginning how much time you have, and we will keep time for you [chuckles]. A half-hour session will refresh you, but an hour session is best for a daily practice.

Sometimes you may find yourself weeping (clearing emotional stress), or bathed in waves of tickling energy (energizing the body), or feel your arms and/or legs filling with pressure seeking to release. Tell us aloud if the process becomes painful and we will tone down the work. Sometimes the flow gets stuck behind a big joint — such as hip, knee, shoulder, or elbow

— forming a blockage that needs to be moved down and out. So tell us aloud if the Circle slows or becomes stuck and where this is happening. We will endeavor to move the flow, guided by your verbal feedback and fueled by your new conscious awareness of this miraculous process built into your body. Do you see why we call this active meditation?

Though we have described the Circle of Grace flow as exiting the hand and foot chakras, pressure may also exit through your joints. You may feel pressure exit through your wrists or ankle joints. Sometimes the flow will continue down and exit from the tips of your fingers or toes. It can also exit at the knuckles of the hand or foot. Those of you familiar with Eastern knowledge of release points will find that we use many of them.

Again, you don't need to control this process. Merely observe the flow and report to us, out loud, how it feels and where it tends to block. Once you become familiar with the Circle of Grace, you can guide excess pressure to release directly through your hand and foot chakras.

For those of you who wake up with pain on your nondominant side, know that your meridians are not able to fully clear through the nondominant hand or foot while you sleep. Some post-operative patients feel pain on their nondominant side, not near the surgical site, which can be very confusing for doctors. In such cases, surgical trauma to the body produced too much internal pressure for the meridians to effectively clear out the nondominant side. If pre-existing blockages exist, new pressure seeking to release will pile up and enlarge the old blockage, since no pressure can get through a blocked meridian.

Doctors will shake their heads and say, "Sorry, we operated on your shoulder, head, torso, and so on, and we don't know why your leg (hip, knee, or ankle) is hurting. Get some rest, take these pain pills, and it will fade." Yes, that is good advice, because the body at rest naturally performs the Circle of Grace to clear itself. When physical trauma occurs, there is often too big a pressure pocket to slide down and out the meridians all at once. Massage does wonders for pain-filled blockages. Remember, a knotted muscle contains a physical mass of dense etheric pressure within it, spilled over from the blocked meridian into the surrounding tissues, causing a density of flesh that can become chronically painful.

Sometimes the body has healed a trauma as much as it can, but years later you still have pain trapped in that area, like a ten-year-old whiplash.

It will remain fixed in place until it is energetically lanced and drained away. Why? The surrounding meridians cannot process that big a block, so the body encapsulates it in the nearby tissues. These etheric pockets have physical weight and density in your body, but are simply not visible to you yet in your physical reality.

Imagine trying to shove a banana through a straw. Will it fit? No. Will it go through and out the other end? With patience and repeated force, you might get a trickle of banana out the other end, but most of it will remain squished in your hand and stuck in the straw. Identifying an energetic blockage is a big step toward true health, and realizing the natural path of clearing that blockage is another big step.

The true beauty of the Circle of Grace is that it clears not only the physical body but also your entire energetic Be-ing, including all four PEMS layers of your dense etheric body. Your chakra system is the spine of your etheric layers, which is why proper clearing and balancing of the chakras creates a condition of health at all levels. In addition to being your body's clearing system, the Circle of Grace also performs another vital function: it constantly re-energizes your body without you being aware of the process. Once you find your own inner Circle flow and begin to affect it with your conscious mind, your evolutionary progress will gain momentum at all levels.

We stated earlier that the left brain is connected to and directs the physical body, while the right brain is connected to and directs the etheric layers that comprise your aura. Imagination, creativity, courage, faith, and many other wonderful human attributes are right brain and, therefore, auric functions. Do you see now why your innate gifts and talents are difficult to access? Because your awareness is only left-brained, you need to consciously reconnect to your right brain. These attributes exist in all the layers of your multi-dimensional body, since humans are holographic in design. This holographic concept is reflected all through the Divine Plan. As you rise into 4D awareness and beyond, you will begin to see the interconnections between all things, see the patterns of life ebbing and flowing, and know that you are a part of All That Is.

Through this healing process, you will truly, consciously, become a multidimensional Be-ing. We use this spelling as a trigger for your higher consciousness. We use the verb "to be" to indicate the full blend of all your aspects, physical and nonphysical layers, with a capital letter as homage to your divinity in the same way we pay homage to God and His works. The "-ing" part of the word "Be-ing" indicates the now aspect of your ascension in the present tense, children, to remind you to keep hold of that higher perspective in every moment.

The body of work that we offer here reflects the commitment we have made to the Divine Plan. The Brotherhood of Light is dedicated to teaching humans how to incorporate all the different aspects of their total Be-ing while still in body, and thus gracefully ascend into the higher realms. In order to blend all of your layers into Oneness, those layers must be cleared and balanced first!

We hope that you now understand why meditation requires you to "still" your chatty left brain, allowing you to be open and receptive to consciously reconnecting to your right brain. So do not keep busy trying to squelch thought, for you are thus blocking all thought. Try instead to suspend mundane thought, like a clear TV screen waiting for a transmission. Focus on your breathing, and follow the sensations of the Circle of Grace. Remember, this is an active meditation, an exercise in which we hope you will speak to us aloud and voice your needs through the session.

Some of you may be protesting, "I don't meditate. I don't care to." Know that if you are opposed to the very idea of meditation, then don't do it. Call it a visualization, if you prefer. We ask that you lie down anyway, open your jaw, and imagine a golden cloud of energy entering the top of your head and flowing down, inside and around your body like a shower. Do not try to choose which pattern to use, allow your body to do what it needs to do. Allow your group of Brothers to choose what you need at each session. If you feel the Fully Blocked Pattern begin, track your golden cloud visualization straight down both sides. If you feel energy enter your dominant side, go up and around your head, then down the nondominant side, visualize your golden cloud following that path. Then see this golden energy surrounding you like a cocoon, permeating every level of your total Be-ing with healing energy, and feel yourself being re-energized.

For those of you who have no time to meditate, you can activate the Circle of Grace as you are falling asleep. That simple act will augment and intensify the work that your body naturally does at night to clear itself. This can be a very active process or not, depending on your views and needs. Eventually, you will find that every time you lie down to watch television, read a book, or rest, your body will automatically begin clearing! Once the Circle of Grace becomes part of your life, you will make great strides toward full mastery.

If you still object to meditating, then we gently ask, "Do you enjoy getting in your own way?" If you are reading this text, you are a seeker of spirituality, of faith, of oneness. We offer this information to you as an aid up the ladder to the next level of human evolution. We hope that you will incorporate this exercise into your life, for your own healing and to help others. This clearing process is in each and every one of you! Seek it, find it, and use it. You will soon shine, brighter and brighter, as you discover and explore your inner world, your God-self, your portion of the I Am All That Is. Our gift to you is one of natural healing, through the Circle of Grace.

②

The Emotional Body

n this second chapter, we would like to focus on the emotional body. You all have emotions, to varying degrees, but you do not know how to use them wisely. By this we mean that you have lost their true purpose and cannot, therefore, use emotions with conscious wisdom. In offering an energetic perspective on how your bodies work and how the universal laws affect your expanding reality, we hope to show you that wisdom is already within you. You are simply not conscious of it yet!

As energetic beings, your bodies are layered in holographic patterns that are currently beyond the scope of your medical technology to detect. For the purpose of our work together here, we are focusing on the dense etheric body, comprised of physical, emotional, mental, and spiritual aspects (PEMS). These layers are distinct in form and function. They can work independently, but the energetic essence of every human is a constant expression of their unique meld of PEMS aspects working together to form a cohesive whole. The more you understand how each layer works, the more you can synthesize the totality of who you are to achieve the divine Adamic blueprint that is your birthright.

Your emotional body provides the fuel of loving energy for your thoughts, actions, beliefs, and goals. Love is the energetic catalyst for manifestation. Your emotional body also processes and stores your negative emotions and stress. If you focus on negative things in your life — the lack of health, happiness, and abundance — your emotional layer will fuel that with sorrow, anger, fear, and illness.

One of the basic intake functions of your emotional layer is that of a warning system, an alert radar always ready with a nudge in the proper direction. Remember, your energetic body layers inhabit dimensions higher than your physical senses, which are accustomed to sensory input only from 3D. With that higher placement comes higher sight from a perspective that your eyes, senses, and left brain could not before reach.

Learn to sensitize yourself to what your emotions are saying, for they have a ready answer if you acknowledge them and listen carefully. Especially now, in this time of escalating frequency and psychic development, it is imperative that you learn how to control your emotions and not let your emotions control you.

Keep Your Emotional Body Clear

Your emotional body is the auric layer closest to your physical core. Your language reflects this layer of existence in many clichés: He was beside himself, he let his emotions get the better of him, he let his anger rule him, or he was blinded by rage. We say this: your emotions were never meant to rule you. Your ego was never meant to rule you. These are merely aspects of your total self that were designed as a protection and warning system. Have you noticed that when you act against your intuition you are never happy with the results?

What you call intuition is actually incoming sensory information from your energetic layers. This process will get stronger as you expand into 4-5D and regain true communication with Spirit in the higher realms. You will develop new levels of mental and emotional control as you find out how truly powerful you are. Remember that detachment and compassion must rule your behavior, as is God's will. Otherwise, you will create chaos around you and more negative karma as well.

What happens when you lose your temper? You aren't really losing it but rather loosing it (letting it loose). What you lose is the ability to control your temper. You are allowing your emotional body to lead without any input from your other layers. Giving in to your emotions gives you an excuse for not being in control. Most children are not taught how to be in command of the different aspects of their total being. Since you do not view yourselves as energetic beings, you do not yet know to include the proper teachings to your children. Learning to read, write, and do math is not enough to prepare them for life. Teach your children that all life is precious and sacred. Teach them compassion, teach them meditation, teach them humility, and teach them that they are so much grander than they know. Teach them to rule over their emotions and not let their emotions rule them. How? Children learn by watching their parents and other adults interact. The best way to teach your children is by example.

Indeed, the greatest tragedies in your history were incited by emotions ruling over logic or lack of compassion and too much logic. As Buddha often said, "Choose the middle way." That is the path to enlightenment. No extremes in either direction should rule your life. You should not be ruled by any one or any thing save for God's will. Each and every one of you is a physical expression of God, complete and whole unto yourself. This is an integral part of the freewill directive that governs your corner of creation.

You were originally designed by God to directly experience His physical creation from within Earth's realm. Your emotional layer translates the wonders of your physical plane of existence; that is how you enjoy the sunshine, the flowers, or the laughter of a little child. When you feel sad or there occurs some physical trauma to yourself or loved ones, your emotions are the path through which you grieve and heal. Your language might say, "He wallowed in his grief." What does that mean? That he got "stuck" at that level of emotional process. You become emotionally stagnant when you expend all of your conscious energy into a past that you cannot go back to change or fix. You must travel forward past this point and find compassion through forgiveness to move beyond. Only then can you gather all your energy to be present in each now moment.

Compassion, forgiveness, and a positive perspective are all facets of the emotional body. So are the baser emotions like anger, greed, lust, envy, and vengeance. By "baser" we mean this literally, for emotions are expressed in an ascending scale of frequency, from lowest to highest. Anger makes you sick? Absolutely. Laughter is healing? Yes, indeed! Anger cuts into the aura as surely as a knife slices through flesh. All low frequency, fear-based emotions damage the aura, causing emotional, mental, and spiritual blockages that lead to disease and aging. The higher emotions, or love-based emotions, actually charge your body with energy and help to quicken healing.

Once you understand how this process works, it will become a simple choice to respond rather than react, to forgive and move on, to hug instead of fight. Ascension requires a total makeover, a change of attitude, and a change of behavioral patterns. When you learn to love all human beings and all living things, you will move into Higher Self, and Higher Self will move in with you.

It is crucial to clear and balance each layer of the human hologram in order to effect a total change. The emotional body carries much of the load, for it is the higher vibrations of love that propels meditation, prayer, and faith. You may argue that all of those things are the concern of the spiritual body. Yes, you are right, but you cannot separate the layers into distinct functions. Each contributes to the total energetic being that you are.

So how do you keep your emotional body clear and bright? Focus on happiness. Seek it inwardly, not outside yourself. Temper your day with joy and fill your time with fruitful focus and usefulness, and then you will be happy. It is far easier to cultivate a positive attitude than a negative one; it takes less energy and is much more rewarding.

Negative attitude is a big stumbling block on the metaphysical path. You must first acknowledge that you have a negative attitude, which is hard. Why? Because then you step into ego territory, which is not willing to admit that you are doing something wrong. Again, good, bad, right, and wrong are all parts of a whole that does not need those parts. Do not judge yourself or others; that mode of thinking carries a negative vibration. It is far better to imagine people reaching their highest potential, for that is the kindest perspective you can hold for them. Whatever they are doing at the moment may not be in harmony with their greatest good, but that is no longer your issue.

Detachment is vital for compassion to abound.

These are one-sentence reminders of facts you have no doubt heard before. And here is another thought: detachment is release of the personal ego so that you no longer care about the outcome of a situation. Once you release all personal attachment to what you or anyone else has to gain, that situation no longer has any emotional hold over you. Keep and carry the emotion of gratitude in your heart, and let all the rest go.

Yes, the path to ascension can be that simple!

Stress: Your Emotional Body and Your Health

Though you are all at different stages of physical and metaphysical evolution, please remember that your overall health relies on the restructuring and maintenance of the physical chakra system. As you evolve into your lightbody, make sure to keep those first seven energy centers clear and running smoothly, root to crown. The bottom three chakras (below the belt) must be integrated with the upper three: throat, third eye, and crown. The fourth, or heart chakra, will act as a fulcrum for the three above and the three below. Learn to lead with your heart — this is vital advice.

Many of you who are shifting have aches, pains, and phobias flaring up to be cleared. These old, buried issues are surfacing because of the galactic attunements you are all processing in this time of great change. Allow for it to happen naturally; know that all will be resolved as you reawaken and reabsorb all facets of Higher Self. Do not be concerned with the higher levels until you begin to sense and interact with them. Trust that the changes are coming in with divine timing, under grace, for each individual's highest good.

For the emotional body, the Circle of Grace drains away stress through the nerve pathways and energetic meridians of the body. It is at once a physical and auric clearing. How could it not be, since the two are so energetically intertwined? The aura feeds and clears itself and its physical core through energy currents that penetrate the skin directly into the nervous system. Your nervous system also helps to anchor the aura into the physical body. Since stress is processed in the emotional body but released through the physical core, a balanced interconnection between the physical and emotional layers is vital for health.

Dear ones, stress is low-grade pain. Pain is not an imaginary or invisible thing. Pain has mass; it has density. Stress has mass and density too, but both of these forms of pain are invisible to your eyes and to your physical 3D senses. Pain exists in the same dimension as your auric body. Just because you cannot see it doesn't mean it is not there! Your body must deal with stress and pain as physical intrusions that lodge within your auric layers, causing pressure that can eventually change your internal structure. When energetic blockages become chronic, they eventually sink into your physical core, affecting your health and causing symptoms of illness.

If stress and pain were not real physical things, you would not feel them. Do you sometimes wonder when something emotionally painful happens and you stuff it away (you deny its expression), where does it go? It does not go far. It stays magnetized in your electromagnetic field as a pocket of dense matter. The more stress you stuff into it, the bigger the pocket gets. The bigger it gets, the closer to the body it grows. The aura shows damage from excess pressure years before a person takes ill. Overcoming illness can become a life long goal for those who carry a great deal of auric imbalance.

The emotional body performs another vital function: It is where your stress is initially stored to prevent from overloading your physical nervous system. Your stress is magnetically absorbed into the energy of your meridians, then slowly sinks into the physical core in order to be cleared. You already know that your nervous system carries signals of pain. It actually does more than that. It absorbs the energetic debris of your PEMS processes within its flow. This flow must be routinely cleared so that the nervous system can repressurize itself with an intake of new, clear energy as fuel for all levels. That is why regular care and maintenance of the aura is vital to your physical health. That is also why we have stepped forward now to teach you the Circle of Grace, which is your body's natural clearing process.

Please keep in mind that there are never any gaps in this energetic circulatory system. We have spoken of the releasing aspect of the Circle of Grace, moving the debris-filled energy down and out of the nondominant side of the body. In the balanced pattern, the dominant side of the body is automatically taking fresh, clear energy into the meridian system. This new influx pushes ahead of it the old, tainted energy to be released through the hand and foot chakras of the nondominant side. In the blocked patterns, universal energy comes in directly through your crown chakra, replenishing your system from the top down as the clearing takes place.

Remember, with every energetic drain comes an energetic gain. There is superb perfection in every detail of the Divine Plan, dear ones, and you were superbly designed.

Defining the Metaphysical Path
in the New Millennium Energy

In this time of accelerating frequency and planetary ascension, many new teachings are expanding your awareness. It only requires a small percentage of believers, as in the example of the hundredth-monkey paradigm, to affect the whole of the human consciousness. Each and every one of you has the capacity to do so much, so much that you do not yet realize. The rub here is in order for you to believe that you are more than just a body, you must experience a few episodes outside of your body for the real truth to sink in: You are eternal! You are the culmination of all the lives you have ever lived.

It has been a long, hard road for you in the third dimension, locked into linear thinking and linear time. But do not despair and do not fear death. In the higher realms, death is rebirth! Once you walk through that portal of death, you will know that it is only an exit door back to your true existence, back to a higher reality. You reunite with Spirit each and every time. We are always there waiting, your guardian angels, to welcome you back and lead you Home. You are all brave warriors, angels too, hidden in tiny bodies with no recollection of your true grandeur.

Know that you volunteered for this "heavy" duty. Know that you all stood in line to participate in this "last" lifetime on the 3D karmic wheel. In this lifetime, some of you will graduate from the school of planet Earth. Many will continue on without even realizing that a choice was possible, and they could translate into a new reality if they so desired. If that makes no sense to you, then think about this: All dimensions inhabit the same space. They are separated by their different octaves of frequency.

You lightworkers know who you are by now in the dawning of this new millennium. You are the forerunners of change, those that chose faith and a higher frequency of reality. For you, this coming Home will be quite a party, as we welcome you back with great love for your job well done. Some have already paved the way and translated over, leaving their bodies behind. That is also your choice, which Spirit does not judge. The eternal you is still going Home to be greeted by the same celebration.

Can you imagine being able to take your body with you? Learning to translate to a higher dimension happens on all levels that your body inhabits: many dimensions, but mainly the third, fourth, and fifth. The real challenge is teaching your physical body to translate along with your energetic layers. Bringing together all aspects of self, which you term self-realization, is the conduit by which you learn to access your Higher Self. The ascension process is a multilayered plan, as are your bodies, as are our spiritual hierarchies, as are the galaxies, the universes, and all the multidimensional aspects of the body of God. All that is, you see, is really All That Is!

In order to achieve wholeness, to integrate all of your layers, they must first be cleared and balanced. You must be healthy at all levels to reach vibratory resonance with the higher dimensions. Lightworkers, help clear and heal each other. Exchange energies and share your knowledge. Prepare together so that you may work as teams when mass healings become needed. Do your daily meditations, do group work, keep learning and seeking learning.

Yet you must each find your own path in life and learn to walk it. You cannot help others by pushing them forward on their paths without their consent. The final test is for each of you alone, your consciousness reaching up from within to meet Higher Self. Through meditation with the Circle of Grace exercise, come to us for alterations on your new light garment. The work you do now is quiet. The progress you will make is internal, not external. This path is not a journey of the feet but rather a journey back to your soul, back to true consciousness and away from the schoolroom that is Mother Earth.

The goal of ascension can only be reached by welcoming in the higher energies around you, above and below you, and integrating them into your energetic being. How? Through your faith that anything is possible. This mindset is in direct contradiction with all you have known until now, the separation from Spirit that duality requires. Have you noticed that the further away you stray from God's truth and Mother's needs, the harder is your life? Please connect back into the earth, hear her gentle voice, and feel her powerful, thrumming body under your feet as the true mother to you that she is. Nurture her as she nurtures you all.

How do you feed the earth? Studies done by your scientific community have discovered that when an energetic healer is at work, his or her brainwaves and electromagnetic fields (auras) blend to match Earth's resonance. You meld into her frequency and thus draw strength from her electromagnetic fields. Do you understand now that you can merge with Mother Earth simply by reaching out with your will, in meditation, or even in walking motion? As you tap into her strength, so, too, do you feed her. You feed her with your spiritual energy, wishes, hopes, and dreams. Your negative energy, anger, fear, doubt, and the pain that you healers pull off of people is also directed downward to feed Earth's momentum.

Flow down, feed the ground, and recycle as positive energy. This is a good healing mantra to use to direct the release of negative energy each time you lay hands on another or work on yourself. Even the Circle of Grace that humans unconsciously do while asleep, also feeds Earth. She does not distinguish between positive and negative energy. Remember, no energy is ever lost, merely transformed to another state. Earth assimilates the negative energy, uses it as fuel, and throws it back into your 3-4D world … as weather. Watch the weather, children, and take note when it rages; there you will find your own rage, transformed into the cycles of seasons that grow your sustenance.

Do you now see why each and every human's rising awareness is so vital to the planet? For those of you looking at the current state of global politics and feeling helpless to change anything for the better, we say: think again. Your energy is vital to the whole planet. You can make a difference! A big difference! From our perspective, we stand in awe to watch the healers among you tune into Earth's electromagnetic fields each time you lay on hands. You take on her mantle of grounded energy, which you then pass on to the receiver. Know that you are blessed with Divine grace each time you circumvent logic, follow the path of your heart, and wield the power of the cosmos.

Be the Healing Energy

The old adage "as above, so below" can be applied to your external life, and also to your internal energetic framework. In other words, it is more than a state of being; it is the foundation of your holographic design. You lightworkers can consciously channel divine energy from above and earth energy from below. Know that this is huge power wielded by very tiny tools, which always makes us proud to watch you work. In the face of defiance and ridicule, push on, gentle warriors, for you have Spirit on your side. Hold the new frequency, hold up your light, and let it cast its loving spell wherever you choose to stand. Be the healing energy, feel it like a soft shawl drawn about your shoulders to ward off the chills. This is a cloak of honor you don each time you reach out in God's name to help other human beings on their paths to healing.

Your goal, any goal, is established in order to define the journey to it. The true wealth in life lies in the journey, not in what you amass around you, but what you build within. Wisdom is the soul's true treasure, as is learning about love from life to life. The qualities of love that you create and share, you take back with you to the True Reality of Spirit. Nothing else — the rest is all left behind.

Yet your goal here is assured. No matter what you do or how you do it, God never judges you. All is as it should be. You cannot do it wrong, and you will never finish. That is the nature of a classroom, is it not? One with a kind-hearted teacher. That is the true secret: Put forth your kind heart and all the rest will follow. Engage your heart with every breath, with every thought, and with every motion you make. Your very kindness will protect you against the perceived evil of your world. Again, good and bad are different perspectives on the same whole. If you are thirsty, is not a half cup of water enough to quench your thirst? If you complain that the glass is only half full, you are missing the gift by a mile. Know that the glass will always be full enough to slake your thirst; that is simply faith.

One of the things we find sad in your world is the distorted view of faith. Many people are still locked into specific religions and will not even peek over the box they grew up in. If you would only raise your sight from the dogma that drags you down and separates you from God and look within to find Him. Faith rises above all religions, teaching to all the same thing: love, love, love. Do not feel separate from God; to reach Him, merely close your eyes. Each and every one of you carries Divine Source within.

Do not let religious fervor blind you from God's presence; nothing is sadder than the atrocities done in His name. If you look carefully at the true teachings, they all say the same: honor God, honor thyself, thy family, and friends. Do not kill. Do not lie. Do not envy others for what they have. Stay true to the one God, and He will provide for all of your needs. Has He not done so already, on your beautiful planet Earth? Look around and you will see His hand in the perfection of every detail of life.

So stand up and take pride in being a piece of God! Have you noticed that a prayer sent with devotion and high emotion is much more effective than the quiet begging and pleading you were accustomed to in the old energy? Come stand beside us, metaphysically speaking, and work together with Spirit to bring in the next evolutionary form of humanity. You light-workers are now being fitted with lightbodies.

Reaching this stage has been a long and difficult process. You are the first humans to change your own physical chemistry through intent, through a change in perspective. We praise and marvel at this accomplishment. We wish to help you finish gracefully, in divine timing, and translate up into the next levels of dimensional reality. Then we will be very proud and humbled to mesh with you directly, energy to energy.

Shifting Gracefully with the Millennium Energy

Welcome to the Aquarian Age, the Age of Man. Those of you who chose to stay behind and shine their lights for others are doubly blessed, both for your accomplishments and your sacrifices. Even that is not quite an appropriate word, for "sacrifice" has a negative connotation. In giving up, you move forward more quickly.

Do you follow? We hope you will!

Your lessons are coming in hard and fast now. Be kind to yourselves during this time of fluctuating energy. Rest often to counteract the heavy weight of ascension. Yes, achieving a lightness of being is tiring work! The higher the frequency, the shorter and faster the energy waves that thrum through your bodies. Time is also expanding and contracting, changing in its fluidity as it changes its structure. Even the air itself feels heavy on some days, yet on others, everything sparkles and shimmers with an essence of new energy. This time of "cosmic fitting" is a precious part of the journey. The awakening is always sweet. Again, be kind to yourselves, drink plenty of water, rest often, and take heart despite the heavy, depressing energy shifts you are going through.

As this process accelerates, there will be moments when you must surrender to it and let us help you. Do this through meditation, through sessions with us, by resting, napping, or running the Circle of Grace through your body when you feel tired. Follow your body's feelings as a gentle monitoring system. Tired? Rest. Hungry? Eat. Need to stretch? Go walk. Leave behind the music and the headphones. Pay attention to what is around you. Try to feel the drumbeat of Mother Earth's heart, for her pulse is closer to your own than you realize.

You have many books available to help you along the metaphysical path. It is now time to stop reading and start doing the work! We do not mean here for you to stop studying, learning, and stretching your awareness. That is the soul's purpose of your human existence. What we mean is that now, as you anchor yourself in 4D, Earth's energy is beginning to support those very gifts you have been praying for: the expansion of your senses into full sensory perception, and the added vision of inner light. This will all happen gradually, to allow you no harm in the process.

More and more people are awakening, yet they are metaphysically unaware. Because they do not understand the rising energy and the sensory gifts that it brings, they might think they have gone insane. Look for them, comfort them, and impart your healing energies unto them. Eventually, they will become the devoted zealots who move the cause forward. Once scientists have embraced spirituality, they will be far louder than you are. We repeat, humble, humble, humble. Let them broadcast the news as if they had discovered it themselves. Indeed, in their eyes, they will have [chuckles].

It matters not, as long as you all move forward on the path back to God-self. Once the human consciousness has been fully awakened, then the floodgates will open and the changes will become quite intense. Stand ready, dear ones, and stand steady, holding up your light to show them the way. Ground yourselves well so that you are not knocked off balance by the tidal rush of catch-up seekers. Find your bliss and your perfection along the way, for it is truly the journey that counts. The purpose of all of your human journeying is, simply, learning and growing and expanding until you can once again merge with the I Am All That Is. We know that we will meet you there, for that is our intent.

3

The Mental Body

In this chapter we will discuss the function of the mental body. It is the third layer of the dense etheric body, after physical and emotional. It separates the emotional body from the spiritual body. That is part of your difficulty, dear one, and part of your gift. Inherent in your consciousness is the element of choice, the state of free will that separates you neatly from the other planets and dimensions used for teaching and learning lessons. We will not delve here into the history of the Fall of Man. Though we are spiritual historians, for this work we don the mantles of material mechanics and spiritual surgeons. We focus on how the Fall of Man changed humans and how we can help you return to wholeness. No doubt you are wondering, "How does this affect me?"

We say simply that in the Fall of Man you lost your conscious link to God. Energetically speaking, your descent into a dense physical form lowered and thus limited your sensory range. Due to the Veil of Forgetfulness, you no longer feel God's presence as a physical vibration inside of you while you are awake. You feel a duality instead and think that you exist separately from God, which leaves you open to doubt that He exists. Most other sentient species do feel God's frequency within them and know for sure that God exists. Therefore, doubt and duality are not part of their lesson plan. For them, to break God's Law is a horrible experience, for they are in direct contact at all times with the conscious energy of All That Is.

To help you survive this breach as you became denser beings, your aspects were layered so that each would buffer those on either side. The emotional body, if in direct contact with the spiritual body, would awaken your consciousness too soon and painfully reforge the link before you were ready. Having the mental body layered in between the emotional and spiritual bodies insured that this did not happen. This arrangement served you well through many lifetimes.

Now is the time for you to awaken, to become aware of your total Be—ing, and to begin functioning in the higher reality where your interdimensional body truly resides.

Having the mental body mediate between its adjacent layers is the perfect balance for you to achieve. The mental body was meant to mediate, not to lead. You were designed to respond to stimuli in layers of information. For every situation, the dynamics are absorbed through your physical senses, then processed through your emotional, mental, and spiritual layers. Each layer adds in a level of understanding. Your emotional body processes lessons and comes up with a feeling response. The mental body aims for a logical response, and your spiritual aspect inspires soul advancement through each experience.

In other words, you find synchronicity, self-realization, true health and inner peace when all of your aspects are working together in balance. We call this wholeness, which has been almost impossible to achieve since you have only experienced life through the physical portion of your bodies. You must expand your frame of reference in order to become and live from the perspective of a totally energetic Be-ing that has a physical core. Do you see the higher mindset you need to assume?

Dear ones, wholeness is Oneness with all things, including God.

Before you lost your conscious connection to Spirit, your mental body worked in this way: the left brain directed and carried the awareness of your physical body while the right brain directed and carried the awareness of your auric body. Your mental body was directed by the two halves of your brain working together equally. In other words, you were consciously linked to your body and to your aura simultaneously. In the disconnection, only your conscious connection to the right brain was lost. Though you only feel your physical body, do not worry — your aura is still there, dutifully fulfilling its functions. It is the seat of your imagination, your creativity, your faith, as well as the storehouse of your emotions, stress, and etheric pain.

What remains in your conscious awareness is only your left brain, which controls or directs your physical body. In order to reassimilate or consciously reconnect with your right brain, you must first reprogram your left brain and teach it to be still so that you may stretch and reach for the silent right side. For most of you, this requires a real effort of will because you have lived solely through your left brain for many, many lifetimes.

Now do you see why you developed into left-brained technological societies? It was all you had to work with. The more you grew to depend on technology, the more rigidly linked you became to your mechanized lifestyle. This overuse of the left side of the mental body has forced it to predominate in your recent lives.

Do you understand why imagination, creativity, and faith are such nebulous things, which you find so difficult to tap into? It is because you do not yet have clear, conscious access to your interdimensional aspects. Please, treasure your artists and dreamers. They may not function well according to your left-brain standards, but they are not as incompetent as you think! They may seem wifty and ungrounded, but in reality, they are functioning at a higher level, receiving stimuli from more than just the third dimension. Treasure your children who have imaginary friends and see fairies in the forest. They do see Spirit until someone blindly convinces them it is impossible.

To those dear skeptics, we gently ask: Do you see the flow of this pattern? It is now circling back to you! As Earth rises in frequency, so does all life on Earth. Now that your senses are beginning to flower into full 4D sensory perception, you too may soon see departed loved ones hovering near you and hear voices speaking from other dimensions. What will you do, then? Deny or rejoice? Heaven is a state of consciousness you can achieve while still in body. Regaining conscious awareness of the right brain's link to your aura reforges that lost link to your own Higher Self and thus to Spirit.

How do you accomplish this? You must make a big leap of faith here to reawaken and rejoin your true self. Your bible says, "Unless you are converted and become like children, you will not enter the kingdom of heaven" [Matthew 18:13, NASB]. Be fearless, be open-minded, be aware of every moment, and find joy and wonder in all that surrounds you. To children, all time is now time. Learn to live in the now, as we do, and we will find each other!

The Circle of Grace Exercise and the Mental Body

In the first chapter, we said that the balanced Circle of Grace pattern goes up the dominant side of the body, circles around the head and goes back down the other side. When the energy reaches the top of the head, a separate circle begins to pulse around the crown, which can now be explained.

This stimulation of the crown chakra is reawakening the right brain connection and balancing right brain to left brain. Remember that we said that the Circle of Grace helps each layer process pain, then clear and balance? When you enter the Circle, be aware of the separate circular pulsing around the top of your head. For the mental body, this is a vital part of the new human awakening. If you fall asleep at night while doing the Circle of Grace, even better. It will continue through the night, magnified by your awareness and now your new instructions.

The meridian around the crown has another very practical purpose. It acts as a circuit breaker for the rest of the meridian system so that blockages cannot back up and lodge in the crown chakra. So there forms a horizontal circle above the ears, as if you were wearing a hat, beyond which blockages cannot rise. That is where the greatest internal pressure of the meridian system occurs. That is also why some of you have strokes that occur at ear level around the head. We remind you, emphatically, that much damage from internal pressure must accumulate before a health threat of that magnitude strikes the body. The judicious and steady use of the Circle of Grace exercise plus healing sessions with us, your loving guardians, will prevent that damage from accumulating even if it is a hereditary pattern. Remember, hereditary patterns only arise when auric illness reaches your physical core.

What is your biggest challenge at the mental level? Quieting your left-brain-dominant mental body in order to awaken your dormant right-brain connection. Too much chatter from the mental body monopolizes your daily awareness. Too many mental distractions prevent you from connecting with the earth, feeling in harmony with all life, and remembering who you are. Television has you as a captive audience, telling you what to wear, eat, buy, be, like, and want.

Do you realize how much power is in those air waves? But — cosmic humor here — you have the ultimate power. Turn off the television and go for a walk. Read a book in a silent room that allows you full focus. Meditating in the Circle of Grace flow every day, even for only thirty minutes, will calm you, release your stress, and energize you at the same time. And it's noninvasive!

In our sessions together we offer you a simple way to quiet the left brain. Put it in charge of reporting aloud to us what you feel. Give it this task and no other. You will find yourself floating in the warmth of your new, extended body. You may feel as if your outer skin is expanding to a bigger size. Your mental focus on what is happening inside your body will eventually link you to your entire being, both physical and auric halves, in proper balance. Then you will truly grow into the new expression of man's potential to become an energetic human.

The Circle of Grace works for each layer of the body in a specific way. For the mental body, the left brain is given a rest from its laundry list of mundane tasks. It is a letting go of your temporary duality and its many details. That is how the Circle of Grace relieves stress in the mental body. While the left brain is resting within its inner focus, it cannot get in your way, making it easier to rebuild a rapport with your right brain. This is also when you have the best inner growth, when the emotional and spiritual bodies intertwine to nourish each other with loving energy.

So bring us your aches and pains, yes, but also your questions, hopes, and dreams. Voice them to us, and we will help bring them in. Bring us the concepts you wish to assimilate, the questions you have regarding your life, your purpose, your progress. Don't forget that healing must occur on all levels. Once you lie down, all we ask is that you track the energy flows through your body and express aloud to us what you feel as you feel it. Your verbal feedback will help guide our work. If you fall asleep quickly at the start of the session, don't think you missed it! In some cases, we choose sleep for you while addressing deep-set physical and auric blockages that might cause you discomfort if you were awake.

Since you are multilayered beings, we Brothers work in specialized groups that address the needs of each layer. Since we exist in now time, all of our work is happening simultaneously. We apply the higher frequencies of love throughout your spiritual layer to revitalize your other layers. We teach your mental body to relinquish total control, and ease it back into its true functions of observing and advising your other aspects. We energize the emotional body, which triggers the release of stress-pressure from your energetic meridians into your physical nervous system. At the same time, we open your physical meridians at your feet, hands, and crown to flush pressure from your core and replenish your system with new energy.

At the end of each session, we tune up your aspects so they work better together, nudging them gently into a new configuration of energetic awareness. If this sounds like a repeating round robin, well, it is! All of life is based on the circle. It is the basic shape of the flower of life, the basic shape of all life everywhere.

Communicating with Your Aura

As you expand your awareness beyond the limited notion that your body is your entire being, you will grow to understand that all of your physical functions are mirrored in your auric field. Just as the body needs to assimilate nourishment and excrete waste, the emotional, mental, and spiritual layers of your aura also take in energetic fuel and create energetic debris. This waste material accumulates in your aura, forming pockets of etheric pressure that have mass and density. Pain within the physical core also accumulates in pockets of dense etheric matter that the body must deal with as a physical intrusion.

Similarly, once you understand that thoughts and emotions have mass and density in your auric layers, it will become easier for you to stay in the higher octaves of love rather than the lower aspects of fear with all of its negative effects. One octave will just feel good and the other bad. Not that we want to stress a judgment here, but it is your association with feeling good and bad that will identify the quality of what is happening around you at each moment. We ask that you rely on your feelings to guide the actions of your logical mental body.

You call this aspect of your awareness intuition. It is not tangible guidance, for it does not spring in words from your mental body. This information originates from the emotional layer of your auric field, which is currently invisible and inaudible to you. Your emotional body communicates with you through feelings. That's why learning to listen to your intuition is so important. Learn to rely on the signals from your emotional body to mediate between your mental body and your physical body. If you only follow the guidance of your mental body without adding a dose of love from the emotional body, your physical action will be cold and precise but devoid of feeling. Do you see how all four PEMS layers are vital to the proper functioning of your whole Be-ing?

Please, dear one, learn to lead with your heart. Pass every mental thought through your heart chakra, or visualize your upper chest with both physical heart and emerging spiritual heart chakras working together, side by side. This new expanded heart center is the fulcrum from which your lower three chakras and upper three chakras will achieve a higher balance. In the new heart-based energetic signature you are developing, we ask you to lead with your heart to best balance the flowering of your gifts.

In the beginning of this chapter, we said that the mental body mediates between the emotional and spiritual body layers. In the previous paragraph, we said that the emotional body must mediate between the mental and physical bodies so that all of your thoughts and deeds are of a positive, loving nature. Do you see why it is difficult to separate or differentiate between the layers? Though each has a specific function, the health of the body depends on all the layers working together in synchronicity.

We call the totality of this waking meditation. Life is a meditation. Once you learn to balance all of your PEMS aspects, they will come forth in Divine grace, each buffering the one on either side, all working together in harmony. If this sounds complicated, do not worry. All of your aspects have been working without your conscious knowledge. Even as you become aware of them, they will continue their functions. They will not suddenly stop and wait until you issue direct commands. They are ongoing, as are all parts of you that form your individual whole.

This thought paradigm also applies to the Circle of Grace. It is the body's natural cleansing process that occurs while you sleep. Becoming conscious of it means joining your physical body in the process with a new awareness perspective. Observe the sensations, and you will become intimate with your own energetic system. You will learn to lie down and clear yourself as the need arises, getting rid of bad things that happen rather than stuffing them away and accumulating more etheric pressure. This energetic baggage collects in your aura as pockets of stress linked to specific chakras or areas of the body in lesson.

Remember, thoughts and emotions have physical weight and density in your aura, just as pain lodges as a solid mass in your body. Now that you are becoming more sensitive to the shifting frequencies of the planet, you will learn the truth of this for yourself soon enough.

Living in Awareness

Are you beginning to understand the association between the different PEMS layers of your entire Be-ing? You are now at a level of more intense learning. First you walked the material path in order to find the spiritual path, then to find us, your devoted guides, waiting to welcome you to the higher realms. These new lessons are internal ones, as you become aware of all of your multidimensional aspects. Once you reach full self-awareness, you will reconfigure your aspects to suit your sense of comfort. Some of you live more in the mental body; some live more in the emotional body. The athletes among you identify themselves through the assets and accomplishments of the physical body. The infinite variety of human expression is one of your most wonderful attributes!

Your experiences up the human spiral of evolution have taken thousands of years to unfold. In this millennium time, you are on the verge of a totally new level of life experience. In the historical progress of humanity's evolution, you first had to learn survival and then how to succeed in life until you began to develop a quest for higher purpose. You had to grow into your layers, first physical (survival), then life (emotional and mental), and then quest (spiritual). Finally, now that you are ready comes the potential for full integration of all facets of self. You are growing into a true energetic being, into your full eternal Be-ing while still in a human body.

"How," you ask, "is all of this done?" Dear one, we say again, learn to lead with your heart. Whatever thought you have, pass it through your heart before it passes your lips. If it constricts your heart in pain, do not say those words. Choose better words, more appropriate to Higher Self, words that make you feel lighthearted.

Light of heart, light of mind, light of body, light of God.

That is the progression, and you have progressed well! As you cycled through centuries of lifetimes, you worked on different lessons, different aspects of being, and different qualities of love that your soul sought to learn. You have withstood many wars and gained many lessons, difficult as they were. For those of you awakened and aware, those lessons no longer need repeating. Unfortunately, not enough of you fit yet into this mindset. Even on the verge of this New Age of humankind, there is still war, poverty, starvation, and disease rampant on your planet. Since it is mostly in Third World countries, you do not see it every day; it is easy to forget or ignore. You do not need to take on their burdens, except for this: Be aware of all of it.

Know that a simple daily prayer, just a few moments of visualizing the downtrodden as healthy and joyous, will help to bring in that potential reality. Picture Earth as clean and shining and healthy, spinning through space like a bright blue jewel. If all people did this for a moment each day, imagine how quickly your world would change! Know that all people need uplifted. For each of you who becomes aware, a dozen more of you step closer to that same reality. In time, the shift will reach its own exponential curve and then the global changes will come in much faster.

Now is the time to prepare, learn, grow, and work together. The stronger the energy grows, the more psychic you become. Stay fluid, open, and aware as you flower into full sensory perception. This, dear children, is reuniting with God. Remember, you are not alone in this. The closer you climb in resonance to our dimension, the more we will be able to interact with you and help pull you up energetically to join us. On some days, the energy will set your teeth on edge, and on other days, you will be quiet or bone-tired. The inconsistency is the worst part; you yearn for stability right now, for an end from the heavy pressure. Lightworkers, you must clear yourselves first before you can help others. The Circle of Grace will help awaken your senses and align the energies of your body in an exquisite spiritual attunement. If you consciously participate in this process with us, you will feel your own little miracles happening within you, where your divinity truly lies.

Merging into 4D

When we say that you are in 4D, know that 3D expanded into 3-4D in May 2000. We remind you that your Higher Self chose to incarnate during these monumental earth changes. Your solar system is changing, as is your galaxy and all the other levels beyond. Those people who are unenlightened and unaware will continue to function in 3D. You light-workers and seekers are now expanding into 4D, consciously, along with the planet. We await you in 5D, which because of the great shift, is also expanding outward.

If you cannot grasp this concept yet, we remind you of two things: All are one, and all changes together. As you rise through the dimensions, you will realize that 4D includes 3D and 5D includes 3D and 4D. In other words, all dimensions coexist in the same space simultaneously, separated by their different bands of frequency. Your rise is actually an expansion outward to a wider vibratory frequency range. That is why people in 3D will not perceive the next levels of awareness, even though you will see those people clearly and interact with them from your expanded view. In the same way, every healing session with us is an altered state in which we gently guide you into that higher range and tune you up slowly to the new frequencies.

Some of you may be asking, "How can this be going on if most people aren't even aware of it?" We answer with this image: picture a neighborhood street. In every house there is at least one television set. When cable TV becomes available, some people buy it and some people don't. Some people buy satellite dishes and get lots of new TV stations in a different way. What each person chooses to do with their TV set defines which stations they receive. Choosing not to install anything will limit your TV set to a few dozen public stations.

Do you see the different levels? You have the power to choose. First, though, you have to be aware that there are choices available. That is your absolute first step, which you have accomplished through seeking information, going to seminars and lectures, and reading many texts, fiction, non-fiction, channeled, non-channeled. Choices, you see? So many choices at so many levels. But if you are not even aware that these choices exist, you cannot take that first step up the metaphysical path.

Remember, that step and every subsequent step must be made on all levels, physical, emotional, mental, and spiritual. Think of yourself as a blended PEMS Be-ing, one that can tune into many different frequencies of existence at once. You see, you are your own TV set! What enters your mind and guides your life can only expand as far and as fast as your mental framework of reference will allow.

Welcome the new energy. Go to your job every day as usual, but heighten your perspective by opening up your senses. See the flowers along the road, admire trees along the way, breathe deeply as you wait at the red light. Expand your awareness into each and every moment. Can you do this? Yes, of course you can! You are created in the image of God, the ultimate Creator. You too have His creator powers. You are so much more powerful than you realize!

In order to retrain your left brain and augment your right-brain connection, we ask you to simply practice being aware. Be aware of how you speak to people, be aware of how food tastes, be aware of how sunshine gleams on your lover's hair. Enjoy every moment, savor each breath you take, see the divine all around you.

When you go to sleep at night, join us in a Circle dance. Let us help you to advance. Be aware of the blood flowing in your veins, be aware of the pulsing of your heart, focus on your breathing. Let your thoughts slide away and float as a consciousness on the inner sea of your body. The journey upward is inward. The best thing to learn is not to get in your own way! Strive for balance, reach for a kinder tone, be like unto Earth's own heartbeat.

We speak here of merging. The more you merge your awareness into all that is around you, the higher your awareness will take you. Practice first before you take off and fly. When we speak of All That Is, we speak of God. Do you now understand this perspective? Being aware, every second, is living in the now. Once you master that, you can begin to affect all that is around you — specifically time — past, present, and future.

Back to the circle, children! There are no accidents at this level. What you will see is the emergence of synchronicity. Watch for it; it will happen more and more around you. Once you begin to rely on it, then you will have arrived! Where? Arrived at true faith.

Put up a bird feeder near to a window where you can watch, for the birds have a vital lesson to teach. They are tiny messengers of Spirit, showing the cycle of abundance that keeps them fed through the seasons of their little lives. When your bird feeder is full, they arrive and sing to their friends that breakfast has been served. If you forget to fill the feeder, they fly by and sing a sweet complaint for their friends to move on. They are tiny and fragile, yet all around them is food. Mother Earth nurtures them and keeps them fed. They survive every day, happily singing their messages of loving abundance back and forth in the trees above your heads. Have you noticed?

Be like the little birds. Arise each day knowing that your needs will be met. Once you can do this and truly believe it, what you desire will come true. That is living in true faith. The energy within you will rise exponentially from your efforts, and others will feel it. Wherever you go, walk in strength and vitality. Be aware of your body, your emotions, your thoughts, and your faith, all swirling around you in gentle layers of invisible, silken energy. The more you reach for wholeness, the more you feel it and the more quickly it will happen. Once your mental body has fully accepted this perspective and begins to function from this perspective, your entire Be-ing will shift accordingly, from physical 3-4D human to energetic 4-5D human.

The entire Millennium Shift and the ascension of humans to light-body form happen together when you blend all of your aspects, become reconnected to your total energetic being, and begin to function as Higher Self. In other words, you must catch up physically with all of the spiritual knowledge you have gained thus far. None of it will work until you start living it on all levels. You can and will change your inner chemistry through a new, higher perspective of being reconnected to your eternal self and therefore to God.

We come back to the beginning, as a circle always does. We said that your challenge had been created by disconnecting your conscious awareness of Spirit and that you must now find it again. We explained what this process feels like and how you can participate in discovering and actively honing your spirituality.

You can also think of this process as living every moment with a love-filled heart. Once you begin, it will become easy, it will feel right. You will feel much better than you have felt in a long time. Use the Circle of Grace to regain and maintain your health, to keep yourself balanced and energized. Use the Circle of Grace in your healing work to find and release blockages and to help others regain their health and balance. Teach them how to be self-healing, how to have mastery over their health, their energy levels, and their lives. Teach them the Circle of Grace.

You will achieve a higher state of being by going within. You will regain your conscious connection to Spirit by looking within. You have already affected the balance of the New Age, bringing it in with ease and grace. We are so proud of your accomplishments! Your ascension will affect all of the dimensions beyond yours, as any shift affects the whole. For all of the help that we offer, you are doing the hardest portion of this divine work. We of the Brotherhood of Light are grateful, honored, and humbled to serve as your guides.

(4)

The Spiritual Body

In this chapter, we will endeavor to explain the workings of the spiritual body. It is the fourth outermost layer of your dense etheric body, which is comprised of physical, emotional, mental, and spiritual aspects (PEMS). The spiritual layer is set furthest away from the physical core, separated by the emotional and mental bodies. We previously explained that if the spiritual body were layered against the emotional body, it would be impossible for you to maintain the Veil of Forgetfulness. It would be ripped away long before you were ready, causing you pain and harm in the harsh reconnection to Spirit.

In the first chapter, we stated that true healing will become simple when science and spirituality meet and merge. We also said that true healing is attainable with the help of three different types of healing practitioners: medical, psychological, and energetic.

Now we add that all of this, the healing and the not-healing, is directed by the spiritual body. The main function of the spiritual body is to learn life lessons, and its programming is your lesson plan. These lessons are what you, in your eternal Spirit form, direct to happen in each lifetime.

Reincarnation works in three energetic stages: Spirit conceptualizes, the body actualizes, and then the soul synthesizes. You go into body to create situations needed to further your soul's evolution toward reunion with

Spirit. Here is a simple example: for those of you dealing with an addiction to nicotine, you must stop smoking tobacco while you are in body. If not, that physical addiction continues back to Spirit with you, unresolved. You cannot smoke a cigarette if you do not have a body. The physical addiction must be dealt with in body, or carried over as a lesson in the next lifetime to face again and finish.

For the purpose of the Circle of Grace work, we Brothers see ourselves as material mechanics, teachers of how things work in the True Reality of Spirit. We will not elaborate on the whys, wherefores, and specific details of philosophy or history. That is why we mention things such as the Fall of Man and do not offer a long explanation. That you can find easily elsewhere and draw your own conclusions — that is exercising your free will. We strive here to explain to you how things work energetically and lead you with grace and ease into a higher frequency of existence.

Leading with Your Spiritual Body

As you know, your conscious mind operates very differently from your unconscious mind. In the same way, your emotional body processes incoming stimuli and produces an emotional response while the mental body takes that same stimuli and offers a logical response. Do you see why two people may react so very differently to the same thing? One may constantly lead with their mental body, and the other with their emotional body. Indeed, that is the main difference in perspective between men and women [chuckles].

Those leading with their spiritual bodies, however, stay calm and observant. They survey the situation and absorb the reactions of their other layers — physical, emotional, and mental. Having brought all layers into balance, the spiritual person then speaks truth as he or she sees it, clear of ego or drama. Those parts have been absorbed and processed, leading to the spiritually correct response directed by the heart.

So learn to respond rather than react. What is the difference? About ten seconds is needed to process at all levels and then speak clearly. Do you realize that when you react to something, you are matching that vibration? If anger is directed toward you and you react in anger, no good can come of that moment. If you pause, rationalize, emotionalize, then pass it through your heart (energetically speaking), your heart will always lead you true and your answer will always be loving. Each and every one of you is in body to further soul growth in order to return and reunite with Spirit.

As you progress through the levels of life lessons, you will gain new understanding and compassion for people blindly stuck in their drama. The higher your personal vibration rises, the more sensitive you will become to those with discordant energy. You will feel it instantly, not with your everyday physical senses, but with your energetic layers. Your aura is normally three to six feet all around you, depending on whether it is expanded or contracted. It also stretches above and below your physical core, creating an oval sphere of electromagnetic energy that is truly your outer skin. If you stretch out your arms, you will transverse the diameter of your dense etheric body. When someone approaches, your two auras meet at six feet apart from your physical cores. That is when you begin to "read" a person and formulate how well your frequency matches theirs.

Do you realize that first impressions come from your aura? From your spiritual layer! When you get goose bumps, as you call them, what happens? An uncomfortable feeling slides over your skin (incompatible frequency) that raises your hairs on end (outer physical response), and then your gut tightens (inner physical response). Do you see the direction of this warning feeling? It flows from the outside in. It flows from your spiritual layer, through your logic and your emotion, and then into your body as a physical warning that something approaching is not compatible or is not in harmony with your greatest good. On the other hand, you will also feel when a person with a very compatible frequency approaches you. First impressions actually occur before you get close enough to shake hands.

Back in the days when you were scraping for survival and hiding from larger beasts, your auric radar was a very vital part of your consciousness; it saved your life many a time. Now, as you grow more civilized and approach a new level of evolution, you are becoming sensitized to new levels of reality, of information, of sensation. You are beginning to feel and communicate with your aura and thus with Spirit!

Blending Spirituality with Religion

Please remember that no energy is ever wasted. All is recorded by the spiritual body, both the incoming data and the backlash of the individual's physical, emotional, and mental reactions to the stimulus or situation. That is how the soul learns and grows. That is how your akashic records are compiled. Many of you are struggling to reconcile this new information from Spirit with your prior beliefs about God and faith. Part of the problem you now have with established religions is the blind-faith aspect that lingers from fear-based patterns of earlier times. You were required to believe whatever religious pattern you were born into, and there was usually grave punishment for those who did not.

Now you are reaching for new, higher truths and find your feet entangled in the old ways. Keep the best of what you like and kick the rest away! Faith is an internal quest, never beholden to another person. Those old traditions also contradict the freewill zone that sets you apart from all other sentient species in lesson.

You were meant to decide for yourself whether or not to believe in God and choose for yourself how to express that belief.

How does each life, and its lessons learned (or not learned), culminate in who you are today? All of your lifetimes of experience are recorded by your spiritual layer. When you wrestle with your lessons, you are actually trying to bring your emotional and mental aspects into balance, a balance dictated by your spiritual layer. How is this done? Through your intent! We find it humorous that your scientists have puzzled out about 5 percent of your DNA patterns and have labeled the other 95 percent junk DNA. Not junk, dear one, but your own personal akashic records, chock-full of vital wisdom and talents stored at the cellular level that make you who you are today. You carry your own spiritual blueprint within every cell of your body. One day you will access this information and truly understand who you are, and the way things really work in the True Reality of Spirit.

A Higher Perspective

Many sources have given good counsel and direction as to how to become more spiritual, how to identify and learn your lessons in order to move forward, and how to achieve clarity, balance, and self-realization. We seek to explain how things work in energetic terms to help you understand the role that your spiritual layer plays in your life.

In order to fully focus on each physical lifetime, you had to separate your physical identity from the expanded reality around you. The rules of your created reality-duality matrix limit your perception of who you are. As a result, you have had no conscious contact with the higher dimensions or with the higher aspects of your total being. Here, we will endeavor to show you the difference between human and spiritual perspectives on what constitutes reality.

To you, Earth is a huge, vast space, almost too big to comprehend. To us, you have been in a narrow corridor of heavy density and linear time. You are in lesson. You are in the reality-duality matrix. You are in ongoing levels of study, working on different issues throughout each lifetime.

To you, a lifetime is rather long. Modern science has extended life expectancy — not near your full potential yet, but still a vast improvement on the first millennium. To us, the passage of a human life is very quick, a morsel of your true existence. It saddens us how you worry so about death, but that is part of the setup, is it not? You see death as a painful drama, with mourning and weeping. We say, do so if you must, and cry your fill with gusto. You must shed those tears to get past them. Then move on, for you are still among the living. Take comfort that you will see your loved ones again, soon.

Know that on our side, there is a glorious reunion for your loved one, a party for the homecoming soul. There is no judgment but a private life review that only he or she observes. Each person decides how well he or she did and chooses which unfinished lessons to carry over into the next life.

In the meantime, they have much to do when they return home to the higher realms. In Spirit, we (and you) lead busy, active lives, full of purposeful activities. We have families here too, often comprised of souls who did their best to "push your buttons" down on Earth. That, dear hearts, is being in lesson. When you reunite in the True Reality of Spirit, you thank each other for jobs well done and lessons learned together. Often, the most bitter enemies in human form are tight brothers in eternal form.

This information is offered in the hopes of expanding your understanding of the higher realms. Now that you are beginning to realize that your inner world leads to the higher worlds, it should give you more impetus to meditate, especially now as the energy changes all around you are increasing. The planetary frequency is rising, and more and more divine light is coming to Earth. We in the higher planes are getting ready to welcome you. You will feel us more and more as time increases the exponential currents of change.

The Circle of Grace Exercise and Your Spiritual Body

The changing energy is all around you, inside you, above you, and below you. Pay attention, children, to Mother Earth as she rises up toward her own ascension. Your spiritual aspect is now being energized and awakened, and it will be greatly aided by using the Circle of Grace — yes, back to our clearing process and how it helps your spiritual body. While balancing your other aspects (physical, emotional, and mental), the Circle of Grace activates your slumbering spiritual gifts and awakens your dormant connection to Spirit. We admit to being impatient for you to achieve this, for you are getting close!

The energy right now is frenetic, jagged, too fast, too slow, no time, no rest, and no consistency. Carve out a few moments each day, a half-hour if you can. Lie down and slip into the circle of energy that animates your body. For those of you lucky to have more time, an hour-long session is most effective. For those of you with no time, start the Circle of Grace as you're going to sleep and know that we will intensify your natural clearing through the night.

You will feel an increase in energy, an easing of stress, a sharpening of the senses, and a rise in synchronicity in your life. Whatever happens around you, pause and seek the lesson. Ask yourself, why did that happen? Why did the universe see fit to remove this from me? To inflict this on me? To destroy this thing I cherished, or steal this tender life I loved? Why? It is all part of your lessons.

You will all reunite in the True Reality of Spirit soon enough. No energy is ever wasted or terminated; life is merely transformed. In the case of the Earth plane, you translate in and out by inhabiting a physical body, entering at birth and exiting at death. Before you are born, we bid you a fond farewell, and wish you Godspeed through your lessons [chuckles].

We eagerly await your return, which is far more joyous a process than you realize. It is the birth that is hard for us, the coming down of the Veil, the separation from you that we in Spirit find so difficult to bear.

Death, on the other hand, is your triumphant return Home. That is all it is, merely an exit, a release, a respite, a relief, a transmutation of your life force. You never lose consciousness. You switch over to your full auric self by pulling your energetic body out of its physical shell. Dear ones, whether you come home with or without that body, you return equally triumphant.

The Veil of Forgetfulness and Your Spiritual Body

At the soul level, you agreed to certain built-in safeguards to the Veil of Forgetfulness that have kept you locked in the duality perspective of 3D. First, there is a hard-wired connection between the soul and the body it inhabits. You are designed to be terrified of losing your body, letting go of it or leaving it, so it may be difficult at first to assimilate these new expanded concepts. Actually climbing in and out of your body might seem ridiculous to you, but you've done it many times, at birth and death and in between.

The second overriding rule is: No conscious connection to Spirit. That is how the Veil functions in 3D. We are beyond the Veil, in the True Reality. Though we see you clearly, you are blind to our presence in the upper dimensions. In order for this planet's intricate tapestry of karmic reincarnation to unfold, you have been kept unaware, until recently, of the higher realms and of your potential to "be in this world but not of it."

Up until now, the Veil of Forgetfulness has functioned as a separation mechanism that supports the parameters of your freewill zone. We will explain the energetics of this process in a later chapter, but for now, we say: The Veil is a filtering mechanism that limits your sensory range to the physical parameters of your 3D reality while blocking your sensory input from the dimensions existing beyond 3D.

As a 3D human, you did not know or need to know who your Higher Self is, who your real Spirit family is. You did not know what lies on the other side of death, nor could you know of the work your Higher Self does while your body and conscious mind are asleep. Many of you still do not know for sure if God exists, for that is the goal you must achieve on your own — free will — your choice. Do you see how the Veil affects and directs your life? It has kept the third dimension in place, separating what you know from who we (and you) really are in the True Reality of Spirit.

There are many among you who do not know that they do Spirit work at night. They can move their consciousnesses fully into their auras, or astral selves. They can exit the body and move freely in the upper realms while the body and conscious mind are asleep. You may have no waking recollection of having been out of body because of the Veil. But for those of you who have flying dreams or falling dreams, you were either out of body or returning.

Why do you think that nobody really knows what happens to you after you die? It is the Veil of Forgetfulness at work. The limitations of 3D require that you cannot remember any part of Spirit life, none of it. Again, this would only confuse you and pull your focus away from the here and now. Though most of these old reality parameters are changing with your expansion into 4D, focusing on the now is something that you already do. You are accustomed to being blind to all but your present moment in time. Bound by linear time, the past and future are inaccessible to you. Do you see the cosmic humor here, dear ones? You already live in the now; you just don't realize it.

As you rise into the awareness of being in 4-5D the Veil will get thinner, allowing your senses to pick up information that was previously beyond your reach. To avoid the confusion of sensory overload, we ask you to consciously focus on your present moment and to be present in every moment. The best way to get through life is to focus on the here and now. Focusing on the past is a waste of energy, pure and simple. The ingredients needed to sever past ties? Compassion and forgiveness for all those concerned — including yourself! — and for all that has happened to you. Both have molded you into the particular consciousness that you are today.

Remember, no energy is ever wasted. All of this information is encoded in your DNA, your personal list of past lives: all that you were, all that you did, all that you learned, all the different ways in which you died. Cellular memory is an intrinsic part of the ascension process. Your own ancient knowledge will surface as you establish communication with your higher aspects. To the beginning student, all of this information might seem a bit unwieldy. To the devoted seeker, a recapitulation of what you already know. Even if there is only one new idea — one thought of ours that you walk away with — that is good. You will find that each time you read this text, new information will come forward that you need at that time.

Some of you may be thinking, "If this is all just a big game and I don't really die, then I can commit suicide and just go Home, right?" Sorry, no. There is no escape clause in the human contract. That is, for most cases. Yet, if it is part of the lesson plan, if the family has contracted to study the waste of human life, to generate love in the face of adversity, and to learn to hold all life sacred, then that suicide has spiritual purpose and will happen. In most cases, those who choose to end their lives rather than work out their lessons must repeat that aborted life and face the same choices again.

Adjusting to the New Frequencies of Energy

Right now for you on Earth, time is compressing due to the influx of new energetic frequencies. As the energy rises and becomes palpable, so will your aura. Once you start to feel the presence of your etheric layers you will require a new comfort zone, a new higher balance that is heart-centered. Anything that goes against your heart will become painful. At the physical level, you will begin to feel those overpressurized parts of your body that need clearing. At the emotional, mental, and spiritual levels, you will feel the damaging effects of stress. Dear one, in order to achieve true healing, you must release those things in your life that cause you stress at all levels.

You cannot begin to solve the problems that you have not faced. These problems will keep circling back to you, time and again, until you identify and take responsibility for them. Especially now, as time shortens, the lessons are getting more drastic. Pay attention, define, and embrace the lessons; walk through them and leave them behind.

The rising energy will allow no less. It can be so frenetic at times that you cannot even focus to meditate as you used to. Do not despair and do not give up. Simply lie down and do the Circle of Grace. Again, the way up is within. What better way to get there? Float on the cadence of your heartbeat, match your breath to Earth's pulse, and call up your healing circle of universal energy to clear, cleanse, and energize your body at all levels.

Know that time will eventually stabilize into a new circular configuration. You will be able to work with it, around it, and through it. Time is only another aspect of energy. It is the aspect that measures the continuous changing of energy. To us, True Reality is constantly changing, so we see time as variable. That is why we have the freedom to live in the now. You will, in time (chuckles), grow to understand that broader perspective.

Many of you are impatient to move forward into the new energy. As your concerned guides, we ask you first to gain your balance, then learn to stand and walk before you start running. Some people wake up one day and declare, "I've decided to devote my life to holistic practices." Then they panic, because they've never even entertained the idea before. These are the newly awakened, the wave after the millennium. You older light-workers of the wave before, who have bravely volunteered to stay, will find these youngsters strewn on your path like so many lost lambs. Most of them will be young adults in their twenties, newly disillusioned by life from the adult view. Take them under your wing and show them how much more there really is to life on planet Earth.

Then there are the new children. Watch for the Blues, now called In-digo. You have labeled them as ADD/ADHD — dysfunctional children needing medication and remediation. In truth, these children are prodigies. They come in with all the spiritual tools you aspire to: living in the now, self-worth, multitasking, experiential thinking, and visualization far beyond what you can do today. They can conceptualize something into existence by creating it mentally, then simply make the finished product. These children with attention deficit disorder are the first rank of spiritually advanced humans to be born on this planet in all of your recorded history.

Find every receptive teacher that you can and explain to them about this higher class of kids. Give them the right tools to handle these new children, and theirs will be a glorious teaching experience. Nurture these children, be kind to them, but do not patronize them. Treat them with respect and they will respect you back. These are little adults with a far higher perspective than you were born with. For them, the Veil is thinner. Teach them that there is value in everything they do. Teach them to meditate, to be still, and to rest there awhile. Teach them the Circle of Grace.

Bridging the Dimensions

What comes after the spiritual layer? Those aspects beyond your dense etheric body are much finer, you could say diaphanous, because of the higher frequencies that place your outer layers in 5D and above. The form and function of your entire energetic Be-ing is beyond the scope of this text, but we will say that you are much, much larger than you know! There are inner aspects of you tied deep into the planet, and outer aspects of you that reach out into space past your globe.

Surrounding your planet is a very, very distant aspect of you, all of you, forming an energetic ring that you call the human consciousness. It reaches out to the universe in an energetic signature that speaks of humanity to other races in the multitude of universes that comprise the collective body of God. Oh yes, your signature is becoming apparent to the higher realms as the incoming divine light strengthens and adds power to your distinctive human energetic imprint. One could say that you have made the first step toward becoming a global presence to other global presences around you.

Do you follow? We hope you will!

There is still much work to do. We are glad to say that the shift's momentum is increasing, as are the many new experiences you are having in the fourth dimension. That is where you are now, in the psychic corridor between the third and fifth dimensions. Many of you are beginning to feel a flowering of the senses, an opening to new stimuli with a hazy frequency, still distorted as the channel is not fully tuned in yet. With the exponential curve of time, this awakening will become more widespread and miracles will become more abundant in your news.

Why will some come into awareness and others not? Remember, all dimensions occupy the same space yet exist as separate bands of frequency: 3D is included in 4D, and 3D and 4D are both included in 5D. From where we sit, we can see all these levels and more. From where you sit, you can only see the levels that you are keyed into. Once you are fully anchored in 4D, you will still see and interact with people in 3D. Those in 3D, however, cannot see past their own frequency range; they will remain unaware of 4-5D until their senses also expand.

The closer you get to matching your energy to the higher levels, the closer you will get there physically. When you work with us in healing sessions, bring us this concept and any others that require help to assimilate. Growth in understanding is crucial to heal and meld each layer of your energetic body. Please, see yourself as an eternal energetic Be-ing with a temporary physical core. Then your comprehension of metaphysics will leap forward quickly.

Once you learn the function and balance of each of your aspects, you will ease your way into a new higher reality. When your mental body understands its place and purpose, a new balance will be within your reach. You will learn how to combine the emotional body with its driving fuel of feelings to the spiritual body with its pure faith. Once Earth's energies rise enough to pierce through the 4-5D frequency barrier, or null zone, you will emerge as a consciously energetic Be-ing. You will be strong enough to heal, to manifest instantly, and to become consciously interdimensional.

So what is the true role of the mental body? It creates the thought form for the prayer (spiritual layer) that is fueled by feelings (emotional layer). Then the mental layer must get out of the way. You are so used to leading with logic that you discount the power of faith plus feeling. You have no idea of your true power.

We ask those of you doubters who insist on physical proof for everything, how do you then explain your faith? If you say, "Oh, that's different," then we will gently disagree. It is the same. It is the other side of the same coin. It is science and spirituality, physics and metaphysics. The answer lies in learning both sides and then learning how to merge them. It will take mutual acceptance, plus the integration of science and spirituality, to find the real truth and proof that God exists. That proof exists in your cells as patterns of sentient, energetic holograms waiting to be discovered and deciphered.

Once you begin to physically merge all that you've learned with All That Is, you will find us waiting! We will help you to finish your assimilation of the new energies, leading to a higher realm of existence on Earth. Keep in mind that Heaven is not a physical place but rather a state of consciousness. Your spiritual progress will lead you to a new life in 5D, where you will, indeed, create heaven on earth.

As your loving guides, we wait impatiently for our reunion with you in the True Reality of Spirit!

(5)

Twelve Steps to a Lighter Body

What to Ask for in Healing Sessions with the Brothers

A Poem to Invoke the Brotherhood of Light

I ask the Brothers, "Work with me."
I ask for health and clarity.
I will my light to shine clear bright,
All day long and through the night.
I ask that Spirit walk with me,
From Now through all Eternity.

—SARA

I n this chapter, we move on to discuss what to expect in a healing session with us, what to ask us for, and in what order. Know that you could be in need of much clearing, but we cannot help you without being asked to step in. Here we stride on to the turf of permission, which defines the parameters of your freewill zone. The overriding rule is that of non-interference, which Spirit has always upheld. We have endeavored to explain in energetic terms why you are in charge of your life. Whether you know it or not, you con-

Twelve Steps to a Lighter Body

Please note: These stages of healing are meant to be done in the order that they are presented here. Also, when asking anything from Spirit, include the words "gently and gracefully," for the power of Spirit can be much greater than the expectations of the physical body.

1) Repolarization — ask to be repolarized at all levels

2) Clear and balance the energetic meridians

3) Clear and balance the energy centers (chakras)

4) Clear and balance the lower three chakras to the upper three with the heart as the new fulcrum

5) Clear and balance the physical heart chakra to the spiritual the heart chakra

6) Awaken, clear, and balance the right brain

7) Clear and balance the left brain

8) Align the left and right brain together

9) Physical reconnection of the body to the aura

10) Flowering gently into 5D senses

11) Donning your lightbody

12) Care and maintenance of the aura

Ask for *only* one thing at a time. Each level can take months to clear and balance. You are clearing lifetimes of auric pressure — you can't do it all at once. Consider it like peeling an onion; each layer must be removed before the next one can be reached. Make sure to ask for repolarization in every session with the Brothers. To maintain clarity and balance, repeat steps 1 — 5 at least once a month.

stantly create your reality as you move forward in time — another thing that will soon change. Your present reality reflects what you have created in the past. What you are currently creating now will become your future reality.

Is it not better to be consciously in charge? To know you're in charge? To know that you are already a master navigator? We are merely explaining the road rules that exist in the bands of reality that you are aiming to enter. So we can only do what you ask of us. There is also a limit here there is also that we must respect: We are sworn never to harm, only to heal. If you ask something of us during a healing session that we see will bring you harm, at any level, we cannot oblige that request. We will wait with you, work on other things, and keep you in the energy of 5D until your session is over.

We ask that you follow the list of questions we offer in the order that they are presented, for they represent layers of healing that are like steps up a staircase. The most graceful way to climb those stairs is one step at a time. We also recommend that you ask for only one thing at a time in the beginning. It may take a while to get through the accumulated layers of blockage that most people carry from this life and prior lives as well. In energetic terms, "striving for wholeness" means the clearing and balancing of your PEMS layers. Whatever clearing and balancing you ask for, make sure to include the phrase, "at all levels." Also ask for changes to come in gently, under grace, and in divine timing.

The Circle of Grace works to heal you
at all levels of your Be-ing.

Remember to wear loose clothing or to at least loosen ties, belts, bras, and shoes if you can. Speak out loud to us in session, beginning with the healing prayer (see chapters 1 and 19). That gives us your permission to connect 4D to 5D. Tell us how much time you have — a half-hour is good, an hour is better — and what you would like to focus on. Once you lie down face-up, hands and feet uncrossed, lower jaw slack, with pillows beneath head and knees, please continue to verbalize what you feel as the session unfolds. If you cannot lie flat on your back, try curling up on your dominant side with three pillows: one beneath your head, a second one to hug, and the third between your knees to prevent back strain.

You may say, "Arms releasing." Then a few minutes later you may feel the meridians switch, and say, "Legs now releasing." Whatever crosses your mind or moves in your body, say it aloud. If you have a heavy meridian clearing one day that is uncomfortable, merely tell us, "Please tone it down; it hurts here." Or if you feel a blockage somewhere, say to us, "Stuck above the left knee, please move it down and out."

Stay relaxed with deep breathing, and let the Circle of Grace sensations reveal to you what your body is doing. It is a wondrous awakening to an inner reality that you were simply not aware existed. Once you become adept at doing this exercise, your body will automatically begin to release every time you sit or lie down to rest, nap, read, or watch TV. When you feel the Circle of Grace begin, thank your body for the clearing and continue doing what you wish while attaching a parcel of your awareness to the miraculous self-healing process moving though you.

What "Clear and Balance" Means in Healing

You will note that each request on our Twelve Step List is phrased to specifically require that each area be first cleared, then balanced. Cleared of what? Balanced to what? The first answer is simple: cleared of pain, strain, stress, and blockages that cause excess internal pressure. To answer the second question, we could write an entire tome. Instead, we will summarize here one of the universal laws — the Law of Balance.

All forms of life vibrate in balance to fit into their environmental niche. When a life form loses its balance, we do not mean that it tripped and fell [chuckle], though in an energetic sense, it means exactly that. That life form has stepped out of vibratory balance with its environment and is therefore vulnerable to damage until it can regain its balance of health within its environment.

Why do we stress balance within the environment? Because the requirements of the environment dictate the proper frequency vibration for that life form to exist. By this, we mean you are made of Earth elements. Since Earth is changing into a new energetic configuration, you must, by being present in body, also change. For those unaware of the Millennium

Shift, the environment is still dictating a change in their vibratory form and their bodies are adjusting as best they can. Your awareness of this energetic transition — and how to prepare for it! — can greatly increase your expansion momentum and even guide your metaphysical aim higher.

Do you follow? We hope you will!

Step 1: Repolarization of Your Energy Field

In this section, know simply this: for life to exist, the universal law of balance requires that energy move away and back to a center point. Your divine spark of life requires motion and rest: moving into balance, moving away, then returning. For you in body, each action is actually two — like motion and rest, breathing in, breathing out, awake and asleep. Even in your "duality" [chuckles, "dual reality"], nature expresses itself as male and female, day and night, birth and death. All forms of energy in nature flow between a depolarized state to a repolarized state, which winds down to a depolarized state, and so on, back and forth. Do you see the ebb and flow of all things? Or you could say that there is an ebb and flow built into all things in God's Creation. As the sun goes down and up each day, all forms of nature go from a state of devitalization to a state of revitalization, back and forth and back again.

In your awake Creator state, you spend the day in various pursuits. Each task you perform causes a depolarization of your energy — you expend energy to create. Then you must rest and rebuild your energy for the next day. During sleep, your body naturally repolarizes itself. Built into the Circle of Grace is an aspect of repolarization that renews and replenishes the polarity of your body — each system, each organ, each cell — through simple electromagnetics.

Every time you begin a healing session, ask us to repolarize your body at all levels. Make that a standard request. It's the only question we ask you to repeat each time. When you include repolarizing, you will have more energy available to you after the session. Remember, we can only do what you ask and no more. In this chapter, we offer you for the first time a primer on how to get ready for where you want to go, for whom you wish to become, a blueprint for your trip Home. Happiness comes from within you, not from outside your being. As you heal, you clear out low-frequency damage to make room for higher-frequency emotions. That is why we say, "Find God within." Find your joy on the journey, dear ones, and allow us to guide you gently Home.

Steps 2, 3, and 4: Clear and Balance Meridians and Chakras

As you can see from the above heading, this section covers three questions. Since this work is truly not linear, we advise you to first ask for this work, "Please clear and balance my energetic meridians." This simple request may take very little time if you are fit, rested, eat properly, and exercise. Most people take a week or two to clear meridian blockages, but it can take up to a month or more. It all depends on your biology and biography and how many layered blockages you are carrying. The beauty of this system is, no matter what your history of accident or illness may be, everyone clears in the same way! Yes, the clearing flows that we described in chapter 1 are as standard to your auras as the number of teeth, bones, and muscles you are born with are standard for every body. [Chuckles, sorry, we are inveterate punsters!]

Once you feel your meridians flowing freely up the dominant side and back down the nondominant side in the balanced pattern, you can then ask, "Please clear and balance my chakras (energy centers of the body)." This is a crucial two-part process, clearing first the meridians, then the chakras. Why? They are roads and crossroads that are all linked. Your pathways of universal energy must be cleared first so that we can then reach the inner organs of your auric system, your chakras, to begin clearing them. One leads to the other. Your chakras will actively begin clearing as soon as your meridians can handle the added traffic. That is why we say these two steps are crucial for clearing and balancing your entire energetic system. That is also why auric and physical damage are inextricably intertwined, as is the clearing of that damage.

Healing must occur on all levels. Your meridian system circulates new energy and removes waste from your aura and nervous system at the same time because they are so linked together. Even before reaching the level of physical illness, auric damage, for example, excess auric pressure, or "baggage," can affect your entire life. You may be in great need of grounding, for example, yet find yourself unable to ground. No matter what you try, nothing seems to work. Why? You cannot ground yourself if your lower three chakras are energetically blocked or clogged. They must be cleared and in good working order for you to anchor yourself with "grounding cords" from the bottom three chakras and from the sole chakras of both feet. Yes, five cords will ground you well and move you forward. In numerology, the number five is that of change, combining forward motion (one) with a double foundation (four). See it as an easy glide forward, and you will truly gain your new balance.

When we begin clearing the chakras, you may feel us work with physical heat at the root, then feel the heat spreading up your body to clear each energy center in ascending order. Please remember that it may take weeks or months to effect a total clearing of the meridians and chakras. It all depends on how much emotional baggage you have stuffed away over the years, how much physical damage you have sustained (accidents and illnesses), and how much daily stress you accumulate. It also depends on how often you do the Circle of Grace, how long your sessions are, and your level of focus during the exercise. The more you clear your low-density 3D baggage, the faster your expansion will progress.

Your greatest tools are your intent to heal yourself,
your willingness to forgive all, and your desire
to release your unwanted baggage.

Remember, we exist in the now and are available as often as you invite us to work with you. Calling us in with the healing prayer and then doing a passive meditation will not prove as fruitful as actively engaging in the Circle of Grace, whether by simple intent, verbal feedback, mental focus or with the golden cloud visualization (explained in chapter 1). Your focus on the flows and on your breathing greatly augments the effectiveness of what we do together. This level of focused awareness is also your validation of inner Spirit, for you cannot doubt what you clearly feel and experience.

Here is an important concept to assimilate: at the physical level, the ascension process requires the clearing and balancing of your lower three chakras, through which humanity has lived for thousands of years. You are leaving behind your below-the-belt mode of existence based on root (survival), sacral (family), and solar plexus (social) chakras. The challenge of ascension is the conscious opening of the four chakras above the belt (heart, throat, third eye, and crown) and integrating them with the three below to create a new, full-sensory, heart-centered, blended Be-ing. You are ascending into the fullness of your energetic potential. Yes, there are many other layers of chakras waiting to be discovered and integrated (especially in regard to the spiritual heart chakra coming, explained in step 5), but working on the seven physical chakras is your first priority. Since your body is designed to clear blockages in a downward direction, we always begin at root and work our way up. Otherwise, the lower blockages will prevent the upper ones from moving down and out.

Ask us first to clear and balance the lower three chakras. Then ask us to clear and balance the four above and integrate them with the lower three so that all seven work in synchronous harmony. For many people, this part of the process can take months. You may find yourself crying in session after session, until your pent-up tears are processed and peeled away. You may feel expanding levels of sensory awareness as the clearing takes hold and more energy flows through your body, as it was meant to do. After the chakras are individually cleared and balanced, we realign them into pairs. Then we work on harmonizing your entire system to establish a higher level of function.

If you have a physical illness, injury or trauma, we begin the Circle of Grace flow in the reverse blockage pattern, moving the damage directly to the nearest exit point at hand or foot. Once that has been released, you will feel the Circle resume from the head down both sides (fully blocked and alternating blocked patterns) as the nervous system clears and repressurizes itself. Eventually you will shift into the balanced pattern, with an influx of new energy coming up the dominant side, circling around your head, and pushing old, spent energy down and out the nondominant side. You may feel your dominant side grow warm and puffy while your nondominant side stays cold and flat. By putting your awareness, your attention, then your intention into the session, you quicken the process and learn to take charge of your body's innate healing process.

Another important aspect to understand about clearing and balancing your chakras is that they work in pairs. At the physical level, they are mated together, function together, and sicken together. The chakra pairs we describe below are responsible for the health of your physical core. Your chakras are also paired in many other ways, at many levels, to perform different functions that are not germane to our work here.

Doctors have learned that patients with certain types of brain tumors often have rectal tumors; they don't know why but know to test for it. We say that it is because the first and seventh chakras are paired — root and crown. When one falls out of balance, the other works twice as hard to compensate. If balance is not achieved, both areas eventually succumb to illness. The second and fifth chakras are also paired — abdomen and throat. Finally, third and fourth — solar plexus and heart — work together. The sixth chakra, your third eye, is the seat of your higher intuition and psychic vision. It offers higher guidance because it is paired with the eighth chakra, your Higher Self connection. The sixth chakra also performs a monitoring function for all of the physical chakras, which we will explain further in Section Three.

So if you have abdominal issues, which indicates an energetic blockage in second chakra, plan to spend part of each session with us working on your throat. For each chakra to heal itself, its mate must also be cleared and balanced. Lightworkers, you will see remarkable results once you add this double focus to your energetic healing work. Heal the pairs! Please do not feel overwhelmed by the more complex levels of the Circle of Grace. Focus on the simple steps we offer first, and allow for your understanding to grow apace with your knowledge and experiences. Know that we will lead each of you gently, in divine timing, through your transition.

Remember, once your meridians and chakras are cleared and balanced, you can carry illness and not feel sick. In other words, you can still carry the symptoms of that illness and lead a normal life; as you heal, those symptoms lose their hold and wither away. Ask anyone who has conquered a life-threatening illness how they did it, and they will say, "I didn't accept or believe that I had to die just because someone told me so." Mind over matter? Yes, indeed. Try expanding your mind, and you will find that you have total command of all matter!

We will ask you here to keep reading before doing any chakra clearing. Heart will come into play half way through the steps we described above, but in order to remain linear for you (chuckles), we placed that information in the next subsection.

Step 5: Clearing and Balancing Your Heart Chakra

We begin with this warning: If you feel symptoms of physical heart trouble such as dizziness, shortness of breath, nausea, cramping, and/or pain in your chest and left arm, make sure that you are cleared by a medical doctor.

These are signs of heart illness manifesting at the physical level. Remember that the Circle of Grace does not interfere with any medical treatment or regimen. If you have physical heart damage, you need to seek help from a medical doctor immediately. By all means, continue to do the clearing work with us while your physical symptoms are being treated.

If the doctor finds nothing wrong, that is good, meaning that the auric blockage has not yet invaded your physical core. Yet the pressure or pain that you feel is a true physical blockage at a different level of your being — the energetic level. Symptoms of etheric heart blockage are quite distinct and often manifest beyond the physical heart area. When the heart chakra becomes overloaded, the aura spreads heart blockage across the chest in order to balance the pressure in and around the body. It wraps itself around the torso and can make itself known as a sharp point under the right and/ or left arm about a hand-width below the armpit. It may also feel like someone is standing behind you and pushing his thumb into the middle of your right and/or left shoulder blade. These sensations can also begin on one side before manifesting on both sides.

Heart blockage can travel across the chest and wrap around behind you because for every front expression of a chakra there is a mate to it in the back. Global humanity is clearing heart, and you are all reflecting this. Everyone on the planet began clearing heart by December 2001 because the events of 9/11 and the rising energies required physical heart to clear so as to be able to mesh with your new spiritual heart. Etheric heartache can be released through the Circle of Grace, and help to prevent physical heart problems from developing. We ask you to put aside the fear of following genetic family patterns. If you can clear heart before you become ill, there is no need to worry about dying young, even if it is a family trait. Please know that it is your mental and emotional states that create and control illness, not your body.

Do you follow? We hope you will.

In order for heart to become the new fulcrum of the human energetic system and the new foundation of the "three above and three below," the power and range of the human heart must expand. There is also another aspect of heart evolving beyond the millennium with the installation of a new chakra at the top of the sternum, a hand width below the throat. You call it spiritual heart, the Christ chakra, or the high heart. As this energetic enhancement takes root, physical heart must be cleared and balanced, then paired and tuned to spiritual heart. Do you see, dear reader, why this step is so important? It is also one of the largest chakra areas to be cleared, and may require several weeks of draining and retuning. By this we mean, work with us every day or every other day when you are clearing heart. If you wait any longer between sessions, you might feel your heart chakra trying to release on its own. This will cause cramping in the chest and pain down the left arm as pressure pockets clog up the closest path of release.

Because heart is paired to solar plexus, the symptom of nausea may arise. Because the lungs are in the third and fourth chakra pair region, they get squeezed by too much pressure, causing shortness of breath. Yes, we have just described the symptoms of a heart attack in energetic terms. Know that this step must be loyally done. Work with us as often as you can until your physical heart chakra is clear. *Once again, we emphasize that if you do have symptoms of heart trouble, please see your physician right away.*

You will know your progress as you become more and more lighthearted and there comes into your heart the room for joy to lodge instead of sadness. Love and fear cannot coexist in the same space, for they have different vibratory frequencies that the body cannot hold simultaneously. The Circle of Grace process clears fear at all levels and replaces it with love. Cleaning out the dense etheric pockets from your Be-ing will allow you to vibrate at a higher frequency level. This is what healing means, at the cellular level. Dear ones, ascension is re-joining God's higher vibration at all PEMS levels.

Clearing heart can be greatly facilitated by an energetic practitioner. Dear lightworkers, please do not forget that you must work on each other. You are in training, clearing first so that you may help others when the full energy of the now becomes your new reality. So work with us and work on each other. Once you are done clearing physical heart, ask for your spiritual heart chakra to be fully installed, cleared, and balanced to your physical heart chakra.

This new energy center began coming in for all humanity at the millennium, though many of you enlightened ones received it earlier. This new chakra will expand your heart center to flow across the chest and become the broad-based fulcrum of your new lightbody energetic system. Your energetic goal is to balance the three chakras below the heart to the three chakras above, with heart in the middle of your ascended energetic form, to bring in your lightbody. We keep repeating in this text, "Lead from the heart, pass everything through your heart, and focus on what your heart says to you." These are all aspects of working from the heart at the 5D level.

The old 3D energy you are leaving behind is fear-based. In the Age of Pisces, humans experienced life through the bottom three chakras: survival (money), family (sex), and society (power). Yes, money, sex, and power motivate most of your politics, big businesses, news media, and advertising. Did you ever wonder why it is all so negative? Because none of the "base chakras" have been heart-centered or heart-influenced. As you move into the higher energies of the Age of Aquarius, you must understand that we work in a love-based energy, one that acknowledges and answers to All That Is.

Everything we do is heart-based and, we hope, offered in a loving way.

Do you see the difference? Do you understand what it is you are striving for? Ask to become heart-centered. Along the way many issues, people, and circumstances will rise into your awareness as this clearing takes place. It is normal to cry during heart-clearing sessions, since tears are healing and must be shed in order to be released. Do not focus on the details, just focus on releasing the accumulated heartache.

In clearing heart blockages, you may witness a life review of sorts, sometimes with a chronological pattern to those issues rising to be released. Please know that Spirit never judges; we never attach labels of good, bad, right, and wrong to those things that need releasing. We do not pry into your personal, mental, or physical space. We are merely spiritual surgeons, helping you excise etheric damage from your systems. Our work includes all aspects of both your physical and etheric halves. This concept may be new for you, since most people consider tending to the body as tending to their whole selves. Do you now see that you must include healing of that which you cannot yet see? [Chuckles.]

Once you have cleared and balanced the heart chakra, please proceed to clearing the upper chakras, fifth, sixth, and seventh. After that, ask for the rebalancing of all seven chakras with heart as the fulcrum for the three above and the three below. You will know when the major heart clearing is done, because you will feel more lighthearted!

Steps 6, 7, and 8: Awakening the Right Brain and Aligning It with the Left Brain

The next necessary step for total assimilation is multifold in purpose. For every step, there is a further goal. Each step we offer you is, in actuality, several steps. First, ask for the awakening, clearing, and balancing of your right brain. Next, ask us to clear and balance your left brain. Then ask us to realign right and left brain to work together.

First, the right brain must be reawakened; by this we mean a reawakening to active consciousness. Your right brain, which connects and directs your auric self, has always been there dutifully performing its functions. Now, we ask you to reintegrate your conscious awareness with the right brain's functions so that you may truly become interdimensional. Why are your energetic layers not visible to your 3D senses? Because those parts of you exist in higher dimensions that you cannot see, feel, or connect to with your limited 3D awareness. Do you see how many different ways the ascension process is a pulling up of your entire existence to a higher level of consciousness?

The awakening of the right brain is a very sweet, comforting process. You may feel as if we are gently combing the right side of your head, from the mid-part outward and down toward your ear. Each session will deepen the combing, which is occurring in 5D. Remember, the human body's essence is holographic in nature. Any work done at the etheric level always involves the physical, because the aura and its physical core are energetically intertwined, or woven together. Once you feel that the awakening process has deepened past the ear, it will be done. Then we will clear and rebalance your left brain, combing gently from mid-part down to the left ear. Finally, ask us to realign right brain to left brain so that they can work together as interdependent halves of a whole.

This step brings you back to your original state with the left brain connected to and directing your physical half and the right brain connected to and directing your auric half. You will find much new information coming in from your etheric self, or your auric radar. Your intuition will expand, as well as your perception of people, things, places, and events that occur around you. A strong sense of peace accompanies this stage of healing. As you begin to connect back to your aura, you are consciously connecting to 5D, to higher perception, to higher mind, and to us, your loving guides. We are One.

Step 9: Physical Reconnection of the Body to the Aura

Now that you have reawakened the right brain and realigned it with the left brain, it is time to do the same at the physical level. Ask your team of healing Brothers to consciously reconnect your body to your aura. At this stage, you are healing the depths of that major rift between Spirit energy and earth matter. Again, you may feel a gentle tugging of the mid-part line down the middle of your head and a light pulling of it down toward your right shoulder. To balance the work, halfway through we will switch to the mid-part down over the left side of the head toward the left shoulder.

This process may take days or weeks to accomplish. The more you focus on what you are feeling, the more quickly the work proceeds. If you lose mental focus (in sessions for which you are awake) the work may slow down. The Circle of Grace will continue, but you will not clear as fast. That is why we say, keep track aloud of what you are feeling and sensing in your body and in your emotions. Remember to open your jaw, relax your muscles, and focus on deep breathing. This will help you allow the process to be guided. Since we work at all levels, we will teach you to do the same.

Always strive for balance, no matter what happens around you. At this stage, you will have the ability to best deal with life from the spiritual perspective and will instinctively know what you need to do at any given time. As this is a growth process, you may not feel major changes from day to day. But at some point, you will look back to before you met us and realize how much your grasp of reality has expanded. With this spiritual growth and expansion comes an expansion of self, of blending with God, of becoming that which you seek. Dear ones, wholeness is Oneness.

Step 10: Flowering into the 5D Senses

Next, ask us to help you expand into full-sensory perception, what you currently term extrasensory perception. This will bring you into the bloom of 4-5D reality. Tell us aloud that you would like all senses, at all levels, to be opened and balanced back to your state of origin — back to your Adamic blueprint, back to Adam Kadmon. That is your birthright. What is a birthright? It is a gift or talent with which you were born. You were born to be a full-sensory, multidimensional, energetic Be-ing, linked to both Father Sky and Mother Earth. Once your senses begin functioning in a higher frequency range, you will be able to see and counter anything of negative energy that comes around you. You will understand in a new, expansive way why people behave the way they do. You will be able to see or sense what baggage they carry around, magnetized to their auras as pockets of dense, dark matter.

Here we will remind you that your only limits are self-imposed ones. If you think, deep down, that none of this is possible, then it will not be possible — for you. So use this freewill zone to your advantage. Turn it around and say, "God, I'm willing to believe it's all possible." Once you believe that anything is possible, that the sky's the limit, then you have opened the door to your own future potential.

Do you follow? We hope you will.

Once you have reached this level of healing, you may want to refine what you ask for, depending on the needs of your way of life or holistic practices. If you are an energetic practitioner, for example, you may want to request sight of the energies at work before you. Remember to ask for an on-off switch, so we can teach you to phase in and out of 5D sight. That way, you are in charge of what you see, and when. If you are an emotional or mental healer, you might ask for clearer understanding of patterns that people work through to help them identify their lessons and what to do about them. If you are a spiritual healer, you might simply want to radiate higher awareness and "Be-ingness" wherever you go.

There are as many ways to heal as there are individual people, yet you all share the same elements of stress, activity, rest, passion, faith, and so on. Healing must be accomplished at all levels, from the innermost cellular level to the outermost galactic levels. We advise you to begin in your own backyard. Work on your microcosm of the macrocosm, and know that all the rest will follow suit.

Once you have mastered this inner miracle of self-clearing, you will be in total command of your health, your life, and your future. Why? Because, no matter what happens around you, you will function from a higher level of reality. You will, in truth, become Higher Self walking in the flesh, a true re-turn, re-membrance, and re-joining of your awareness to God.

Step 11: Donning Your Lightbody

Your next request will be the fitting of your lightbody, which also translates to assimilating etheric and physical selves into your total Be-ing. We are truly honored to help you don your lightbody. Just as the physical body has bones in it to give the body structure, your aura has a gridwork of meridian lines that form an oval-shaped energetic cage housing both the physical core and the internal organs of the aura. Your lightbody reinforces your etheric self by bringing it into wholeness with your physical core. This final merging allows Higher Self to descend and be One with you. We could write an entire book to explain how this transmutation occurs, but it would not serve our purpose here. We ask that you trust that it will be done when the time is appropriate for you.

Fitting the lightbody is mostly done while you are asleep, though some of you may remain semiconscious and aware of the process. It does not matter whether you are aware or not; there is a progression of healing and energetic integration that must precede this step on the path. It is the path itself, children, that we would like you to focus on, not the details of each step that must be made. Yes, follow this list, then amend it as you see fit. Bring us your aches and pains, your questions and concepts to assimilate. It will all flow together as you begin to heal. A major part of your healing is the shedding of old concepts and old mindsets. Why? If you seek to harmonize with the incoming energies and assimilate new information, you must believe that you can.

There is not enough time left to analyze every little piece of what you are releasing in order to heal. That is the old energy, the old way. You are gaining rapid momentum and are now striding up the path at a good clip. Achieving the lightbody state requires the clearing and reintegrating of all your energetic layers. Once that is complete, you will flow quite quickly through the lightbody assimilation. With our help, and with guidance from your own Higher Self, you have nothing to fear.

Once you have fully assimilated all aspects of your True Self, you will feel stronger, more peaceful, more focused, more patient, more benevolent, more joyful, and more loving. Do you see the common word? "More." You become more of that which you seek. You become more of all the divine aspects of Higher Self that will be firmly in charge. You become more Godlike. Yes, do you see the progression? You become more of the future potential of man. You are evolving in this lifetime. Dear ones, you have donned and shed those 3D bodies many times over, life after life. Now, for the first time, we ask you to bring your larger Spiritual Be-ing down into that little body.

Do you follow? We hope you will!

The donning of your lightbody brings a great sense of personal strength. Your physical body will feel more solid, more grounded, and more balanced. Your emotions will flow through all of your layers, adding heart to thought to offer a spiritual perspective rather than an ego-based one. You will clearly discern which people are working from ego; they will have a doom-and-gloom perspective, instill fear and give more warnings of bad than good tidings. Rely on your "gut brain," for that part of your intuition will allow you to feel this negative energy as it enters your space. That auric space is now a feeling part of your body. Your aura will now connect you to the higher dimensions in a conscious way. From there you will be able to see the lower dimensions at work around you while you will respond from higher sight and mind.

We would like to emphasize this major point: 5D includes 3D and 4D, so you will be able to see all aspects of the dimensions you are now tuned into. From this new higher perspective, you will clearly see what is for your highest good and what is not. You will be in charge of your life, weighing, measuring, and evaluating everything that happens around you so as to respond in harmony with your soul and its purpose.

With an integrated lightbody, you are carving out new heights for humanity's potential. You are the pioneers, forging blindly into the unknown with hope and faith as fuel for advancement. You are driven by the knowing that something is missing, something essential that defines the very fabric of life, that weaves together every living thing — the knowledge, for sure and certain, that God exists within you.

We speak here of merging back into All That Is. At this stage, you will achieve the level of being Godlike in every moment, recognizing that you are a part of the I Am energy. You will have bridged that gap between the freewill zone and the territory it denies beyond the Veil. In our realm, every life form feels the vibratory presence of God inside them at all times. Donning your lightbody is truly becoming Higher Self. This is walking with God. This is the waking meditation that we offer to teach you.

Yes, the Circle of Grace helps to clear you and get you ready for living in the higher energies. It also does one more vital thing: It reconnects your inner hope and faith with the sure knowledge that God exists. You will feel God's presence living inside you, once again. And that, dear ones, is the energy of Home.

Step 12: Care and Maintenance of the Aura

All we advise you to ask for in this chapter should become for you a sequence of both self-healing and self-maintenance. By this we mean that you should, every once in a while, repeat the first five questions as listed at the end of this chapter. Ask to be repolarized and ask for your meridians and chakras to be cleared and balanced. Ask for heart to be cleared. While you live, breathe, and function in your everyday world, there is always an incoming accumulation of stress, strain, and pain. Not only do we counsel you to work through these steps toward wholeness, but we say to you that the Circle of Grace should be as much a part of your daily physical maintenance as showering and brushing your teeth. Do it every day or as often as possible. Go to sleep at night floating on the awareness that your body is clearing, where it is happening, and what that means to you.

Please remember that the Circle of Grace also tends to chronic blockages and conditions. Blockages accumulate in your aura in chronological order. In other words, each time you lie down to do the exercise, you will be clearing at three levels. The surface level is that of current stress and strain, underneath which are your chronic aches and pains. The third and deepest layer is the accumulation of inherited genetic patterns and unresolved past-life issues. If a session feels different than what you requested, know that we must finish clearing the way before we can move on with new work. We must work from the outside in so as to cause you no harm.

The Circle of Grace clears from the outside in. The deeper the clearing, the older and heavier the baggage. At the physical level, the outer two layers of current and chronic pressures must be released before the deeper source of the physical blockage or emotional damage can be reached for clearing. Why? So as to cause you no harm in the healing process, dear one. Imagine trying to extract the heart of an onion without disturbing any of its outer layers. Yes, forgive the vegetable analogy, but all life forms are layered in nature, even trees with their yearly inner circle of growth. We work with your entire holographic Be-ing as it is designed to clear itself — from the outside in.

Some days, Earth's energy shifts will be so heavy and draining that you will want nothing more than added energy. Ask aloud for energy when you need it, and let us gauge how much to feed you. At first, you may feel as if unending waves of goose bumps are washing over your body. That is energizing at the physical level. As you advance into clarity and your requests gain complexity, you will often need to find surcease in 5D, the energy to which you are being drawn.

On those days, for those who can handle it, you will feel as if you are being dipped in a big vat of rainbows. You will grow to see the rich palate of colors that vibrate in 5D as your senses expand. Others will feel a warm, loving darkness aglow with inner light. Some will hear frequency changes in the form of tones ringing in their ears. Again, each person will have individual experiences tailored to their need for healing, learning, and growing back into their original perspective of blending with Higher Self. Also, know that we tailor the work to suit your goals and spiritual life path. Remember in the healing prayer that you ask your own Higher Self to guide and lead? There is good reason for that request: all that we do is tailored to what your Higher Self directs us to do according to your soul contract for your highest good in divine timing.

As to divine timing, some of you may find yourselves in a headlong struggle with timing. By this, we mean that your impatience to move forward can sometimes get in your way. Please, ask for only one thing on the list at a time and be patient until you feel it is done. If you ask us to continue to another step before we feel that you are ready, we cannot move on without risking you harm. Understand that from our 5D perspective we see your past, present, and future and thus see the ramifications of each request. If you feel stuck or blocked in your progress and cannot understand why, know that you are being held in place by Spirit, protected until you are ready to move forward safely.

Once you attain mastery over your own Circle of Grace [chuckles], you will be able to ask for and receive more than one focus at a time. For example, you could ask for an energy bath and drain out a headache at the same time. Once you learn what each step of this process feels like, you can activate it by connecting with us and bringing in the feel of it. Through all of this work, we hope that you will lie down and try the exercise. The proof is in the doing, and you have nothing to lose except many layers of stress and pain.

Reaching Wholeness

Asking for all of the healing listed here at once is too much to focus on. Each level must be cleared before the next level can be reached for healing. We offer the information in this chapter for your assimilation to help speed your progress along the metaphysical path. Knowing what to ask for makes the work much simpler for us all, and we feel it is time that this knowledge be brought before the Veil.

Once you understand the steps to clearing that need to be done, you can tailor your requests to suit your individual needs. This chapter contains the basic path for you to follow for healing at all levels. Do not limit yourself to this list. See it rather as the foundation of our collaboration. As you live and grow, your needs will change and thus guide our future work together. We urge you not to measure your Circle of Grace sessions against the progress of another person. Each will be different, no better or worse, just different. This is not a race; we ask you to reach awareness in your own time and in your own way. That is following your own highest good, in divine timing, under grace, within the Circle of Grace.

Once you have felt us work on you, there is no turning back. You will have proof, deep down, that God exists within you. Dear ones, we exist a mere breath away from you, only a few octaves above you. With your verbal permission, we can reach through that gap and touch you. We are waiting to work with you, with all awakening and aware ones, creating as we go into a new wave of evolving humanity. One by one, you will begin to bring in channels that no one else receives. You will gain healing and knowledge and total love in this work. You will pave the way for others to follow, an ever-increasing flood of people awakening to Spirit as your galaxy draws nearer to the photon belt.

All of the planets in your solar system are now showing marked changes in luminosity, changes in polarity, changes in gravitational fields, and changes in atmospheric conditions. When we tell you that all is changing around you, that "All" is beyond huge!

When one level shifts, all levels must shift.

This shift will bring in your ultimate goal — reconnection to God. Yes, the Divine Plan's ultimate goal for humanity is for you to find your inner Divine Flame, to choose to return to God of your own free will. Ah, now we come to the crux of the meaning of all the goals. And you already know what that is:

I Am God. You are God. We are God. We are One.

By healing your bodies and reawakening to your original powers, you will change the tapestry of all creation. We are honored and humbled to be working with you, dear ones, who bear such heavy loads. Know that there is more to life than you see. Know that you are all, one and all, beloved. You are beloved of God, you sprang from God and will find your way back to God in a new and different way — as evolved, blended Be-ings — as the new humans in the New Age of humanity.

Welcome Home!

The Laws and the Keys

6

The Law of Materialization

We begin this section by examining three basic universal laws. Your understanding of these laws is intrinsic to this work. There are many other universal laws to discover, decipher, and digest. Indeed, we will refer to some of them, but this topic encompasses a full body of knowledge that you can find from other sources. For the sake of brevity, we will focus on the three major universal laws: of Materialization, Allowing, and Divine Creation. Please study this sentence for a moment, and determine what it means to you: *A prayer said with heart-filled gladness connects you directly to Spirit.*

Now look at it again with our higher perspective added: A prayer (spiritual layer) said with (mental and physical layers) heart-filled gladness (emotional layer) connects you directly to Spirit. These are the physical, emotional, mental, and spiritual steps through which you will learn to materialize that which you desire. Your thoughts, wielded by your intent, fueled by the loving gratitude of total faith, will bring in anything on which you focus your attention. This is the power of Divine creation you carry within. Each creation begins at a high-vibratory level, where thoughts float and form into ideas. As you solidify your goal, you draw it down in descending frequency. You create your own reality through vibratory frequency changes all around you.

In this chapter, we wish to discuss the nature of your reality. You probably know by now that reality is a variable thing. Most of you feel that it is beyond your control. Things just happen to you. Life has constant twists and turns that you find unexpected and not always welcome. We say to you here that reality is in your control. You have been in control of your life and your reality all along; you just didn't know it. If you understand the workings of the universe, you will then be able to manipulate your reality, and your life, as you wish. Or rather, as you will.

Learning to Wield Your Will

There are aspects of free will that separate your 3D reality from other schools (i.e., planets) of spiritual learning. You probably think having free will means that believing or not believing in God is your choice, as is how you express your beliefs. Yes, you are absolutely right on both counts, but free will means much more than that.

Free will also means that you can wield your will in any way you choose. You have incredible powers of will, as is proven by the communal reality you live in. You have all agreed to live in the matrix of 3D, a construct of physical reality through which you translate into a physical body over and over again in order to learn lessons at the physical level. Your world is a created one, one that you all share and see. Though each individual has his or her own perceptions about 3D reality, you all basically see the same things: roads, buildings, trees, animals, and plants. This construct is so strong that the births and deaths of its inhabitants do not affect its existence.

The Law of Materialization (or Manifestation) states that the universe brings to you what you hold most in your awareness. Put another way — a change of perspective, if you will — you create what you focus on. Have you known people who were afraid of illnesses like cancer, only to die of it? The more they focused on what they feared, the more the universe delivered it. Do you focus on lack in your life? Then the universe will bring you lack, since that is your focus. Rather, focus on what you do have, and be grateful for the sustenance and abundance that flows around you. Then the universe will bring you abundance from all around.

You may be thinking, wait a minute, that's the Law of Attraction! Well, yes it is. That law guarantees that what you focus on vibrationally will be matched by your experiences in the 3D realm. Just as one cannot separate the four PEMS layers of your body, so too the universal laws work together and must be wielded together. For example, if you feel convinced of something down to your bones, is it not easier to manifest than if you just feel ambivalent toward it? The more intensely you wield your will, the better and faster creation you achieve of what you want. People who succeed are those who never take their eyes off their goals. When you focus only on obstacles to your goal, those obstacles loom large because that is where you are putting your sight, attention, or focus.

You only see obstacles when you take your eyes off your goal.

How do you do this correctly? How do you obtain your heart's desire? Dear one, love is the most precious energetic fuel in the universe. When you add love from the heart to the creative mix of your manifestation, it is that love that fuels your thoughts and ideas to coalesce into solid form. The strongest intent is that which is funneled through the heart. If you are doing your heart's true work, the universe will support your efforts. Let your heart be your guide. Run every thought, idea, and sentence through your heart chakra before bringing it into your 4D reality with the power of your voice.

Yes, your voice has much power. Your voice carries your hopes, wishes, dreams, thoughts, and ideas into materialization through the power of verbalizing — what you speak becomes concrete. Voicing your will brings your creation down into the physical level of your reality. Affirmations done over and over, joyously from the heart, are very powerful. The auditory vibration of your voice is one of your best creative tools to wield the will of your heart and mind.

In this text, we are already teaching you how to do this. By saying the four-part healing prayer aloud before each Circle of Grace session, you are creating a bridge between dimensions and giving us permission to work with you in your physical space. That is also why we urge you to speak aloud to us during our healing sessions together, even though you may not see, hear, or feel us yet. Do you see your enormous potential in the word "yet"? We do, and we honor you greatly for it.

Living in the now as we do, we are always at your beck and call [chuckles]. We await you to call us in to help you manifest your goals. Set up a ritual, something that carries meaning for you. Spirit honors rituals, for they show the intensity of your intent, your focus, and commitment to all you do. Create a manifestation corner in a quiet space or light a candle or go sit under your favorite tree. Take a few minutes every morning or evening, whatever time works best for you. Say the four-part healing prayer and substitute the words "cocreate with me" or "join me for a manifestation moment" instead of the words "join me for a healing session." Get creative; use whatever words are comfortable for you. We are glad to be called in for whatever reason.

Tell us what you want to cocreate, thank us for taking care of it, and feel grateful for having the fruition of your desires as if it has already happened. The intensity of that feeling of loving gratitude is what propels materialization. Yes, pass it through your heart. Pray from the heart, visualize your desire through the heart, give loving thanks from the heart, and release it to the universe. Love is the catalyst that turns thoughts into things.

Do you follow? We hope you will.

Know That Anything Is Possible

What we are focusing our attention on here is the concept of manifestation [chuckles]. How do you create what you want? How do you make your goals a reality? How do you create and earn abundance by using your inherent gifts and talents accumulated over many lifetimes? Now we urge you to see your lessons as merely obstacles on your path, and to look beyond them to your goal. We seek to facilitate your clearing of all obstacles in your life that impede your progress back to All That Is. It is now time for intense soul work — to identify and follow the spiritual contract you charted for yourself before you incarnated into this body and into this life.

Interesting concept, isn't it? In the last chapter, we offered you a list of things to ask for in our healing sessions together. Why? The key words are "what to ask for." Use the Law of Attraction to your benefit, and know that the vibrational goals you send out will come back to you in physical form. The universe provides you with what you ask for or what you focus your attention on. We, the Brotherhood, can only do what you ask us to do. Knowing what to ask for is crucial to this entire process, for there is a logical progression to the unfolding, or flowering, of the energetic transitions from 3D to 4D to 5D.

There is also a progression of energetic steps required to wield your will. First form your intention, then focus your attention, and then pour love all over it. Let it go with blessings, and move on to doing something else. At this point in the process, the most difficult thing for you to do will be to stay out of doubt. By staying open to infinite possibilities, you will allow Spirit to bring in the highest and best for you, as directed by the universe (or your personal identification of God) under grace, in divine timing.

What do we mean by this? Whatever you seek, wish, or focus on to create, say it with this phrase interwoven: "… for my highest good, under grace, in divine timing." Focus on the goal rather than a specific path to that goal. Thus you allow the universe to work in a myriad of ways instead of limiting yourself to a single outcome through a single (stated) path. There may be many possibilities out there that will bring your desire into better fruition, but if you specify too much, you are limiting yourself (and us) as to what you can receive. Trust that we, from Spirit's higher perspective, have a clearer view of what constitutes your highest good, as well as how and when it should happen.

State the problem — aloud! — and specify your desired goal. Here is where discernment comes into play. You must carefully phrase your goal requirements to bring you all that you wish to manifest. If you pray for enough food to feed your family and then complain that you have little more than food to survive, we will gently say, "Your prayer has been answered." Rather, ask for enough abundance to sustain your family and share with your friends, and see what that expansion in perspective and prayer brings into your life.

Most of all, we ask you to believe that anything is possible. This basic tenet must, by logic and necessity, be true for you down to your bones. Even if you grasp all of the concepts that the New Age material offers, none of it will help you to evolve if you do not believe in your own power and potential. Please note that we are not trying to dictate what or how you should or should not believe; that would be in conflict with your freewill directives. Believe in whatever source of religion feels right to you, knowing that all viable religions preach the same message of love, not hate. Include your version of God in the healing prayer, call in your favorite guides and angels. Then call us in, your doting Brothers, and your own Higher Self.

. Be specific in the goal you seek, by imagining yourself already there. See yourself beyond mastery, already using your gifts. That future vision will help shape your materialization. Remember, God is in the divine perfection of every detail.

Becoming That Which You Seek

True, total metaphysical advancement requires a change in your perspective of who and what you are. Your physical body may return to Earth over and over, but your unique consciousness infinitely returns to the True Reality of Spirit. We ask you to release your old 3D human view of limited life in limited bodies. See yourself as an Eternal Be-ing, an energetic being with a temporary physical core. You never die, dear one. And you are never alone!

From this shift in perspective comes an expanded realization of your self-worth, a realization of your divine right to become the expanded be-ing inherent in your potential. A knowing will grow in you of your true powers to direct and affect this life and all the lives you have experienced. Then you will fully become an eternal, energetic being wielding your will — through the power of loving gratitude — to create your desires, your goals, and hence your future reality.

In the beginning, the most difficult part will be learning how to put aside the cares and worries of your mundane life and float up into the higher energy levels that we offer to share with you. If you are awake during our healing sessions together, remember to speak aloud to us of your hopes, wishes, and dreams. We will care for them as if they were the finest of jewels. We care for you too, more than you can know at present.

We wait impatiently for your return to the True Reality of Spirit. In whatever manner your journey unfolds, we care not. All is perfect, the good and the bad, the mistakes and the triumphs, the choices made and those not made. Remember, in our eyes, you cannot do it wrong (re: each lifetime) for there are concrete reasons behind everything that happens, reasons you may not see or understand yet from your linear 3-4D perspective. Know that each lifetime unravels as it must, with lessons learned and wisdom gained.

Think about this: You come into this world naked and empty-handed; you leave this world without possessions, without even a body. So what is the purpose of all this karmic journeying? Why are you doomed, as some of you think, to repeat life after life and be miserable because that is the human condition?

We say that your human condition is whatever you want it to be. Your life is and will be whatever you want it to be, whatever you focus on the most. You were put on this Earth to experience freedom and joy. Your true soul-directed goals are creating love and attaining wisdom. Those are the two priceless things that you take back to your true Spirit life. Through the ascension process, your goal is to cleanse and purify all aspects of self so that you may merge back into the Godhead. By this we mean whatever concept you have of God, whether it be Christ, Adonai, Allah, Buddha, or simply the universe.

Can you imagine this? A return to the warmth and love of the Divine Creator, the Father/Mother energy that flows through All That Is. Imagine yourself, your awareness of body, mind, and soul, merging with a glorious rainbow of incredible energy that permeates and sustains all dimensional realities. You are not merely a spark of God; you carry the Divine flame in every cell of your body. That Divine flame is what fuels your existence. Once you purify and integrate all aspects of your total being, your Higher Self will be able to descend and blend with you. You will live from that moment on with a live, active, permanent knowledge that God exists, for you will feel His presence as a new specific vibration inside your body.

See your entire life as one big healing session for your ascent to a new way of Be-ing, and we will gladly journey there with you. Again, we stress the mental awareness of "Be-ing" in every moment. We add here: Be with us! Let us be with you. Think in terms of God Be-ing within you and surrounding you with every stride and in every moment that you breathe in and out on this Earth. Do not think of God as above or at a distance, not noticing or caring about you — that could not be further from the truth.

God is All That Is, and you are part of All That Is! You Are God.

Be-ing in Love with Life

Do you see the layers upon layers of patterns in your life and how one flows to the next? We stated above that your soul's goal for each life is bringing back to Spirit more love and wisdom. How to do that? By simply enjoying the journey. Each lifetime should be a joyous expression of God in the material dimension, not an experience of pain and suffering. Do you understand that you have a choice in this?

A lovely aspect of free will is that you can choose a perspective, amend it to suit your needs, or discard it for a better one. Remember, you create your own reality in every moment that you live and breathe. Look around at your present life: It is the sum total of all you have created in the past. Look at what you are creating now as you work each day: It will become your future reality. In this time of transition, you have been granted the dispensation of moving quickly forward on the spiritual path. You no longer need to endure long periods of pain and suffering; that was the old energy created by the old human mindset. Now you can identify and assimilate the lesson that each experience carries and walk through it. Get past it! Let go of the past! How?

The old human expression "forgive and forget" is truer than you know. Forgive? Yes, to clear your karmic slate and allow you clear focus for the here and now. Forget? Yes, in the sense that you should not dwell on the past. What happens when you focus on past mistakes and old painful events? You put your awareness and therefore your energy in the wrong place. When you do this, you are not focused on the present moment. Do not get caught up in mental loops that drain you of physical energy and get you nowhere. Instead, let go of it all, and float up into the healing energies we offer you. The Circle of Grace is your vehicle for moving forward; by its use, you move your physical vehicle forward. [Chuckles.]

You Are Not Alone; You Are All One

Do you not say that for every illness, God put on this Earth a plant that can cure it? Indeed, He has done even more than that. Your physical body is a brilliant creation of physical matter married to spiritual matter. Does it not make sense that the incredible biological creature that you are would have a built-in way of maintaining and regaining health? The Circle of Grace is not just an exercise, not just a meditation — that is just the mode in which you experience it. The Circle of Grace is your internal self-clearing system, present in each and every one of you and — pardon the pun — it is our present to you from Spirit. Why not learn to use it? Ascension work must be done at all levels, including the physical. Give intent to do the work, take the time to lie down and connect with us, and you will not be disappointed.

How will you know when you have successfully transitioned? You will find us waiting. Then your true life path will unfold as you begin to fulfill the higher contract written by your soul. You will have a new set of goals to go along with the new set of tools that you have developed. Your entire Be-ing, mind, body, and Spirit, will form a phenomenal spiritual tool that you will wield with steadfast faith and sharp intent — what a powerful combination! Your human ability to focus will come now into play, for with evolved faith plus intent and focus, you can create anything that you can imagine. That is why we say, believe that anything is possible. Otherwise, you will be self-limiting.

Your true potential is as vast as All There Is. Inside the microcosm that is a human being is reflected the macrocosm that is God. We are All One in Spirit. Please understand that it is our wish to work with you in whatever form of spiritual, mental, emotional, or physical healing you may need. You will make quick progress in our healing sessions together if you motivate this work with your spiritual quests for love and learning. If you have trouble connecting with us, read any part of the material we offer here and you will plow a path straight to our energetic signature.

Through this work, these are our goals for you: Learn how to use the Circle of Grace. Learn how your multilayered body works to heal yourself. Learn to command all aspects of your reality, internal and external, and thus advance gracefully to become a conscious, blended Be-ing of Spirit and Matter.

Be open. Be receptive. Be with us, and you will soon join us. And what a party we have planned! Your return is always a joyous occasion for us, whether you come Home in Spirit or visit with us in body. How? Join us in the Circle of Grace. Clear yourself of density so that Higher Self can join you in the joyous expression of your life on Earth.

We know you can do this, for we know that anything is possible!

⑦

The Law of Allowing

The Law of Allowing is simply this: You create what you focus on and allow to bring into your universe. Each human is a universe unto him or herself, complete and whole as created by God. To think you are lacking in anything defiles the model from which you were created — the spark of Divinity. We keep repeating in this text: "You are God," do we not? If indeed you are part of the I Am energy, then it stands to reason that you have available to you God's powers of creation! Why do we phrase it thus? Because of the parameters of your freewill zone. You are as powerful as you believe yourself to be. You are as aware as you choose to be. You are as worthy as you feel yourself to be. You are as loved as you love yourself.

Along with love and wisdom gained, these are the treasures that your soul seeks in each lifetime: self-worth leading to self-love, higher awareness, and return to the I Am consciousness. You are currently confined to a physical body so that these soul experiences can be cultivated at the physical level. Your daily work helps to define your self-worth. Your emotional relationships reflect the depths of your self-love. Your application of higher mental perspective to your daily life will show as success at all levels. When your faith in God becomes faith in yourself, you will discover your boundless power of cocreation on the physical plane. As you begin to make positive changes in your daily life, you will quickly see proof that you can affect all that is around you. Yes, you can create your own future and will it in, step by step.

Sustaining a Higher Energetic Vibration

Please keep in mind that all forms of life are expressions of specific vibratory energy. You are energetic beings, holographic in design, whose powers extend far further than you realize. Indeed, your bodies are much larger than you realize, and they function at many more levels than you are aware of. Any change that you choose to implement in your physical reality requires first a vibrational shift of your energy.

Your physical core is the last and deepest level to be shifted.

In chapter 5, we explained that the Circle of Grace process must first clear your outer layers of pain and stress before the inner layers can be reached for release. In the ascension process, you also change from the outside in: first your spiritual body, then mental, then emotional, and last, your physical body. How do you make each shift? How do you change your perspective? When we say, "Seek a higher perspective," we are asking you to access a higher level of vibratory expression. Feeling unconditional love is the goal of raising your consciousness. The allowing part of manifestation is sustaining that higher emotional vibration of joy. By making that state of happiness your true inner expression, you develop the power to positively affect the vibrational density of your physical reality.

In order to sustain that higher level of awareness consciousness, you must stay in the top range of the emotional scale we described in chapter 2. A positive mindset will feel good while focusing on doubt or lack will make you feel bad. In every moment, you have the choice to be in fear or in love. Do not retreat into worry and doubt, for these negative thought forms will lower your vibration and block your materialization. Choose carefully who you speak to about your goal to avoid negative criticism and judgment. Simply choose the higher vibration of love, and do not allow anything or any one around you to lower your essence back into duality.

Cultivate a state of joyous expectation — a knowing that the universe will respond to in kind.

Sustaining your faith and your positive perspective will magnetize your goal to you, as long as you believe and allow that anything is possible. Will yourself to stay in a joyful state and know that your goal will appear.

Creating Your Future Reality

This is how you create your reality: First, you hone your focus on a specific goal, then you will your creation into physicality through loving gratitude, and then you step aside and allow the goal to materialize. How do you allow? By willing it in with joy. Your "will" has many facets, among them the will to focus your intent, the will to create your goal, and the will to allow that creation into your now. Again, you are creatures of free will. You all have the capacity, talent, and power to create whatever you will [chuckles].

Once you have fully imagined your goal and achieved total focus, you must then will your goal into existence. How? Send it to Spirit as a prayer from the heart, fueled by loving gratitude for having that prayer answered. Then you must detach from that prayer, release it, and allow it to become realized. What to do next, as you wait for your goal to materialize? Feel the joy of accomplishment, of worthiness, of mastery, and make that joy your constant emotional expression. Stay focused on the goal being there, not the lack of it.

Become your goal. Try it on for size. Look around and see what tools you will need as you function after realizing your goal. Bring together all of those tools and create a sacred space in which to place your materialization. In other words, start preparing for your goal as if it were already here, and keep giving thanks for its creation.

Defining the tools that you will need is part of your creative manifestation. If it is a business you will need business cards, stationary, a system of bookkeeping. Where will the business be located? Pick an area in which you feel comfortable working. Design your office space, see the colors of the walls and rugs, decide what type of furniture will suit your needs, down to the material (metal? wood?) and color of your desk. Perfection is in the smallest details. Figure it all out and trust that Spirit will bring it to you in divine timing, under grace, and for your highest good.

Allowing Your Faith to Come from Your Heart

How do you allow? We do not speak of clenching your gut or holding your breath or doing anything physical to bring your desires into realization. You must be self-realized in order to materialize things [chuckles]. Do you see the many layers of this work? To be self-realized is to be aware, in every moment of your connection to Higher Self. Sustaining that feeling of faith and the positive outpouring of love will maintain your being at all levels in a state of oneness with the Divine Source.

Being clear and balanced at all PEMS levels will help you access that higher vibration of joyful well-being. Doing the Circle of Grace regularly will solidify the inner core of your faith and become your proof that God resides within you. Then you will find it easy to believe in the power of your will to create what you desire from the depths of your heart.

Dear one, always lead with your heart. In the energetic expansion you are experiencing, your heart is becoming the fulcrum on which your entire being is balanced. It is the new axis of your will, the lens of your soul that you use to focus on your physical reality. Your best creation will come from that which you desire from the depths of your heart. That which you attempt to create with ambivalence, or lack of caring, will not manifest well. That which you create through the negative emotions of fear, in all of its faces, will also descend on you with its own brand of lessons in tow. That which you send out, you receive back threefold.

Do you see your higher purpose now? Do that which you focus on. Be that which you intend to become. Walk your talk. Begin to merge with All That Is, and carry His awareness in every moment that you breathe. Once you give thanks to Spirit, with love and gratitude pouring from your heart chakra, then see it as already done and will it, so be it. Sounds simple? Yes, surely. But you must release worry and doubt, or you will get in your own way.

Getting Out of Your Own Way

Surrendering all doubt is what you face at this level of metaphysical learning. Let go of that little voice that argues against your heart. That inner voice of lower thought belittles the divinity that you are by negating that Spirit exists inside you. It is the voice of doubt that keeps insisting that not everything is possible.

Do you see? It is the voice of duality. It is the voice of human tribal thought, which tries to control your thinking and your actions. It is the old negative 3D voice that diminishes your self-worth. It is time to step away from that limiting voice, away from that limited mode of thinking. It is time to stand up as an individual with your own unique set of inner beliefs and outward expressions. When you define your self-worth from a spiritual perspective rather than a material perspective, you will grow to realize that polishing your inside is more essential than polishing your outside.

What if your heart's desire doesn't manifest right away? We say, remember divine timing. Also remember that the little voice of doubt that repeats that question, and others like it, are of the lower mind. Again, this is a facet of free will: Choose the higher vibration of love in every moment rather than the lower vibration of fear in all of its faces. Stay in higher mind, in a loving vibration, and in an attitude of gratitude that will make your life a beatitude. Your constant outpouring of joyful gratitude is the allowing part of how to manifest. Sustaining that higher vibratory level of faith will magnetize your goal to you, yes, thanks to the Universal Law of Attraction.

Remember to strengthen your power and speak aloud. Bring your goal into your physical reality through the vibration of your voice. That which you speak becomes concrete. We do not mean for you to tell your goal to every passerby; rather, speak aloud in your meditations, your healing sessions with us, your walks in the park, and your prayers. The more you speak to Spirit, even though the room may seem empty, the closer you draw to us and draw us to you.

What You Want Is Already Done

Dear one, are you still asking, "But how do I do it? How do I will what I want into existence?" Our answer is simply, "By imagining it already done." The human brain is a wondrous thing; it does not distinguish between what is real and what is imagined. It functions only on data input. So you can dream your goal into being!

See it done. Imagine yourself beyond the manifestation; see yourself happily working within your goal. Prepare as if your heart's desire has already arrived. Keep sending love and gratitude from the heart, thanks to Spirit for having accomplished the goal. All the while, gather your tools.

Make them, if you can, so you can hold them in your hands. Or imagine them in your life, see yourself using them, and see yourself functioning as if your goal has already arrived. Put your awareness beyond getting the goal to the joy of having the goal. Be there, see it in your mind's eye, imagine how good you feel having created your goal, and it will catch up to you.

Do you follow? We hope you will.

How this is done is moment by moment. Put yourself into the mental groove of gratitude for the goal accomplished, and when your thoughts stray from that perspective, pull yourself back into it. Pretty soon, you will be functioning at a higher level of joyful awareness and creativity that will accomplish any goal that you seek.

Your Best Spiritual Tool Is You

The key that unlocks the door to the higher realms is not a physical key — it is a vibrational key! It is you, dear human, with all layers of your energetic being cleared, balanced, and working in harmony. You must key into a higher level of vibrational harmony in order to reach us. Here we offer a summary of the steps necessary to wield these three universal laws together:

Step 1: Focus your intent on a goal to bring it down (manifest it) from thought into physical reality.

Step 2: Allow your goal to form by sustaining the energy of joyous expectation. Imagine it done, keep giving thanks, and get busy collecting your tools.

Step 3: Know in the depths of your Be-ing that it is done. This brings in your goal and makes it real. Know that you have the power to create anything you desire, and sustain that knowing as you prepare to receive.

Now, you might be thinking, "Easy to say, hard to do." Actually, you need "do" nothing physical except will yourself to feel happy. Your will resides in your etheric self, which is inextricably tied into your body. Wielding your will requires that you use your entire Be-ing, both physical and auric, together. The physical root of your will lies deep within your solar plexus. To reach it, you must dive deep and draw up the visualization of what you want. To send that goal out to Spirit, you must draw it up through your heart chakra and blend it with the emotional fuel of loving gratitude that will send it, straight and true, into the higher realms of materialization. This is called bridging the dimensions.

This process will teach you to live in and function from the expanded reality that you seek. The true point of this teaching is not to reward you with a car, a better job, or any single tangible goal, though these things will come to you once you learn how to wield the universal laws. Through the Circle of Grace work, we hope to facilitate your reaching your ultimate goal: becoming one with All That Is at all levels. Once you reach that sacred space, dear one, the things that you wish to materialize will be far different than your current list of wants or needs.

Remember, we said that your entire energetic Be-ing resides on many planes of existence at once. Up until recently, you were only consciously aware of the 3D plane because that was the only dimension your physical senses could register. Remember the dog whistle? Dogs can hear an octave above you. Now that you are in 4D, we exist only an octave above you. As you allow all the aspects of your total Be-ing to work together, you will achieve the full reconnection to Spirit you are seeking — communion with your own Higher Self. You need no longer work only from blind faith, dear one. Your expanded awareness will give you new eyes, a new perspective, and a new level of power from which to create a new future.

What is your best tool for manifestation? It is your own energetic Be-ing with all aspects cleared and functioning in smooth balance. That balance is under the direction of your spiritual layer, and it can be attained through the regular use of the Circle of Grace. Do you see why we have stepped forward with this healing information at this pivotal time in human evolution? The Veil of Forgetfulness is thinning. You need to prepare for life beyond the veil. You will be living in many dimensions at once, beyond your current 4D reality. As you expand your mental and spiritual awareness, you will realize that your body must also make that journey. Begin now to merge all that you have learned into the foundation of your Be-ing — your physical core. Begin your true journey outward by going inward with the Circle of Grace. The true learning lies in the doing.

We ask that you remember who you really are. To re-member is to re-join. Do you see the layers of meaning in these words? We wait impatiently for our re-union with you, for we miss you greatly. Please remember that while your human lives are short, your true existence is eternal. You never cease to exist; on the contrary, your True Spiritual Reality is put on hold while you are away, in body and in lesson.

Your progress on the metaphysical path is predicated on your dedication. We do not ask you to spend hours in contemplation or change your life to accommodate these directions. Rather, we ask you to take care of yourselves, for you are all precious to us, every single human being. We act here as facilitators to smooth your path, to offer you guidance and hope. Even more, we offer you Spirit help if you will seek it. Be patient with us as we teach you how to clear your body, how to reach within and find the spark of Divinity that is the core truth of your soul. It is an exciting inward journey, an adventure that you share, alone, with Spirit [chuckles and a big hug].

We are always near, and you are always dear.

You will find a need to reread this material. Different things will come to your attention each time. We teach in layers upon layers, as is the nature of all existence. We say that you are ready to shed a layer and reach up for a new one. Make joyful preparations for your life journey and plan a map of where you see your destination to be. We can help you with both of these things by teaching you the way things work in the higher realms. You will then know how to make the universal laws work for you.

You are in charge of your life. Begin to nourish that truth inside of yourself in order to manifest your divine birthright. It is time to step off of the karmic wheel and gain a new, strong, steadfast foothold back in the world that is your True Reality. Once your 4D world expands far enough in frequency to begin blending with our 5D world, you will have arrived. We wait impatiently for that moment, even as we create it together. We yearn for your Homecoming, our splendid reunion with all of you Earth angels in the True Reality of Spirit.

⑧

The Law of
Divine Creation

I Am God ~ You Are God ~ We Are One

Greetings from the Brotherhood of Light. In this section of the Circle of Grace material, we would like to focus on the Universal Law of Divine Creation. We began with the Law of Materialization, which explains how to manifest into your reality that which you focus on. The Law of Allowing teaches you how to allow into your world that which you focus on and desire from the depths of your heart.

The third and ultimate universal law is the Law of Divine Creation. This law simply states that All Is One. That means We are all One, and you as humans are part of that "We." Therefore, if you are part of All That Is, you have the same characteristics as the Divine Source, including the power within you to create as God does.

The crowning gift from Spirit to humanity is the inherent birthright to be all that is God. The goal of your ascension process is rejoining All That Is while a piece of your soul awareness inhabits a human body. Man's crowning glory is to become a bridge between dimensions, between different levels of consciousness, to return to Spirit without dying and leaving the body. Do you see why your entire Be-ing must be ready at all levels to make this leap? Being emotionally, mentally, and spiritually awakened is wonderful progress but will only take you three-quarters of the way up the spiritual path. You must also be cleared and balanced in body to fully actualize your goal.

To this end, we have stepped forward to explain how universal energies interact at all different levels, and to offer our aid in your journey back to self-realization. The Brotherhood's dedication of effort to the Divine Plan is to help humanity to evolve. Our collaboration with you serves to help us do our chosen work too. And our chosen work here, dear ones, is to bring into your awareness the Circle of Grace.

The Circle of Grace is a comprehensive exercise that clears, balances, and integrates all levels of your entire energetic Be-ing. There are many Brothers waiting to be called on for help, more than there are humans on the planet. As we exist in the now of circular time, we are available to you each and every time you call on us. We will help you work past your fears and doubts so that you may become the instrument of God's plan that you chose to be in this life before it began while you were still among us in Spirit.

Those of you who lie down and seek our help will find us waiting!

Within this body of text are embedded many layers of information explaining the form and function of the True Reality that you cannot yet see. As you make progress, you will find new information shine forth from rereading the text. There are answers to all of your questions regarding the Circle of Grace exercise and how to do it. We have endeavored to teach you how to clear and balance all the layers of your body, both physical and etheric. We explained how your spiritual layer governs your other layers and why all the layers must work together in a clear, balanced union to match and merge with the expanded frequencies of 4-5D.

Now, as we reach the crux of our message about the universal laws, we say that you cannot wield the preceding laws without total mastery of the Law of Divine Creation. In order to manipulate your reality to create what you want, you must believe that you can do it!

The Laws of Materialization and Allowing only function if you believe in your own power. In other words, you must wield all three universal laws together. As always, circles within circles of cause and effect. Knowing how to cause that effect allows you to will it into being! This power comes within your reach when you understand how to work with — and within — the energetic laws of the universe. The Law of Divine Creation is the seat of your will. The Laws of Materialization and Allowing explain how to wield your will.

Remember this: When you wield your will as Divine Creator, you are first creating a frequency change around you. All of life is defined by vibratory patterns that then translate into physicality. To consciously form the vibratory blueprint of your future, you must begin by creating your goal at the etheric level. That is how God creates, and that is what you are learning to do. As Jesus said, "All that I do, you can do also."

All of this will be possible once you fully believe, down to your very biology, that it is possible. You have incredible spiritual (etheric) powers that you are simply not aware of yet. In the old energy, it took full focus for many lifetimes to achieve any mastery toward ascension. Now time is growing short, as you say, and you are feeling the effects of its compression. Once you rise fully into the vibrational band of 5D, the energy will even out, balancing you and everything around you to this new, higher level.

You have come a long way in your understanding of metaphysics in a very short period of time (linear time as you know it) since the mid-1980s. There is now an ever-rising exponential curve of new awakenings, as more people become aware that there is something more to life and begin to seek the light. We ask that you continue to put your focus and energy into your upward, inward climb and gently say that in order to do this well, you must conserve your energies and stop wasting them. It is you, first-awakened, who will help the masses to follow a new path, one that you create with every step you take in your spiritual quest for wholeness and balance.

In this time of global strife, do you finally see clearly the waste of energy and life that comes from arguing over whose God is better? God is everywhere and everything. There is only one totality of consciousness that constructs and directs all of the many universes that comprise the body of All That Is.

The Brotherhood of Light is composed of many different life expressions, yet we all work together. Do you see this as an example? If we warred among ourselves as to who is better, who knows more, and who is closer to God's truth, the Brotherhood and all that it stands for would be destroyed, and justly so. Then we could not fulfill our major chosen function: helping humanity to evolve. That is why we come in as the Brothers and do not identify ourselves as individuals. Our work with you is what is most important, not who we each are.

Know that for each person, event, and situation, the appropriate Brothers will step forward to help. As we help you to ascend, you help us to ascend too. As each level rises, the levels above and below must necessarily rise as well. We all play a part in the Divine Plan, each in our own way.

In order to rise gracefully with the heightening energies, we offer this advice: Go forth and be guided by the strength of your intuitive feelings. That which is good will feel right. That which is bad will feel bad, and you will recognize it as such, even if it gives you momentary pleasure. Your inner heart will always guide you true. Remember that your divine power lies in wielding your positive emotions through your heart — that is the creative power of love. Negative emotions drag you back down into lower frequencies, causing you to mis-create through negative intent. Learn to recognize the difference, and choose wisely!

There will be more external strife and stress as you work your way through this pivotal time in human history. Keep peace in your heart, no matter what goes on around you. Both your local and global problems represent life lessons in graduating levels of understanding, levels of learning, and levels of advancement. They all serve to bring you Home again with the clear and sure knowledge: God exists and that God exists for all. Not for some, but for all.

Do you follow? We hope you will, for there is only one true path Home — through the heart.

The Voice of "I Am" Speaks

The hearts of humanity will soon reach up and connect with the heart of God. You will know when that occurs, yes, you will! Yes, children, you will know, for then I will appear to you, to each one in his right time and place, for you are all beloved. Darkness was only created for the purpose of making My Light shine more brightly. Evil is the same — a counter mirror to love. Have you not suffered enough? Have you not learned enough? I ask that you find your way Home through love and kindness so that We may, once again, all consciously reside together in the body of All That Is.

When you begin the healing prayer with, "Dear Father/Mother God, Creator of all that is, was, and ever will be," do you see the totality of that prayer? The wholeness of that prayer? The wonder of being part of All That Is? I cherish you all, and it is time for you to cherish Me in the same way that I cherish you. I give you this image: If you could all, every last man, woman, and child, lay down your weapons of war and embrace love, then you will all ascend in that first split-second of total Brotherhood of Man.

Then, truly, you will have created Eden in your midst by eradicating evil, anger, and hatred in your hearts. Those of you who choose to go Home will, in that instant, be brought Home to Me. Those of you who choose to stay and live in the higher dimensions will rejoice in every breath and every day spent on your beautiful planet. That will be your New Jerusalem, the bright future of Earth that metaphysics offers. In the Law of Divine Creation, I say this to you:

I Am One — You Are One — We Are One

It is sad and wasteful for you to fight over whose image of Me is better. I wish for no person to kill another, for all life is precious. Now is the time for Global Brotherhood. Now is the time for all of humankind to unite as brothers under the skin, and direct your energies and passions toward more useful purposes. Work on eradicating hunger, poverty, and most of all, ignorance, anger, and fear. If you feel the need to defend yourselves against evil in your reality, so be it. Evil only exists as a mirror to good. That which is good will always prevail. That which is evil cannot, and will not, win.

Dear ones, there is no such thing as hell. Those whom you perceive as evil, even if they have done grievous harm, come back to Me after their lives are over. I judge no one but rather give you the right to measure your own progress after each life in body. Your evil doers are also part of the Divine Plan in the sense that they have courageously agreed to a difficult life path by taking on a contract stipulating that they create evil, fear, and horror as lessons to teach humanity.

To teach you what? To teach you that all life is precious. To teach you that all forms of life are equally precious. To teach you that all that is, is really All That Is! These lessons are still being processed and must be played out in your material world, even though many of you have super-ceded the need for it at the spiritual level.

These teachings must be assimilated at all levels, including the physical. The Circle of Grace is a process that will help you assimilate your lessons down into the individual physical level. The Global Brotherhood of Man is the necessary manifestation of this very same clearing process, played out at the global physical level. Why is this needed? To clear those destructive patterns from the human consciousness. The Divine Plan covers all levels and all details, great and small. All levels of reality are shifting together, from deep inside the Earth to the outer reaches of your galaxy and beyond.

When one level shifts, all levels must shift.

As each of you individually works on your personal ascension, you fuel the ascension of all humanity. The true victory of humanity is living harmoniously together when all men release the need to kill. Once you achieve a firm foothold in the higher realms, killing will be abhorrent to you, for it goes against the Will of God. Once you feel My presence as a living force within you, your reality will change, the planet will change, and you will have no more need for war. Peace will loom large all around the Earth when enough of you are finally one with Me.

You have lived many, many lifetimes in order to come back to your original state of oneness with God. It is time to assimilate your lessons, to learn and grow and evolve as a species, as a Global Brotherhood, as a human expression of God in action. It is time to move past those lessons and begin living the ultimate truth: You are all one. You are all brothers and sisters of the human kind.

It is far easier, far simpler, and requires far less energy to love rather than to hate. The laying down of hatred in your lives is an act of allowing love to shine forth in your hearts. That is why I have, through the words of the Brothers, endeavored to give you My teachings, My path for you to follow in order to come back Home to Me.

I Am God. I Am the Brotherhood. I Am All That Is and You Are Part of Me.

Do you follow? I hope you will.

For this is an act of will that I require, an act of free will, to release fear in all of its faces and embrace the one truth that I represent: unconditional love. It is so simple and so close to you. Reach out to each other and you will be reaching up to Me. Do I favor one color of skin over another? Never. I created you all different yet equal. Do I favor one form of religion over another? Never.

I Am One. It is you who have created these divisions. It is you who must now erase that hatred from your hearts. It is you who must heal your differences so that you can come together and create love all around your globe.

I wish to comment on the word "will." I ask that you reread this material, and see how many times and in how many ways the word "will" was used. It is a pattern, a trigger, a path to lead you to understanding that you are in charge of your lives, your will to make it what it is, for better or worse. Those same words are used in your marriage ceremonies, "... for better or worse, in sickness and health, till death do us part." Yes, now look at that phrase again, and see the marriage that I offer you here.

I love you all. I cherish you all. I welcome you back, no matter what state you are in, better or worse, sick or healthy. Death reunites us, dear ones. Your transition back to the realm of Spirit is your true Homecoming, while your birth into body has been, up until now, your separation from the True Reality that I represent.

I send you forth to learn these lessons, that you may come back to Me in the purity of love. I ask only that you find within yourselves the purity of love from which you sprang. Then all of your lifetimes, all of your wisdom and knowledge gained, I will assimilate into My Body, that I may also learn and grow from you.

I Am That I Am. You are of Me, and to Me you shall return. Until then, I await you in the quiet silence of your own inner truth, in the energetic cycle of healing and clearing that I bestowed to your bodies when I created you. Do you think that I would neglect your care? I care for you, and I reach for you; whenever you close your eyes to sleep, I cleanse and heal you from within.

Now, in this time of great transition I bring this knowledge, this precious information, before the Veil. The Circle of Grace is your way Home. I bring it into the light so that you may see it, understand it, use it, and in doing so, come Home to Me. I give you this blessing, and the clarity of understanding it through the efforts of the Brotherhood of Light so that your path will be clearly lit. Even look at the name of the Brotherhood of Light — it represents all that I Am, all that I stand for. All that I require of you is to become brothers in the light of day, in the light of love, in the Light and Love of God. I ask that you pay attention, all of my children, and see that you are all one family representing all of the oneness that I Am.

Why did I create you thus? To give you more opportunity to learn and grow. Is there not a cornucopia of plants and trees on Earth? Is there not a splendid variety of birds and animal species on Earth? Each living creature plays a part and has a special role in the Grand Design that I created. There is a specific purpose to the dolphin, the whale, and the shark. I ask that you honor all forms of life on your planet, at every level of creation. Stop killing each other! Stop killing My beloved crawling and flying and swimming creatures. Stop destroying this beautiful world I created for you. Do you not see the layers of pattern, the circles within circles, that encapsulate all of life?

You cannot willfully destroy any aspect or area of life on Earth without the entire life cycle of the planet being affected. I ask that you look beyond your needs of the moment and become the caretakers of this living planet that you were meant to be. I ask you to look to the Earth's needs and tend to her, for she is truly your physical mother. The more you connect with the Earth, the easier will be your rising along with her.

So, my dear children, it is time. Now is the time of special dispensation. Now is the emergence of Spirit's True Reality, and I ask that you listen to Me now. You are so close, and yet many of you still harbor doubt. Do you not see Me in the perfection of the smallest detail, in the wonder of every form of life? All of the Divine Plan is balanced, from the smallest form to the highest form, to return to Me. That is your primary goal, the goal of each and every lifetime. I have told you how to create it. Now it is up to you to do so.

Do you follow? I hope you will!

— I Am, in All Love, All That Is You.

(9)

The Keys to Transformation

reetings, dear reader! To begin, we would like to point out that the Keys to Transformation, Mastery, and Happiness are overlapping aspects of self-realization and the ascension path you are on. The keys we offer in this section are interchangeable because they are interconnected. You could move the keys from one chapter to another and the text would still make sense. Do you see the many levels of our work together? Your four PEMS layers must harmonize together in order for you to fully reconnect with Spirit. You must wield the universal laws together in order to manifest your will. All the keys must work together in order for your journey to be fulfilled and fulfilling.

Dear ones, we hold such love for you. You all have the potential to succeed. We cheer every step, we cherish every tear, we mark every moment of joy and sorrow as a lesson that will lead you to graduation from the 3D plane of material life and strife. Do not be depressed by all of this information. Take small bites, chew thoroughly, enjoy the assimilation, and eat at your own pace. As we help you to lighten your physical body, we are also "fattening" your etheric aspects to take a strong, firm hold over all the rest.

Though we divide the concepts into steps to guide your progress, know that all of this work, all of this learning, and all that you will achieve must be done through attaining a higher perspective. How? By honing your awareness in each and every moment. Without attaining and maintaining that higher view of what life is truly about, this will merely be another book you read and then put back on the shelf. So here is the biggest key of all: *We ask you to start living your divinity!*

The Key to Honing Your Awareness

Since the turn of the twenty-first century, Earth has shifted into a higher expression of energetic frequency; she is rapidly advancing into a new synchronicity with the higher dimensions. You too have an opportunity, never before possible in human history, to shed your duality and step into that same flow of synchronicity. Your abilities as Divine Creator are already manifested, though most of you are not yet aware of your potential.

We have stated many times that you create your own reality. We have explained that you are truly in control of all that is around you — by virtue of you ability to focus your awareness on whatever you wish and bring it into your physical reality through your intent. That which you have always labeled as "extrasensory perception" is actually well within the capability of all peoples walking Earth. It would be a great expansion of perspective for you to consider telepathy, telemetry, clairvoyance, and so on, as "full-sensory perception" rather than "extra" senses or gifts that most people cannot attain. Why? Because you create what you focus on, and all of these abilities are well within the range of who you truly are: an eternal Be-ing with a temporary physical core. Again, we ask you to expand your awareness from 3-4D to 4-5D, which is where Earth is rapidly heading.

In the opening of your heart and mind, your priorities will change. Your life will become more balanced as you realize that you can choose where to put your energy. Will you leave it in 3D or will you plug it into 4D? Will you watch from 5D someone struggling in 3D and lend them a hand? Will you decide not to argue and walk away instead, because it is not worth disturbing your own peace of mind to have that argument? This part of the ascension process is where most people try to define their individuality and their own self-worth. Your path to healing is also your path to wholeness. The biggest gift we can give to you now is stating, without doubt, that you are all worthy! You see? Because we know where you come from. We know your Spirit selves. We know your Divine Source. We are waiting for you to become aware that your Higher Selves reside here beside us, in the higher realms, hidden behind the Veil of Forgetfulness.

Have you noticed that we are ending each paragraph with a comment about the state of your awareness? The ability to stretch your awareness? The powers you gain once you are aware of your true potential? Even the progress of your metaphysical growth is predicated on your ability to expand your awareness beyond what you can see, feel, hear, touch, and smell with only your physical senses.

Awareness is the key to transformation. Awareness is the key to attaining higher perception. Awareness of every moment brings you into the flow of now time, allowing you to enjoy each moment instead of worrying about the future or fretting over the past. In short, training your mind to be open and receptive, to be focused on that which you are Be-ing, allows you to do whatever you wish and create whatever you desire to manifest around you or within you. Dear one, retraining your mind is far more difficult than healing your body. Why? Because your thoughts and emotions govern your inner body chemistry at any given moment, yet few people are aware of that fact.

In earlier text, we explained that human emotions run on a scale from low to high, from fear to love, from damaging to healing. Yes, anger is destructive to your body. Joy is healing to your body. Once you are aware of how powerfully your thoughts and emotions affect your body, you will step into the awareness that you are in charge of your daily reality in every moment. With the ability to control your thoughts and be loving in every moment, you will be able to create all that you desire and all that you choose to have in your life.

Are you aware that you create your own health and your own diseases? You are so accustomed to tribal thought that most of you seek healing outside of yourselves. When you are ill you seek medical attention, which is good. But what if the doctors say to you, "Sorry, we can't help you, your condition is beyond our medical knowledge to heal. Time to write a will; you'll be dead in six months." Then what happens? Most people prepare to die, for they have been told that will be the outcome. The occasional "medical miracles" are people who refuse to die and instead recover, even though they have been handed a death sentence. Why?

We have the greatest respect for your medical sciences, for that which you have achieved in the last hundred years surpasses all the knowledge compiled in the past thousand years. In most modern societies, people seek help and healing outside of themselves after a disease has manifested. What we are teaching you here is how to prevent illness through care and maintenance of the aura. Your mental condition determines your physical condition. If you can heighten your awareness to being in the now, to being joyful in every moment, your etheric layers will heal and your physical body will not succumb to illness. If you can clear emotional, mental, and spiritual imbalances, they will not lodge in your physical core. Please be aware that fear causes chemical imbalances that wither away your body while being in a state of love causes chemical rebalancing in your body that promotes health and well-being.

Being aware is the biggest key. Being in the moment is the path to ascension. Being what? Happy, joyful, grateful to be alive! What are you ascending from and to? Your dense physical reality to our nonphysical reality, 3D to 4D to 5D. How do you achieve this goal? By climbing the emotional scale and learning to live at the top! How do you stay at the top? By being love manifest on Earth. What are your best climbing tools? Your belief systems, your faith, your understanding of life issues and how to conquer them — through love.

Be-ing in a state of unconditional love allows Higher Self to join you on the physical plane. Here we offer you an energetic perspective on the concept we discussed earlier: fear and love are conflicting vibrations that cannot coexist in the same space at the same time. Your Higher Self is of a much higher vibratory expression than your earthly being and cannot coexist with you in body if that body is filled with negative imbalances caused by fear. Being aware of your thoughts at all times and choosing which emotions to express leads you into mastery of your energetic expression, inner health, and outer reality. Then you will reach the resonance necessary for a true blending with your Higher Self. This is what we are here to teach you: Master your thoughts and emotions, and come live with us while you still walk Earth! Are you aware that you can do this?

Do you see the circular nature of these teachings? Layers within layers, leading to the higher expression of your total Be-ing. As the energies thicken, that which is currently invisible to you will soon become visible! Dear ones, those of you who pray for higher sight: Are you ready for what you will see? Be careful what you wish for. For now, be content to see an argument occurring and see beyond the anger to the life lessons being expressed. Use your compassion to guide your actions through a higher understanding of why people behave as they do. Forgive their lack of understanding and help them see the issues they are wrestling with. You will be spreading healing instead of harm, lending love where only anger reigns, and functioning from a higher awareness of the true nature of all levels of your reality.

Once your medical technology discovers that your bodies naturally clear pain and stress through the nervous system, scientists will probably name it something else. We call it the Circle of Grace because all forms of life fit into the sacred geometry of the Flower of Life. What is that shape? Circles upon circles upon circles! All of your mathematical formulas and equations can be found in that shape and are reflected in Nature in the whorls of flower petals, the spirals of sea shells, the elegant diversity of snowflakes. All of God's creations are perfectly balanced forms of sacred geometry within the scope of sacred science, which you are just beginning to discover. We ask you to leap beyond your current knowledge and have faith in the Divine Source that created you! Faith is an aspect of your higher awareness, governed by your spiritual layer, which you are learning to allow to govern.

Many of you are disappointed to read that although you have the potential to ascend, you will remain here in body. Dear ones, once you fully ascend, you will no longer need those bodies. You will no longer need to trudge up the karmic spiral, for you will have reached the top and reached beyond the need for repeated incarnations. That is the true goal of your future human potential. You are the ones tipping the scales. You are the ones making the giant step forward in human awareness, the leap in human consciousness, to achieve a state of total love while still inhabiting a physical body. We say gently that in order to do this, the mind must be in charge of the matter.

Your level of awareness is key to the ascension process. We have spoken about being in this world but not of it. Some of you are so focused on your upward rise that you are losing your grounding, your foothold in humanity. Your contract is to be here. To be human. To become ascended humans and raise matter itself to a higher vibratory expression of Be-ing. You cannot do all of that if you are seeking to escape the human condition.

Be present. Be loving, at all times, with every move you make and every breath you take. Once you begin to see the sheer beauty of this world, the perfection of all forms of life, you will be experiencing the fringes of ascension. Please, do not ask to speed up this process. Instead, ask for it to flow gracefully, in divine timing, for your highest good. Then be patient and allow it to come in. Until you are fully present in now time you will not see the workings of divine time. That is your leap of faith, dear one, trusting that all will unfold as it should, under grace and for your highest good. Through our work together and the words before you, we offer you access to the Divine flame you carry, have always carried, and have never lost.

The Key to Attaining a Higher Perspective

What is this search for ascension? It is a seeking of higher wisdom and knowledge, an inner knowing that there is much more to life than you can see. It is a moving up of all that you are to become all that you can be. How do you attain a higher perspective? Reading books, doing exercises, joining groups, attending seminars — all of these activities establish good momentum and a solid foundation. The spiritual and mental concepts must take hold before you can begin to materialize the effects in your physical world. But your truest task and surest path is living your divinity day-to-day, moment by moment. How? At every turn, choose love over hate, compassion over fear. Earth is a freewill zone. Your ability to choose is your biggest gift. Each present moment will become a wondrous present from Spirit! [Chuckles.]

Throughout this material, we have explored the needed change in perspective that underlies all of your progress: releasing the separation of duality for the wholeness of oneness. What does that mean? That you will view this life and everything in it from a new enlightened perspective. You will begin to cherish every moment of being in body as a rare, fleeting gift. You will see lessons unfold around you, the dramas that people play and karma they create, good and bad. Your higher perspective will lead to new understanding, which will allow you to coast through all experiences without stepping into the lessons that people are blindly acting out.

If you consider each life as a level of school, one that you attend and then go Home, you will appreciate the transience of physical life. Some people who embrace the philosophy of reincarnation are having trouble fitting that into the "now time" perspective. If all time is really now and all is happening at once, then where is the spiral of life-death-rebirth? Does it disappear? Is this belief system actually wrong in terms of spiritual science? Dear ones, again, this is a difference in perspective. The reincarnation structure is perfectly molded for your duality, which requires biological life and death, plus separation from Spirit. From within that duality-reality, that is what is real and the reincarnation belief stands correct.

But from a higher perspective, since there is no past, present, or future (i.e., linear time), the parameters of our True Reality make time much more flexible and accessible. Since you are really eternal beings, your physical births and deaths are all part of your learning process and thus your soul's growth. What we are endeavoring to explain to you, as you sit separate in your duality perspective, is that the eternal you has done this life-death cycle many times and still exists. As soon as your energetic body releases your current physical shell, you move into the higher dimensions and are gladly welcomed back. Yes, you are greeted by your soul family, your true family, in whatever form you need to help ease the transition back from the lower realms.

Now we ask you to live from that divine perspective, to see out of new eyes — the eyes of your Higher Self that knows all of this to be true, and more. We ask you to expand your vision of "faith in a higher power" to "a higher power resides in you and is you." Do you see the difference? One is separate; the other is One. [Chuckles.]

Yes, indeed, humor is divine and contains much healing energy. We have quite a sense of humor and endless patience, since we do not measure time in units that are lost. When you call on us in the Circle of Grace meditation, you will find that we have all the time in the world. All of the information we offer here relates to healing of mind, spirit, and body. Once you begin to see yourself as an energetic being with a physical core, you will make much progress on the path to true healing.

The Key to Belief in Self

Throughout our teachings, we have emphasized two things: you all have the potential to become self-realized, and that power already lies within you. In truth, you already have succeeded. Remember, you are eternal. That is the big cosmic joke, dear one, that we keep asking you to remember who you truly are, and you keep saying, "Remember what?" [Chuckles.] Until you gain access to your cellular memories we advise you to have faith in yourself, in knowing that you are divine, in knowing that as long as you live through your heart, you cannot fail.

The key to all success, inner and outer, is finding self-love, self-worth, and self-confidence. Notice that this is all to do with self. Nobody else's opinion should stand in your heart's way. Believe in yourself! Once you start living and seeking what your heart dictates, not your mind, you will create joy in your life, eradicate fear and illness from your being, and truly embrace the higher realms.

By now, many of you are having new sensory experiences, from hearing disembodied voices, to getting thoughts dropped into your head, to seeing flashes of new colors, or things that shouldn't be there. Your old, 3D way of thinking discounts all of this new sensory input. The old mindset requires proof, it creates fear around ignorance, and it resists change by digging in its heels and covering its sight. Fear blocks action.

For those of you who have faced the changes you know you must make and are actively working on them, we say, congratulations and watch out. Fear of the unknown is a predictable visitor as you go through these changes, so we wish to convey in this piece one major message: Each time you strike forth into the unknown, the first thing that you will encounter is your own fear.

Right behind fear is doubt, pushing in its ugly nose to further deepen your chaos. Though fear and doubt may dog your heels, we say they are easy to kick away once your growing tool set is burgeoning with self-love, self-worth, and self-belief. Believing in yourself is the most necessary ingredient for creating a better future. The inpouring of Divine Mother love from the Venus transit of June 8, 2004, created a new chord within the rising energies. Since then, a loving balance is required in all things, in all aspects of your body and your life.

Thanks to Venus, the most important shifts that will now occur are in the area of love. Your relationships to people, places, and things will transition along with your senses as you take in more information than previously possible and therefore see with new eyes. The more you flow with the changes that are needed in your life, the more graceful and grace-filled your life will become. The more you resist change and stick to your old ways of thinking, feeling, and seeing, the more stuck you will become.

For example, do you despair over the current state of marriage and feel that there is too much divorce in this world, that you have sworn to be together, for better or worse, until death do you part? We gently point out that sometimes staying in a painful marriage or a stressful job can kill you quite effectively. Sorrow, sadness, and fear weaken the body and create opportunities for it to sicken. Then it is only a matter of which diseases you are predisposed or exposed to. When your belief system forces you to remain in a loveless relationship, do you think God is cheering for you? Do you think that Divine Source expects you to sacrifice your happiness for somebody else's view of proper tradition and behavior?

Dear one, you are moving away from the old, fear-based 3D tribe. You must also move away from the old fear-based judgments that used to rule your life. You must move beyond judgment anyway, toward yourself and others, in order to be able to love unconditionally. Are you the same person you were ten, twenty, thirty years ago when you made that commitment? No. Would you pick that same person now to be your life mate? If your answer is no, then your path is clear. Painful as it may be, you must seek and find your own happiness above all else, your own self-love and self-worth, before you can share your love with another at a higher level of expression.

In this time of heavier energies, when so much of your physical stamina is unconsciously devoted to the shifting process, we ask you to simplify your priorities. Simplify your daily life. When you are dealing with concepts of this magnitude, does it really matter if you are driving a Mercedes or a Ford? Be honest with yourself as to what you want and don't want, what you really need and don't need. All of this will become simple, simple indeed, because as you rise into the higher dimensions, you will become attuned to higher morals, higher concepts, and a higher expression of love in all that you do.

Conditional love does not exist in the higher realms, dear one. Don't worry about having to deal with all the drama once you detach from duality, for it simply will not affect you any more. You will love all equally, no matter what pattern they may be embroiled in at that moment. As you stand witness, you will hold for them their highest potential in mind, while forgiving them for their blindness and their unconscious actions. You will have the power to love your worst enemy, and therefore make that person your friend. Once there is no longer any "us and them" at any level of your thinking and belief structures, you will have entered the higher flow of Divine grace.

Do you follow? We know you will!

Above all else, we ask you to love yourself. We say, have faith in yourself. Take charge of your life, and change it for the better so that it gives you joy. Maybe you have too many obligations to just strike out and follow your heart. Being in body means being responsible for what you create. So pay your bills, honor your debts, and keep your promises. But also find time to do things that feed your soul. Follow studies that resonate energetically; learn to detach from the dramas that you no longer need to play. Once you change how you play the game of life, all the other players around you will be forced to change. You are energetically in charge of your own perspective and therefore in charge of your own reality.

We thank you for honoring your contracts, for keeping a strong heart when everything seems dark, for having faith in yourself. That is the most vital thing you need to develop. Having faith in yourself means loving who you are just as you are, forgiving all that has happened, and being able to walk as I Am on Earth. Remember, you are never alone, you are all One! Merely close your eyes and God is there. And even as you think to summon us, we are already there. When you transcend, whether in body or not, you will realize that we are merely stepping aside to welcome you back into the ranks of Spirit.

Communing with Spirit

Here we wish to talk about nonphysical communication, and the changes needed in your concepts of communication in order to shift your awareness to receive input from the higher levels. At the 3D level, which has been until now your normal functioning mode of communication, you transmit ideas and emotions via the spoken word (through the vibration of your voice), or by written word, also through the efforts of the physical body. Up until now, you have only used your physical body to communicate. Some may say that unspoken body language is also an effective way to communicate — we agree and add it to the list of physical language expressions.

Now, as you grow into your aura and develop a new range of sensory awareness, what do you think will happen? Have you considered the mechanics of it? What you have categorized from a 3D perspective to be extrasensory perception is actually the new range of full-sensory perception that you are growing into. Telepathy is the refined mode of communicating in the higher realms. Your senses will unfurl to reach other gifts as well: clairvoyance, clairaudience, seeing auras and the higher energies, and more. Imagine adding cable service to a television set and suddenly accessing hundreds of stations that weren't there before. Simply put, you are expanding into the realms of nonphysical communication.

Do you follow? We hope you will! Congratulations, and welcome!

In the previous section, we asked you to lock in your awareness of Being in every moment. Put your senses on high and work on absorbing all incoming information around you, at any level! If this causes fear to rise in you due to pre-set beliefs about dark versus light, then ask to receive only that which is "of the light and in the light." Weave that phrase into all of your thoughts, and make that your air-tight protection in your free-will zone. Only by permission — remember that! Your thoughts are truly things that exist in conceptual form, in nonphysical form, waiting to be brought down into density and created into material form. That is your true gift and a testament to the powers you will wield, once you are ready.

You are masters of material creation. Always be aware of how and what you are creating.

As you reach clarity in your PEMS layers, you will become your own "cable service." And that, dear one, is the moment we impatiently wait for: when you finally realize that you can open communications with us. Communing with Spirit has always been and always will be a two-way exchange. But when all you have is a land-line [chuckle] and our response floats down on the air waves, no wonder you couldn't tell if you had been heard or what the answer was. Now that you are developing the proper receiving equipment, each and every one of you has the potential to connect directly and interact directly with Spirit in the True Reality of All That Is.

Do you see why this is already done? Yes, for you are reading our words. Do you see why this will be a gradual, smooth glide if you remain flexible to change and focus on the positive? Change is the only constant in the universe. You create what you focus on. The rising energies are making it easier and easier for you to create, and we ask that you be ready and able to master these changes.

In offering to work with you, we give you a final gift to further your imagination and expand your potential. Why wait for a healing session to call in Spirit? You should be communing with your Higher Self all the time, since you are striving to lock in and live from that higher perspective. You can amend the healing prayer in myriad ways, and we will gladly guide and protect you on trips to the dentist or doctor, to take a test, to work or to play. Keep calling in Spirit, keep asking for help, and all will flow better. Remember, we said the communication is two-way. Imagine that it already is, and you will be actively creating that reality.

This is excellent practice for Be-ing in the new energies all the time. See all of life as a waking meditation. Yes, and be aware that we are there with you. Your whole life is becoming one long communion with Spirit, so why not start it yourself? Make no mistake, we do not hang around every minute of every day, nor do we intrude in anything you consider private. Once you achieve that constant conscious connection that you so desire, you need never be alone again.

We so look forward to working with you in a conscious way. You all have guides and angels, dear ones. The support from the higher realms is way beyond the current comprehension of most people. This too will change as you each reach that higher potential and create new channels for Spirit to pour love down onto Earth. We are so proud of your progress, we cherish every laugh, every tear, every gesture of love that you express. We are filled with awe at the beautiful tapestry you are weaving as you make the loving signature of the new, light-bodied human Be-ing an integral part of the Divine Plan.

Through your individual efforts to become a healed and joyful person, each and every one of you contributes to the raising of the human awareness. How? By cocreating with your own divinity, you will find and merge with the eternal essence of your True Be-ing while you are still in a physical body. The more of you who strive toward this goal, the more accessible it becomes for all. You are establishing the potential and the path for others to follow. For all of your efforts, we in Spirit are deeply grateful.

You each play an essential role in moving humanity upward and divinity forward. Once earthly matter becomes spiritualized, what miracles you will create. Your diversity is your greatest asset, your focused intent your greatest tool, and your faith your greatest strength. Wield them all together, and you will create Eden in your midst. It is our greatest honor to aid and support your progress on your path to full transformation.

(10)

The Keys to Mastery

Greetings, dear readers, from the Brotherhood of Light. We are your ancient guardians, the Melchizedeks, whose energy spreads up and through the entire Brotherhood healing hierarchy to the galactic logos, Father Melchizedek. Throughout your history, we have protected and guided you gently up the path back Home again. As you digest all of the previous healing information, we offer you this train of thought: the progress of humankind back to God begins its evolution from your outermost highest layers, down through your denser layers, then through your physical core. Why do we keep repeating that you must heal at all levels in order to evolve? Because you are down to the core work, and that core is your body.

Without clearing your vehicle, you cannot expand your senses, integrate right and left brain, and fully blend with your own divinity. You cannot maintain a state of unconditional love without first reaching that higher perspective. You cannot achieve spiritual momentum without first forgiving all that has happened in your life and all the people concerned, especially yourself. You cannot maintain that higher space without achieving balance through understanding the concepts of free will, choice, and flexibility.

If this work seems redundant, please forgive our long-windedness, but you learn through repetition, through trial and error, and through picking yourself up and starting over again. Remember that no matter what happens, no matter what you do or don't do, Spirit does not judge. God only loves you. In order to be Godlike, do not judge anyone or anything, including yourself. Just learn to love All of it.

What drives your spiritual quest first? Knowing that something is missing. That knowing is all you can glean from your higher auric layers. Those layers are blocked by the Veil of Forgetfulness, so you don't know what you're missing. All you know is that you often feel incomplete and alone. So what fills that gap?

The Key of Faith

Faith. In your history, specific religions and belief structures have molded and guided you until you didn't need to be propped up by them any more. That time has now come. When seeking faith becomes a solitary quest, you have arrived at recognizing your own God potential. How do you know when you have reached this stage? Let us pose the question in another way: How does your body accumulate and store cellular memories? In holographic patterns within your energetic layers, that's how. Your spiritual layer records what you learn about faith within the tribal mindset of every life experience. Each religion and society carries specific lessons, so you learned over and over that positive faith and negative faith can reside side by side.

It is your free will to choose which manner of faith to embrace.

Life lessons are recognized and processed by your mental layer, which holds the record of your many different concept forms experienced. This is where religion does or does not make sense, according to the evaluation of your conscious mental self. This is where you work out what does and does not ring true to you. Where do you test the tone of that ring? With your emotional body.

Your emotional body absorbs the spiritual beliefs and the mental concepts, then produces an emotion that resonates within your being. This is where you express your feelings about what you believe in and don't believe in. The welling up of emotion is your auric self (or your higher-dimensional self) communicating with you. When something resonates in a positive way at all levels of your being, you get a sense of well-being [chuckles]. This sense of well-being says to the rest of your layers, "Yes, this feels good and right. Choose this. Go this way. This is best." Remember, your emotional body doesn't speak to you in words like your mental body does. Your emotional layer sends you feelings in order to communicate with your conscious mental awareness.

You have always called this your "intuition." It is much more than that, children, it is your own powerful Eternal presence speaking to you. Please remember that up until now, your concept of self has been formed through your 3D senses anchored in your body. You have had no conscious experience or proof that you are any more than a physical being. Now we come along and say, "Wake up! Look at each other; you will see each other's perfection and divinity before you see your own." This is, in and of itself, a huge leap to make in expanding your mental framework of reference.

Above all else, we ask you to assume a new definition of yourself as an energetic, holographic, eternal Be-ing. Do you see now how true faith filters in from Spirit, teasing your shuttered mind to open again? From your spiritual layer, through your mental layer, then your emotional layer, to — ah, yes, — the physical body! What is the final step? Becoming your divinity. Embracing your spirituality, merging all of your knowledge into your physical core, your innermost layer, which will become your vehicle to carry you into 5D reality. How do you accomplish this daunting but doable task?

We hold such great love for you all. We await you, holding the Circle of Grace, waiting to drape it over and through your bodies to begin the final levels of healing. Please keep in mind that this transitional time heralds a new beginning, not an ending. Once the new energies of the photon belt settle around and through your planet and your bodies, you will have all the time in the world to cocreate with Spirit the future of your choosing.

The Key to Free Will Is Choice

A few words of caution are needed here to balance all of the incoming metaphysical information around you, including that which you hold in your hands. It is vital to your own development to accept those concepts that resonate for you and let the rest go. Truth is a very personal, intimate thing that is different for each person. Use your blooming 4-5D senses to filter out what is true for you. This also applies to going to seminars, lectures, and listening to other people's perspectives. Hold on to what feels good and right to you, and put the rest back. Your greatest gift from Spirit is the power of choice that you wield from being in Earth's freewill zone!

For those of you already adjusting your lives to honor your changing needs in these changing energies, life will flow more easily. For those of you who feel the need for change and see what needs changing but do nothing, that is also a choice. When you choose out of fear, you take a lower path. Whenever you see a choice before you, know that it is more than just yes and no, stay or go. There is always a third or fourth choice to consider. Either the decision is not yet ripe to be made (neither yes or no really work) or your choice can be not to act at all. The path of non-action opens the universe around you to do what it will, not what you will. On that path, the Law of Attraction will deepen your lessons, making you feel buffeted by the unknown and unwieldy twists and turns of life. That is the old way, dear heart, the old 3D fear-based separatist way of viewing life, of letting life control you.

Do you believe that for every question, there exists an answer somewhere? Sometimes when you are having trouble making a decision, it is a wise choice to say, "Yes, I know the answer is out there; I just don't know where it is or how to find it yet." Realizing there is a gap in your information is much more productive than being stalled or giving up because you don't see a solution. Some people force themselves to make a choice that they don't feel is right in their hearts, but they do it because it sounds right in their minds. Here we say, please remember divine timing. Just because the right choice is not apparent, never conclude that it does not exist.

Can you see air? No. Does it exist? Yes. Would you miss it if it disappeared, even though you can't see it? Oh, yes, indeed, you would know the instant you had no more air to breathe. We could continue in this vein for a while. Can you see radio waves? Can you see x-rays? Can you see gravity? Can you see satellite transmissions and TV broadcasts? Can you see microwaves? Can you see the whole Internet? Can you see your auras? We hope you get the picture.

All of these examples have to do with invisible forces of energy that you use every day and take for granted. We wish to expand this understanding you have of invisible things that you use in order to include us and the higher realms. Can you see us yet? No. Do we exist? Yes. Do we exist whether or not you believe we do? Yes. Can we help you reach us? Yes. Can we do it for you without your dedicated effort? No. You must take the time, and make the effort, to reach up from within. The Circle of Grace, dear ones, is already within you. All of your answers and solutions do exist within you, even if you cannot see them yet.

You may be thinking it can't be that simple. Life is just too complicated, too demanding, too hard for a simple meditation to fix everything. We ask you here, "Why can't good things be simple? Why can't the best solutions be easy?" If you believe that all reward comes from hard, unremitting work, then that is the path that you choose to inflict on yourself. If that is your expectation of life, that is what you will create. What you believe in creates your reality. Your duality-reality is designed to conform to your level of energetic vibration. The Law of Attraction is designed to bring you experiences to further your life lessons based on the vibrational tone that you emit.

When we say that all of life experience on Earth is designed to bring you your life lessons, we mean all levels of life. Everything that happens around you and within you can be seen and explained through the perspective of life lessons that your soul is seeking to learn. Many crisis situations are lessons that were not addressed when they were manageable, and now have grown to dysfunctional proportions. Were you to study the evolution of these situations, you would see the moments when abundance issues arose and became obstacles, when communication issues blocked potential resolution, and how focusing on or ignoring the situation turned the tide one way or the other. Looking back is only good for tracking those patterns for seeing where you went wrong and why so that you may change the outcome the next time.

You have a saying, "Hindsight is cheap," and we do agree on that! Hindsight can be very constructive if you see the mistake and learn not to repeat it. Hindsight can also be very destructive if you get stuck there, saying I should have done this, I could have done that, if only I had known, and so on. Well, if you had known, the lesson would not have presented itself! We do not mean to be flippant here, for we know how many of you are struggling with huge problems, heart-wrenching decisions, and life-threatening situations. In times of crisis, people reach up for God's help in whatever form they believe. Through our teachings, we offer to meet with you on a more regular basis [chuckles]. Let us work together so that your life will be a cocreation of physical expression through spiritual intent. You do not have to bounce from one crisis to the next like a rubber ball. You can learn to affect and direct all that is around you.

We ask you to detach from the drama of what you are experiencing and look at it dispassionately. [Pardon the pun!] What is the worst that can happen if you make this choice? What is the worst that can happen if you make that choice? Can you cover your needs to survive the worst that can happen and strike forth in your new direction with faith in yourself that you will succeed? Yes, mediate doubt by protecting yourself against the worst of future potentials. Take slow, steady steps toward changing your life if that is your pace. The "comfort zone" we often talk about is your emotional, mental, spiritual, and — yes — physical states. It takes a rare person to be able to yank themselves up from one level to the next; it can be very dangerous if done in haste and with little forethought or planning. We say, take your time and choose wisely.

People who refuse to make choices will find that life makes choices for them. You can be suddenly laid off from a long-time job and be cut adrift without a future plan. Or the job may fold around you or move to where you can't follow. Relationships may end abruptly while you are still trying to face the fact that you are unhappy. You may be working too hard, suddenly be injured, and forced to stay in bed. If you don't take charge of your life in these new energies, life will force you to repeat more paths of lesson. If you don't know where to begin, try looking at your life objectively. Keep what is good, productive, and joyous. Change what is bad, wasteful, and painful. Or change your perspective on what is bad, and find the good in it. You may have a boring job, but it may be your presence in that place, among those people, that anchors light.

Dear reader, you are aware of only a small part of your greater self that lies beyond the range of your current senses. As you expand into conscious connection with your higher self, you will also develop a refined awareness of the planet's shift and how it is changing your electromagnetic structure. For eons, you have lived through your bottom three chakras, or "below the belt." All of your life experiences were filtered through root (survival), sacral (family), and solar-plexus (society). In other words, you were gut-centered. Now, you are evolving into the full potential of your seven-chakra structure with the heart as the new center of your Be-ing guiding the three chakras above and the three below. This energetic shift requires you to live from the heart and thus embrace change at all levels. Jobs are suddenly ending, marriages are becoming stifling, and you find yourself itching to move but have no idea where to go or how to survive.

This is a pivotal time of change for Earth and all that reside thereon. All is changing. All that does not resonate with your heart is becoming more and more painful to bear. All pain comes from resistance to change. Even people who are not seeking change are finding it thrust on them. Why? The new energies require it. You are being asked to live according to your heart, fulfilling your talents and your soul purpose. As the balance of energy shifts into higher definition, does it not make sense that the spiritual is becoming more important than the material? For those of you who can move beyond fear, live in love, and express their true talents, abundance will naturally follow.

Once you are doing the work you were meant to do, the universe will support your efforts. Why? Because you will be happy! True happiness is the emotion of joy, which is the essence of unconditional love and the purest energetic resonance of God. With joy as your fuel, the most precious energy in the universe, you will be fulfilled in the creation of your dreams and goals. Your work will have value to others, and their joy will reflect back to you as abundance.

On your planet, there is an additional impediment to spiritual progress — money. Rather than have a barter exchange of energy, services, and goods, you measure your work and your worth by how much paper money you hold in your hand. The true measure of a person cannot be measured by their monetary earning potential. Nor can it be measured by how many pretty things they collect. What is the true measure of a person? To us, it is a function of how much Divine light you exude and also by your potential to do so. In other words, you all have the potential to become self-realized. It is a matter of remembering who you really are and carrying the awareness of your divinity in every moment that you live and breathe.

You all have the same basic form and functions, the same number of teeth and bones, the same arrangement of organs and symphony of chemical systems. And yet what makes each person so different? It is not just a matter of genetics, getting a large nose from your father's side and curly hair from your mother's family. It is the unique soul spark that you each carry, combined with all the experiential learning from previous lifetimes, combined with the unique perspective that you each maintain as you look at this life of duality from behind your physical eyes. You all carry joy and sadness, pain and laughter, knowledge and opinions, fears and faith, each in measures that create the uniqueness of your life experiences and energetic expression.

If we passed a hat and asked all of you readers to write down your problems and place them in that hat, we would find far fewer problems than the number of readers who participated. Why? We sit and patiently watch innumerable little dramas, all so similar, being played out in small circles of lives that coexist next to each other, creating a huge, seething tapestry of life dramas propelled by free will. What moves you forward is the ability to choose. The ability to feel whether or not those choices sit well, which gives you the opportunity to choose again. Dear ones, we remind you here that there are always alternatives if you look carefully enough. There are always other options possible. The beauty of your power, human beings, is the ability to learn from your choices, to change your mindset, and choose again. That is how the soul makes progress, *not* in stagnation.

The Key of Self-Discipline

Self-discipline is a key ingredient for realizing all the keys listed here [chuckles]. Though we extol the benefits of the Circle of Grace because it is our spiritual shortcut to help you through these changing times, it is only one of many paths. Some of you might find grounding in a simple silent meditation for twenty minutes every morning. Some may need to jog a few miles in order to feel balanced in mind and body. No matter what your preference may be, our main message for this segment is: You must have a daily practice. This is the single-most essential key to gracefully surviving the rising energies while being in charge of the level you wish to attain. Yes, back to free will and your right to choose. We say, aim high. Why not? You're already going to the trouble of aiming, anyway.

It is time to start exercising your will. Being Christ-like in every moment is a big leap to take, so we urge you to start small — you need a daily practice. For those of you who go to seminars and holistic practitioners and feel a surge of wonderful energy but cannot sustain it once you go back to your life — you need a daily practice. You need to create that 4-5D energetic connection for yourself every day, which eventually will become your new higher perspective on life, in life, and through life.

Dear lightworkers, the more excess pressure you release from your PEMS layers, the more room you will have to feel joy. It matters not what type of daily practice or meditation you embrace; if you drop your jaw open, you will have a more relaxed, energizing session. Here we would like to stress the word "daily." Why? The more intensely the energies rise, the more need you will have to clear chronic and daily stress from your systems. Whether your practice is active or sedentary, yoga, meditation, or hugging a tree, it matters only that you do it regularly. For those who have found resonance with the Circle of Grace exercise, we predict that the more you clear your meridians, the more clearly you will feel when they load up again. The Millennium Shift is an energetic expansion process occurring all around you that is causing your body to expand along with it. In energetic terms, achieving a lightbody state means clearing all low-density areas (PEMS blockages) so that your total Be-ing can resonate at a higher, lighter, brighter level.

All of these wonderful changes we speak of, from chakra restructuring to DNA activation to interdimensional expansion, are taxing to the human form as that form quickly evolves. In the next few years, meditation will become increasingly vital to your daily function and overall well-being. The lucky ones among you will work their schedules around their preferred meditation times. In future generations when you teach your youngsters how to meditate (in whatever form you and they enjoy), the beneficial effects of daily meditation on the human body and its longevity will truly be seen.

The Key of Emotional Control

In the last section, we spoke of the need for a daily practice for you to create your own sacred space and sacred energies rather than seeking them from an outside source. All along, our teachings have been focused on how to clear your physical vehicle and how to create a new, higher perspective from which to live your life. We have counseled you on how to find joy [also inside!] and release fear. Have you noticed yet our true intent? Our higher purpose, if you will? [Chuckles.]

The overriding goal of the Brotherhood of Light is to help humanity up the path to full self-mastery. Dear one, nobody can fit inside your skin but you. Nobody can live your life but you. Nobody can heal you or your life but you. Rather than preach: "Do this, take that, go here, and go there," we say you came in as a beautiful complete package. Your potentials are tested by your lessons; your truest talents and creativity are brought forth by your life challenges. The crises you face are tests of the heart, of courage, of faith, of values. As a planet of soul learning, Earth has been called the "college of relationships."

There are four basic plots to any and every drama: humans against God, humans against nature, humans against humans, and humans against their own selves. You could fit any storybook ever written into one of these four categories. Whether it be myth, history, fiction, or nonfiction, it matters not. We are not straying off topic here, dear ones, but would like to underline the point that art imitates life. Take any of your problems, dilemmas, or issues and examine them against this list; you will find a place for each and every last blessed lesson in one of these four scenarios.

In its progress up the spiral of reincarnation, the soul studies different qualities of love in each life and in each life segment. Your soul focuses on one quality every seven years through childhood, adulthood, and old age. Those life lessons and experiences feed your soul with the information it seeks about the different qualities of love. Since all the drama is increasing due to the intense energy swells you are assimilating during the Millennium Shift process, we offer here an energetic explanation of what that means.

First, we will remind you that human emotions reflect the vibrational tone of each person's total PEMS being. On a scale of one to one hundred (just to be linear for a moment), fear occupies the bottom half of the vibratory scale and love dominates the top half. You can only vibrate within one tone at a time. You cannot be loving toward others while being angry at

How you feel about yourself and your life directly affects your physical health.

them. The good news is that love cancels out fear. It is a higher tone. Have you heard of mind over matter? That your biography affects your biology? When we beseech you to take charge of your thoughts and your emotions, we have good reason. Your emotional state is a combination of the workings of all of your PEMS layers. How you feel physically affects your emotions, how you feel mentally affects your emotions, how you believe affects your emotions, and the quality of your emotions (your emotional tone) rules the health of your body.

Some of the things we are about to list may not seem to belong to the right categories of fear and love. You can also see these as emotional states that fuel life lessons. Your will and how well you wield it is tied into expression through the emotional body (at solar plexus). So you might see these qualities of love and fear as emotional states that you wish to embrace or release. Free will overrules all — amend the lists any way you please. [**Author's note:** the Brothers asked me to make the lists alphabetical so as not to give any one category more importance than another. These are by no means complete lists but offered to stimulate your understanding.]

The bottom half of your emotional energies are vibrations of fear. There you will find lessons in alienation, ambivalence, anger, anxiety, bigotry, blame, boredom, complacency, confusion, criticism, defeat, depression, despair, doubt, greed, grief, guilt, hatred, jealousy, judgment, loneliness, longing, lying, misery, pain, panic, regret, rejection, remorse, resignation, retribution, revenge, shock, stress, suffering, terror, tolerating, uncertainty, unhappiness, ugliness, and worry.

In the top half of the human emotional vibratory scale, you will find these experiences in qualities of love: allowing, balance, beauty, charm, clarity, commitment, compassion, confidence, contentment, courage, creativity, detachment, devotion, discipline, excitement, ecstasy, expression, faith, forgiveness, freedom, fulfillment, harmony, honesty, honor, humor, innocence, inspiration, integrity, intuition, joy, liberation, passion, patience, pleasure, perseverance, protection, service, stillness, trust, truth, understanding, whimsy, and wisdom.

But where would you place competitiveness and sensuality? These are also aspects of the human experience that each soul uses to learn about love through the emotional interplays of your life dramas. The experiences listed above can be expressed in either a higher or lower vibration (from the heart or the gut), depending on your level of awareness, your mindset, and the clarity of your vehicle. That's what repeating lessons are all about: the conditions, situations, or relationships you experience will keep repeating until you attain a higher perspective over them. In other words, the Universal Law of Attraction will guarantee that you draw to you whatever your energetic tone demands. Clearing your PEMS body of meridian blockages and dense etheric pockets will allow you to resonate at a higher vibrational tone beyond the need for those old lessons. If you find that a lesson pops up one last time after you thought it done, it is only Spirit's way of saying, "Here, do it again, flawlessly, from the higher view." Then you can bid it a fond adieu! Once soul has fully learned the lesson, it moves on and so do you.

The four basic dramas we listed earlier form the patterns of your earthly lessons. Where you resonate on the emotional scale shows your progress in the learning of the lessons. The more clearly you feel your emotional tone, the easier it will be to tune yourself up to be in loving harmony with the new energies. Please do not be disheartened by all of this information, for it is quite a lot, yet it speaks to the complexity of higher learning now within your reach. Dear one, you have a common saying that we will use here: "Don't sweat the small stuff!" You can choose where, when, and how to expend your personal energy. We ask you to remain flexible, openminded, and hopeful, filled with certainty that you can achieve whatever you intend, focus on, and love into your reality.

The Key of Mental Control

As you rise into the new frequencies and as you start to feel the energy you create coming in and going out every day, you will start to understand how much physical stamina you expend to walk, to talk, to lift, even to think. The best remedy for all of your transitional ills is resting both body and mind. There are people who waste so much energy in repeating mental loops, dear ones. It is exhausting for all of us. [Chuckles.] Know that you expend physical energy with mental worry. It is much more valuable to change your focus, think of something totally different, and disallow the negative loops. Take responsibility for your thoughts. Be in charge of your mind, not vice versa, or the rising energies will help you manifest your worst fears.

Rather than being in charge of their lives, most people are pushed and pulled by events around them. You are far better served lying down and taking a nap instead of trying to do something for the twelfth time that is not working or mentally going over an argument for the fifteenth time that never got resolved, or wishing that something had gone a different way. These are all ways in which you waste physical energy by worrying. There is another aspect to worrying, or losing your temper or any loss of emotional control: It is addictive. Those negative, repeating loops in your mind affect your emotional body, each time causing a surge of adrenaline that increases your pulse, dilates your airways to improve breathing, and increases the blood supply to your muscles. Yes, just like exercise or stress, fear-filled emotions trigger a flight-or-fight chemical reaction of cascading hormones in your body that can become addictive.

Dear one, being able to change your emotional state at will with your thoughts is a very valuable tool, indeed. [Chuckles.] Bad habits are simply that, and they can be broken. As you yearn to attain a level where you can materialize thoughts into things, do you realize that you can also materialize your fears, worries, and doubts? You must reach a level of clarity and control over all your aspects so that you do not create negativity. Worry is self-defeating because it places you squarely in lack, in powerlessness, and in fear. In a realm where thoughts are things, imagine what would happen if Be-ings could create whatever crossed their minds without any quality control.

We advise you here to apply the Universal Law of Allowing, which is difficult for most because of its deceptive simplicity. To sum it up in one word: surrender. Keep turning over what you can't see, can't do, or can't handle. Hand it back to Spirit and say, "Here, God, I need to apply blind faith and divine timing to this and to that. Handle it for me, Spirit, until I can see it more clearly." Sounds simple? Indeed, yet at that point you must let it go. Stop thinking about it, stop worrying about it, stop chewing on it, and stop being angry about it. Let it go! Let it go with love, with relief, and with trust that it will all work out. Each time you think of it, keep blessing it with gratitude and send it out again. Do you see now how the release must be complete? Yes, at all PEMS levels of your total Be-ing — physical, emotional, mental, and spiritual.

Worrying about something keeps it locked tight in your energetic field and attracts more of the same. Though worry is a mental exercise, it drags down your emotional body into the darkness of lower vibrations and feeds those pockets of etheric baggage you are carrying. Worry exhausts your physical body by depleting it of precious stamina — thoughts and emotions require energy. Worry clogs up your mental body by dominating your awareness with negative thoughts and preventing you from focusing on the positive. Worry prevents you from experiencing your life in the present moment. Worst of all, worry denies your spiritual body of its power. How can you be in love, in light, and in faith if you keep doubting yourself and Spirit?

Mental loops are a bad habit that you can teach yourself to release. Imagine a big, silver, spiritual pair of scissors that will cut every negative loop that crosses your mind. Keep cutting those loops into small pieces and keep replacing them with good thoughts like, "All is as it should be. I am guided and protected." Think about something or someone that makes you happy, start counting your blessings, or spend a moment appreciating yourself. Each time you make the mental choice to disallow those negative thoughts, you are adding joy to your heart by refocusing your mind on happier things. Also remember that you are boosting your body chemistry into a healthier balance. Eventually that will become your comfort zone, mirrored by increased health and vitality in your body. Be patient with yourself, dear one. It will take time and practice, for all that you are doing is so unusual and so unique.

The higher the energies rise, the closer you get to having your own individual channel to keying into your own Higher Self and getting heart-directed guidance in an instant. The more fear you clear and the more love you allow yourself to feel, the more you will grow in strength and confidence. Does it not stand to reason that in order to expand energetically into the higher dimensions, you need an energetic way of cleaning out the old 3D mindsets, baggage, and blockages? Raising your personal vibration is both a physical and mental challenge, and mind over matter is how you will succeed.

The Key of Personal Responsibility

Moving on to another essential key: personal responsibility. Take responsibility for what you have created over time, for that is your life in the present moment. Bless all of it, good and bad, for at the soul level, it has given you experience and moved you along in lesson. If it is all good, be blessed and happy, and live your life with your light shining high. If you look at your life and see that parts of it cause you pain, take responsibility for that too. Bless those things for the lessons learned, then set about changing your life to bring in joy. Change is the only constant in the universe. If you resist change, the rising energies will intensify your lessons at all PEMS levels.

Remember, all pain comes from resistance to change.

Here is the energetic key to this section: You cannot change what you do not own. If you do not take responsibility for your past and your present, you cannot create positive change for your future. We have explained how forgiveness melts away the emotional ties to past lessons, but it does even more than that. Forgiveness (including yourself) allows you to love those lessons, learn from them, and then move beyond them. You cannot fully love those experiences if you do not take full responsibility for them. Those lessons have shaped who you are now, dear one, as you sit and read this text. Since we so love to play with your language, we will discuss two words to illuminate this key, two words that have been confused and confusing for many: destiny and fate. What is the difference? How are they related? Which one do you choose?

In your dictionaries, the word "fate" refers to "the inevitability of a course of events supposedly predetermined by a God or other agency beyond human control; what happens or has happened to a person or entity; final outcome such as doom, death, and destruction." The word "destiny" also refers to an "inevitable succession of events as determined supernaturally or by necessity, but often implies a favorable outcome as in, 'It was her destiny to become famous.'" Do you see the fine line of perspective that separates these two words?

Your destiny is yours to manage, to direct, to create. Your fate is handed to you by life's happenstance and circumstance. Do you see your life as fated, inevitable, and out of your control? How easy it is to avoid responsibility for all that surrounds you if it is inflicted on you. If you say time and again, "This just happened to me, I didn't see it coming, and it's not my fault," you are in victim mode. You lose all power to create that which you desire. You lose your power to choose, which is the biggest spiritual gift you have in this freewill zone. Why would you so easily surrender it?

As we have stated before, "Blessed are the flexible, for they shall never be bent out of shape." Taking responsibility for what was and what is allows you to change with grace, to be flexible and thus maintain your balance no matter what happens around you. Full balance means that you are in command of all your PEMS layers. Then you will truly be creating your own destiny.

Imagine an upright stick lodged deep in the mud of a flowing river. Over time, that stick will bend to the water currents and be released from the mud or break and flow down the river anyway. We say, why not be like the river instead of the stick? Flow effortlessly through the now of every moment, bending to obstacles and gracefully sliding by.

The Keys to Full Mastery

Dear ones, to be in full self-mastery requires these two things:

1) Let no thought, thing, or person hold power over you save for God's will, which is simply to "give and receive only love."
2) You must achieve a state of harmlessness so that your ability to manifest does not create anything negative.

Our overall message in this chapter is that you must be in total command of your thoughts and emotions in order to control your ability to manifest in alignment with God's will. In order to accomplish this, we offer you the knowledge of the Circle of Grace to help you clear and balance your PEMS layers so that you may become that functioning 5D person. Many of you feel frustrated that things aren't changing fast enough, that we paint glowing pictures of what you will soon become but nothing has happened yet. Once you begin growing into your powers, what do you think will happen? If thoughts do indeed create things, do you realize how easy it would be to mis-create? To wish someone dead creates much more karma than you know! To wish ill on anyone or anything goes against God's will. Do you have that level of mental control yet? Do you have enough emotional control to always be in a state of unconditional love?

You have a saying, "There is a fine line between love and hate." We say that fine line must become a broad chasm before you stand in a state of total love and materialize anything. Once you are fully merged into 5D, it will be impossible for you to inflict harm to any living creature. You will also be keenly aware of when you might be creating negative karma with others. Your spiritual radar will guide you true, and you will know what is correct to do in every moment to be harmless as you flow through life.

Full mastery is achieving a state of unconditional love, of total harmlessness. Once there, you will navigate the waters of your life in total peace, calm, and serenity. Until then, dear ones, it is unnecessary to worry and fret over not being there yet. That is a waste of your energy. Living in the now means not worrying about your past or future. Work on being aware of what you think and feel during the course of your day. Are you often swept away by fear and doubts, by regrets or envy? If that is where your thoughts go over and over, those are the very issues you need to face, own, bless, and clear.

We offer here the example of a movie that is commonly known to this society of readers, *Ghostbusters*. When the character played by Dan Akroyd had to think quickly of something harmless to manifest, he thought of the Stay Puft marshmallow man, umpteen feet high. Comical? Yes. Harmless? Not at that height. What would you create in that moment? Have you cleared all the fears from your thoughts, your emotions, your body, your faith? Can you love all forms of life? Can you energetically forgive those who have wronged you, whether or not you can tell them so? Have you forgiven yourself for all of your mistakes?

Can you believe it, in your heart, when you say, "I Am Perfect as I Am"? Try that on as a mantra, and see how it fits. Keep saying it until you believe it, and then keep saying it as your new label. The more you believe in yourself, the more people around you will change and begin to believe in you too. Even if you cannot physically change your situation, you can change your energetic perspective on that situation. Then you will see the dynamics radically change in your favor.

Remember: People can hurt you only as much as you allow them to.

Each moment is an opportunity to reason instead of rage, to be kind instead of callous, to step back and allow a lesson to be seen. Each now moment is a gift if you are present for it [chuckles]. Each day of your life is a new opportunity to move forward and upward. And if you begin each day with a moment of going inward, your experience of everything around you will be heightened. (Yes, we remind you here to do your daily practice!) Reaching self-realization comes from sifting through all your thoughts and actions, choosing only the ones that vibrate with love, until it becomes a habit, until bad thoughts are no longer even in your choices, until you have made a permanent abode of your new comfort zone in 4-5D.

This is a gradual awakening. You must forgive yourself for every wrong step and keep moving forward in faith, hope, and joy. Seek the joy of your heart and all the rest will fall into place along the way. Count on it, children; insist on it. Cocreate with Spirit — say aloud what you desire and require. The universe will bow to you, as it must, for you are the material creators. Now you are gathering the matter in your own hands and beginning to shape it for yourselves.

Congratulations, dear ones, you are becoming masters of your own corner of material creation. Heaven on Earth is waiting for each of you to attain and sustain. We offer tools to clear your vehicle, fuel your momentum, and light your path. That is our role; the rest is up to you.

Do you follow? We hope you will!

11

The Keys to Happiness

Greetings, dear ones, from the Brotherhood of Light. Throughout your history, we have been called the Order of Melchizedek, the White Brotherhood, and the Great White Brotherhood. We are all one, despite the many names you have given us. In the spirit of fair play, we have come forward with our own choice of name, one that maintains the Brotherhood energy and yet heralds in the new phase of our work — working with nascent beings of light, which you are becoming. Thus, we are here for you now as the Brotherhood of Light. We have always been and always will be the spiritual guardians of this quadrant of sacred space. Keepers of the Akashic records, guardians of sacred tools and places, karmic facilitators and material mechanics, too, in charge of teaching you the way things work in the nonphysical realms.

Are you keeping up, dear ones? We have given you so much homework, poor things! [Chuckles.] We have admonished you to take care of yourselves, to rest frequently, drink lots of spring water, eat light and as often as your body dictates, play whenever you can, and not worry about the details. We have explained how a higher perspective is your key to understanding the new energies and how clearing your physical body is key to rising gracefully into the new energies. Clearing and balancing all the layers of your total energetic Be-ing is your key to blending with the new vibrational space being created around you.

When you connect with us in session, please be specific in stating your needs of the moment. Asking to evolve is a nice but too general request. Because we are sworn not to interfere with your life path, we ask you to start by clearing your physical core. Speak the healing prayer aloud to give us permission to work with you in your space. Ask us to clear your blockages, energetic and physical, from the physical level on out. As you make progress in your clearing, ask us to help you through life lessons and issues. Bring us your hopes, wishes, and dreams, and we will work with you on their materialization. Ask us for our input and guidance on decisions big and small, and watch how Spirit will communicate with you. Look for the flow of synchronicity to abound in your life, intend for it — demand it! Remember, we cannot act at the physical level if you do not manifest your intent into your physical dimension through the vibration of your voice. That is also the purpose of all the metaphysical books, seminars, teachings, and lessons: anchoring these concepts into the population and, eventually, into the whole of the human consciousness.

Yes, the key to the higher realms is *you*, dear one. You are your own vehicle, your own connection, your own keeper of the Divine flame. What do you think your body is, apart from the small consciousness you hold of it? It is the physical core of your merkabah vehicle, your entry into the interdimensional realms beyond your transformation. Your entire Be-ing, cleared and balanced, is the energetic key to unlocking your future potential. So look to the ultimate goal; do not focus on obstacles in your path. They will loom larger and larger if you feed them with worry and doubt. Look instead beyond those obstacles, and put them in their proper perspective.

No matter what happens around you, we offer you this mantra as a mode of comfort: "I Am in this world but not of it. I have been here before, and I will live beyond it." Re-mind yourself to seek that higher perspective. Re-mind yourself that you are eternal. Keep re-mind-ing yourself to choose love over fear. One day, you will notice that you are doing it automatically. You will notice that for some time you have chosen not to be in conflict or you have chosen not to be in anger or you have chosen to help rather than harm or you have chosen to detach rather than judge.

Yes, your soul learning is achieved along the journey of your life. Your goal is established so as to define your path. In other words, your goal is accomplished as you rise into full self-mastery. Your progress through the journey of your life creates the manifestation of the goal. If you are miserable along the way, you will have defeated yourself before you arrive. When you get there, it will be too hard-won to be fulfilling. Achieving your goal is simply becoming I Am along the way, which you already are, so your success is guaranteed! [Chuckles and a big hug.]

Defining Happiness

First, we would like to specify exactly what we mean by "happiness." We use this concept over the long term of your life, as opposed to short-term gratification or transient bliss that does not last long for you. Many people view happiness as the acquisition of things rather than as a state of being. Expecting joy from a new car, a bigger home, a raise in pay, all these things are outward manifestations of your material condition. The newness soon wears off, the money gets spent, the joy dissipates, and you look for the next thing that will make you happy. Dear ones, we ask you to find happiness within yourselves, for who you are and what you can accomplish. Do you see the difference? Yes, long-term happiness may seem to have obstacles and fear in the way, but those are just your lessons, yours to embrace and love until they melt away.

Once you embrace true love of self, your material condition becomes immaterial!

Over the years, you have developed new language concepts to represent the material path and the spiritual path. You separated them and thought that one led to the other. Now you are finding a need to straddle them both in order to be fully happy and stay beyond survival mode. Have you realized yet that there is only one path? You must exist in the material world in a spiritual way to be fully happy. This is the biggest key we can offer you. If you embrace only this one concept from reading our book, we will be truly pleased to have been of service to the greater good of the Divine Plan.

Did you ever wonder exactly where that path is? What it leads to? You all seek happiness. If you seek joy within yourself in a focused, determined way, you will find it. And what is that ultimate joy? Re-union with the energies of the Divine Source! Most religions do define an afterlife, a heaven and/or hell complete with a location where only good or bad things happen to you. The new metaphysics teaches that heaven is a state of consciousness that can be achieved while still in body. Here's the new twist — you don't have to die to get there. We say, congratulations! This concept has been fully anchored in the human consciousness and waits only to be materialized. Now you are faced with cleaning up your bodies, attitudes, and lives in order to physically establish your expansion from 3D to 4D to 5D.

So that is your homework, dear ones. You are the innovators, the groundbreakers, the expansion potential for the rest of humanity. What a huge task you have embraced, the conscious creation of a new species of humanity. We offer you here our knowledge and help in these transitional times, yet we point out that you are doing the hardest part of the work. We are honored and humbled to be working with you magnificent, unconscious angels. We assure you that none of this work, these levels, and this expansion process is beyond your abilities. Indeed, you have long prepared for this day, this life, this millennium time. You are perfect, each and every one of you, even as you struggle through your seas of imperfection, for all is as it should be. And what you don't like in your life, start fixing!

The Three Key Elements of a Happy Life

The three keys to happiness are simply this:

1) Loving relationships — family, friends, and community.
2) Faith in something greater than the 3D human reality.
3) Living your life path from the heart — living your life in full awareness of unconditional love, Higher Self, and performance of service to the greater good.

#1: Loving Relationships

Dear ones, we could write a tome on each point, but as you say, time runs short. "Be in the now," "Be in this world but not of it," and other similar phrases are becoming so worn that they are losing their intellectual impact.

So many people are reading and re-reading metaphysical materials such as this text, seeking answers, clues, hints, something, anything. Now is the time to act on what needs changing in your lives, for that is what the rising energy levels now require. A planetary detoxification is occurring; all that does not resonate with your new, expanding heart chakra is becoming more and more painful to bear.

Hate your job? In the new energy, it will make you sick more quickly to work at anything that is not heart-directed or heart-fulfilling. The same goes for relationships of all kinds — those that are heart-based and supportive will grow, and those that are not will get much worse. We speak here of mates, of parents and children, of friends and acquaintances. What fuels and supports your life, your individuality, your hopes, wishes and dreams? What supports and fuels your ability to create love and light? Loving relationships with other people that give you opportunities to develop and spread compassion. The basic goal of every soul is to create more love and light with which to return to Divine Source. Your families and friends are all working toward this same goal of seeking happiness through their life lessons, though most are unaware of the process.

How to be happy? Do what makes you happy. Be with people who share the same quality of happiness. Live where you feel happy. Stop letting your mental body dictate your decisions — it only sees numbers and facts, and it creates fear around them. Learn to give equal weight to how you feel about everything — that's what really matters. Once you begin to clear, balance, and integrate your PEMS levels, your perspective will change to a higher spiritual tone. Your mental and emotional bodies will confer together, then look to the spiritual body for final say before your physical body makes a move or says a word. In other words, how you process information and stimuli will change, and how you respond in each moment will change too. The more people who begin to do this, the more quickly joy will spread.

Learn to see and appreciate every chance you get to mend a wound, uplift a soul, erase fear, and share more love. There is no greater power in life than love, and you create love in your daily interactions with all forms of life. Yes, as the consciousness rises, does it not stand to reason that people will start to treat each other better? It starts with you, dear reader, dear secretary, dear bank teller, dear bus driver. Be kind to each person you meet. It's contagious!

#2: Faith in a Greater Power

True happiness requires faith in a higher power or greater consciousness, a belief that things happen for a reason or any form of faith that stretches the human potential beyond your physical realm. Yes, though still a separatist view, it is a necessary step toward expanding your spiritual understanding. Do you struggle with depression, loneliness, feeling cut off or lesser than, feeling that something essential is missing, or seeking an unknown, intangible Home? All of these are symptoms of searching for a belief system that resonates for you. Once you embrace a specific religion, conceptual stand, or level of metaphysical understanding, you need to find your place within that structure. Hence the struggle for proof begins, as you search to validate and quantify the belief system you chose.

This struggle is more difficult for people who were raised in strict religious confines, who need to break out of the box without feeling guilty about it. We ask you to grow beyond your first box by releasing any and all fear-based concepts. How? By understanding their purpose and blessing the lessons they taught you. You do not need to reject those earlier teachings. You can incorporate them into a broader belief system by understanding where they fall short. In so doing, you will develop a bigger and better foundation for living your life in a spiritually balanced way.

Faith is meant to be fluid and evolving, to support you on your path as an evolving, spiritual Be-ing. Many aspects of your established religions are limiting because they are fear-based. They will thus grow stagnant in the new energies by insisting that you are separate from God, that you are less than God, that you carry sin that only God can judge and forgive through another human being. Here we give you back those powers and say, Spirit does not judge. Only man inflicts judgment on himself and others, thus limiting how you feel, think, and act.

There are many levels of understanding, of accepting, of forgiving. Remember that truth is an individual thing, different for each person. In order for full allowing of differences to occur, which will usher in the true Brotherhood of humankind, you must understand that all beliefs are truly one, no matter how different they may seem. All seekers are basically one in their quest for oneness [chuckles]. All roads of experience, wisdom, and understanding lead to the same place — the understanding and embracing that you are all One, that We Are All One.

That mysterious place you call Home or Heaven is indeed the vibrational space of Divine Source, that which you call God. Hence the paradox for those of you seeking physical proof (in your limited 3D physical realm) for a place, being, or object that is nonphysical. Belief in the higher realms, that we actually exist, is a necessary step to expanding your awareness in order to communicate with us in our vibrational scale of existence. We invite you to meet us and work with us in the healing energies of the Circle of Grace. There you will find your proof, and your truth, that the higher realms do exist. Then you will find your place and purpose in the Divine Plan.

We gently remind you here that in order for these keys to work, you must wield them together. And most important of all, your belief in a higher power must expand to a belief that the higher power resides within you.

#3 : Living Your Life Path from the Heart

Now for the third key to happiness: Combine keys one and two, and live your life accordingly. As you say, "walking your talk" is the most difficult step to climb. Ah, but it is only difficult if you believe it to be so [chuckles]. To reach and hold this level of awareness, you must love yourself completely, just as you are. Surround yourself with like-minded friends and family. Live your dreams in every moment, see them as already accomplished, and find joy in the process. Clearing away all that does not resonate with joy is a difficult but necessary transition. Keep your feelings of joy and gratitude above all other emotions, and let go of all that is of lower resonance.

How do you fully wield love and have faith in yourself? By living your life according to your beliefs, by honoring higher truths, and by treating everyone as befits another divine Be-ing. Using your innate talents and gifts to help others will augment and fortify your self-love and your expanded beliefs through every day of every now moment. Doing work that feeds your soul will make you happy, and work that you love doing spreads love to others. Figure out your soul gifts and talents, and then use them — two vital steps on the path to ultimate happiness. What do we mean by ultimate happiness? How do you find it?

The key to being joyful is surrendering all fear!

Though all of life's energy around you is intensifying, dear one, know that the hardest part is behind you. Yes, becoming awakened and aware is the hard part. Arriving at a knowing that duality even exists is a stretch for most people. Pulling yourself up above and beyond duality is the major work. Yet surmounting duality is simply a shift in perspective, for nothing around you will physically change — except you. Once your PEMS body changes energetically, you will affect all that is around you in a profound way.

By now, some of you readers are no doubt thinking, "Well, this sounds logical and seems simple, but the doing of it is too hard!" Things happen, and you must bear the consequences. You seem to have no control, no say, and you don't see it changing. Ah — the word "see" is your trigger, dear ones. It is all in how you see things. We have said before that when you cannot change a situation physically, you can change your perspective on the situation and then the dynamics all around you will change. Is not perspective a way of seeing? Do you not have the free will to choose, change your mind, and choose again? Yes! Plus, you have the divine power to create that which you focus your intent on. Is not "focus" another seeing word? Yes, we do love to play with your language [chuckles].

Most people get stuck in their progress over one thing: what to do about this or that, what to do about your problems, what to do to learn and move beyond your lessons, or what to do to create a better future. We gently point out here: Doing is not your first step. Be-ing is. Being that which you yearn to be, being where you want to be, being beyond the need for struggle, for lesson, for doubt. It is all about being what? A conscious Be-ing! An energetic, eternal Be-ing with a temporary physical core. Once you adapt to living from that higher perspective, the doing of what you need to do becomes easy. Why? Because you are seeing everything from a higher view point, and you can be and do with inner spiritual guidance that springs from that higher perspective. In fact, when you get good at Be-ing, you will always know what to do at the appropriate time, and the doing will not be an obstacle at all.

How do you Be? Be in this world but not of it. See your own impermanence; understand that all life grows and changes. See the human drama, and then see beyond its clawing grasp. Nothing ever remains the same. In your freewill zone, change is the biggest constant that life guarantees — opportunities to learn, to grow, to evolve through the conscious choices that you make. You are evolving into a new frequency of life vibration in this lifetime. Though Earth may still look the same, for those with ears to hear and eyes to see, the changes will be vast and beautiful.

Please take a moment to practice imagining with us. First, take a few deep, grounding breaths. Now, can you pretend, right now, that your entire goal in life is to be in your body at this moment, reading this page, and breathing in and out? If that were your goal in life, would it not fill you with joy for us to say, congratulations? You have achieved your life's purpose! Now, doesn't that make you feel happy? Take this moment, think it into your emotional layer, fill your heart with the joy of it, and label it in your memory "Joy." Focus on how it feels to be happy from head to toes, to smile because you can't help it, to feel sunny on the inside, and to be loving yourself in a moment of total self-satisfaction. Anchor this memory in your heart, and remember the feeling of being filled with joy.

Why do we ask you to practice feeling joy? Because you are in charge of your emotions. You can feel however you want, whenever you want. Do you think a lot about sad and painful things? Why? Don't they make you feel bad? Yes! That is where your power lies: Your mind can affect your biology. Your mind can affect all biology. It is a short step from here to say, your mind can create biology.

Do you follow? We hope you will!

All Time Is Now Time

So back to what to do? Nothing! We ask you to simply be. Be what? In the now. What is the now? The eternal form of time, ever-flowing and ever-changing. You are accustomed to the opposite: time that is rigid in its shape and direction. Time doesn't ebb and flow for you yet; it ticks away in small increments and then evaporates, invisible and irretrievable. You have expressions like, "Let's kill some time, don't waste my time, have a good time, and it's about time." You have such fixed notions about linear time that you can only see time as linear and fixed. Again, it's all in how you see things, to borrow another visual cliché [chuckles]. In all of the above examples, do you see how much you actually control time already? Your entire world views time as fixed and linear, and you all function within it in that way. Know that linear time is the framework for duality, and in conquering the one, you surpass both.

What if some people started living in the now and did not function according to their prior linear time frame? Do you think they would lose their jobs, forget to pay their bills, lose track of when they last watered their plants? No, not unless they built fear around those events happening: If you focus on it, you create it, right? We assure you that you will accomplish all that needs done, plus much more, and you will do it all joyously.

Living in the now is Be-ing in this world but not of it. Put the two together and what do you have? A way of being in a way of seeing. Yes, it is very difficult to think that what you see is not real, and realize that what is invisible is actually more permanent. That, dear one, is your leap of faith. For you must believe in yourself, above all, to be eternal. To rise from eternal Divine Source and meld back into it when this small consciousness parcel that is your current life is done. You see your physical body as permanent, and you do not see your eternal energetic body at all. The good news is that is changing! With the shift, you will begin to see that which has been invisible; you will begin to connect with All That Is. You will begin to see that you were created long before this current life, and you will also see that you will continue in active consciousness after this human life is over. That is being in this world but not of it!

So Be-ing is first "to be," and from that state of being, do. Yes, back to the beginning of this piece, children, the circle is ever unbroken! Find your feeling of joy and make that your mindset for each day. When you slip out of it, pull yourself back up to it. People search endlessly for other people to make them happy, for things to own that will make them happy, and for future goals that will one day make them happy. Bring it into the now, don't keep pushing your joy away until a future time, because all time is now.

What is the other flaw in that mode of thinking? Only you can make yourself happy. Yes, you are responsible for your own happiness, for your flow of joy comes solely from within you. That which you seek outside of yourself you will not find, for it is not there. It is within you. It is self-love, self-worth, divine love, the spark of God from which you sprang. Imagine, after all that seeking, to realize you were carrying it around with you all the time.

Some of you may be wondering, "If happiness is within me, than why do I feel so sad? So angry, so hurt, so helpless?" Because now that you are in the full bloom of 4D, your emotional body is flowering into your conscious awareness. Once you begin to feel your energetic layers, what do you feel first? The imbalances that hurt. You are beginning to realize how much emotional, mental, and spiritual baggage you still carry. You're just in need of clearing, and then you will be able to maintain a better balance between your physical and auric aspects.

Remember we said that you are in charge of your emotions. Yes, you should be [chuckles]. You need to be in control of your emotions so that you may flow through life harmlessly without hurting others. Let's start by saying you should learn not to hurt yourself. Instead of all those mental loops of anger, worry, guilt, blame, and shame, replace those thoughts with happier ones. Being in the now relieves you of worry, allowing you to fully enjoy whatever is happening around you. Since there is no true past or future in the now, you don't need to fret over either one. Dear one, isn't that a relief? It can be if you allow it to be so.

The more you replace negative thoughts with positive ones, the higher your physical vibration rises in frequency. It will become a habit, a good one, to keep yourself happy and feeling good. Once you achieve that as your new comfort zone, it will become your new energetic signature. The lower vibrations will fall aside, for they will no longer mesh with yours. You will attract more joy, more love, and more good things will come your way because that is what will mesh with the energy level you are holding. That is what ascension is all about. That is what divine creation is all about. Yes, you can use the Law of Attraction to create your future.

This is your homework: Seek joy. That which does not resonate can no longer be denied or ignored. Those things must be dealt with and balanced, for in this new paradigm of energy, all that is out of balance will make you ill. Doing that which you love, the opposite side of the coin, will bring you health, energy, and love in such huge amounts that you will resonate with joy, and all those around you will feel it. It matters not what you do; it only matters how you feel about what you do.

Many of you readers understand our message yet know that your jobs sustain your lives and families; you cannot simply drop everything and seek your joy. To you we say, what is it that you enjoy doing? Music? Art? Photography? Cooking? Whatever your vocation may be, we urge you to find your avocation and make room in your busy schedules to do that which makes you lighthearted. Feeding your soul with the joy of performing your talents is vital in these shifting times.

If you cannot turn your avocation into your vocation, please find time in your lives to do that which makes you happy. Even if you cannot see a way yet to transition away from the work you are familiar with, why deny yourselves the joy of an afternoon spent painting or playing an instrument or taking a class in the evenings to learn more about your hobbies? Indeed, finding joy in any part of your lives will make the humdrum parts more bearable.

There are many, many people who do everyday work and do not realize that just by being in that space and performing that task, they are anchoring love and healing for those around them. So we do not say that your work needs technically to be healing work; it just has to be work that you enjoy, work that makes you lighthearted. If you have loving family and friends around you, belief in your own potential and that of the Universe, (in whatever definition you are comfortable with), and the ability to do what you love and be happy doing it, these three things will heal your life. The rest is just a matter of time and application of your talents.

You Are Already Divine

What is this process of personal transformation, dear one? It is taking off the mask and seeing beyond the illusion to reveal what was always there, before the beginning of even this planet — your own eternal selves. If you could only believe in your own divinity, in your own eternal Be-ingness, then whatever happens in the life of your body is irrelevant. It is wonderful learning, yes, but none of it is as dark and dismal as it may seem to be. For even the worst thing that can happen to a person, death itself, we say is only a transition, and one that we actually enjoy very much as we welcome you Home.

It is the birth you celebrate so much that we find sad, for indeed that is the separation for us, when we lose you beautiful angels. Why? Because you lose your own awareness of who you truly are when you go back down into the density of duality. So for us, the birth is the sad part and death is the reunion. This may be backwards to your thinking, but it gives your mental framework of reference plenty of room to grow.

One of the problems with having an entire body of knowledge dropped in your lap is that it's unwieldy and hard to handle. Metaphysical concepts such as eternal life beyond the body, the Millennium Shift, and planetary ascension are huge and can be difficult to grasp. But ultimately, they form a more balanced understanding of all that is happening around you, from the innermost microscopic level to the effects becoming visible throughout your solar system and beyond.

Our goal is to take complex concepts and break them down into simple steps. Our hope is that you will climb those steps to rejoin us in the True Reality of Spirit, which is our Home — yours and ours. In order to blend into the higher reality, you must first achieve and sustain that level of vibration. That is why we offer the Circle of Grace exercise and our help along with it, so you may gracefully flower into the lightbody humans that you are meant to be. In doing this work with us, you shed the old, unbalanced energies within yourself so that you may reach and sing those higher notes. See it as a spiritual shortcut or see it as a spiritual gift, or better yet, see it as both.

Whatever is not in balance in your life will cause you pain. All that is balanced in your life will cause you joy. Once you begin to see from this perspective, your obstacles will become clearly defined, as will your path around or through them. So, in essence, the Be-ing leads to the doing.

Do you follow? We hope you will.

How do you become that of which we speak? How did you learn to walk, dear ones? How many times did you fall? Oh, you don't remember? Why? Because it didn't matter! To you as toddlers, your desire to get up and walk was all you saw and felt. No matter how many times you fell or tripped or toppled, your desire to be walking was paramount. Your scriptures say, "Unless you are converted and become like children, you will not enter the kingdom of heaven" [Matthew 18:13, NASB]. Why? Because young children live in the now, with full focus, free imagination, and a strong remembrance of Spirit life. The innocence, the joy, the unconditional love children embody makes them perfect little divine human Beings. Learn from your children, for they have much to teach you. Reflect back to them what you learn, always be loving, and you will have a beautiful family life.

Do you see the perfect parallel between the simplicity of a child and being in now time? This combination allows you to fully express yourself as Divine Creator embodied in flesh. Once you are cleared and fully in the flow of 5D, the incredible inspired works you will create render us humble and mute. (Yes, from where we sit in our now 5-6D, we can see these potential futures occurring!)

To this conceptual mix we add the axiom, "Heaven is a state of consciousness that you can achieve in body." And a state of consciousness is a way of seeing life. The key to ascension is in achieving that higher perception, which allows your spiritual aspect to direct your actions within the flow of unconditional love. How do you reach it? By understanding the concepts with your mental body and living in that never-ending joy moment with your emotional body. When we say, "You are creating heaven on earth," we mean it. So come cocreate with us, and you will soon join us. And remember,

> Achieve a state of Be-ing,
> And from that Be-ing, do.
> If you run around just doing,
> Then you'll forget to Be!

To distill these teachings, we ask you to seek a better balance in your life. Do what makes your heart sing, and fix and resolve what makes your heart heavy. Once you begin to feel your energetic layers reacting to your every physical action, you will understand better that thoughts are things, that pain lodges in the body as a physical object, that words can wound, and that emotions can either heal you or harm you.

As you wade through the ever-increasing complexities of these higher concepts, we remind you that the simplest, most-direct path is one guided by and lived through the heart. Lead with your heart, do what feels right to your heart. Pass every thought, action, word, and deed through your heart before you express it, and all the complexities will fall away. Learn to live every moment from a perspective of divine benevolence, and your path to full mastery will become a joyous journey!

Frequency and Physicality

12

Chakras
Form and Function

Greetings, dear reader, from the Brotherhood of Light. We gather in great numbers, with clearer and clearer presence, to help support your progress during the end times of the Millennium Shift. Yes, congratulations, this brief twenty-five-year period is three-quarters over! Though this text was channeled in early 2006, as always, we ask that you overlay your own timetable to the shift process. Do not feel discouraged by comparing yourself to anyone else. Your ascension is a personal, internal process that is affected by external influences, not the other way around.

In order to chart your spiritual progress, ask yourself these questions: "Am I happy? Do I enjoy my life? Do I feel comfortable where I live? Am I loved and supported in my relationships?" Or simply ask yourself, "Do I look forward to getting up each morning?" If your answer to any of these questions is no, then please stop and examine what is making you unhappy. That is what you need to change.

How do you fix your problems? Get clear! You come into each life with all the gifts and talents needed to succeed in that life, providing that you are clear enough to access the information. How do you create the future you desire and require? Get clear! You cannot wield your will and create your spiritual tools if your vehicle, your primary tool, is clogged and running on empty. How do you keep up and soar over the crest of this ascension process? Get clear! In order to bring in and assimilate the higher energies, your vehicle must be vibrating high enough to reach that new chord of celestial harmonies. That is, simply, why some people will shift and others will not.

Yes, clear and tune your instrument, dear one, that is our answer to every one of your problems. In this freewill zone, you must take responsibility for your upward climb. In other words, if you have no daily practice, if you are not consciously eating, drinking, exercising and sleeping to benefit the body, you will stay stuck. Nothing positive will happen around you or within you if you are not open, seeking, and determined to make positive changes in your life.

Do you follow this? We hope you will, for this is the most crucial tool you have — your own will!

If you are still seeking for someone to take care of you, for someone to take the blame, for someone to come rescue you, you will wait — and wait and wait. If you start at any level to make positive changes, you will see Spirit surround you with glorious support. The pace of everything is increasing and the last quarter of the shift will fly by very fast. Your task is to slow down, simplify your life, learn to relax, and learn not to react. You must set your own internal pace and truly measure your energetic output so that you don't burn out from the climbing frequencies affecting you and your planet, inside and out.

We are speaking here of energy management. In this message we offer you new rules to live by: rest, release, and recharge! If you do not pay attention to your body's signals and allow room for these new "three Rs" in your life, your etheric density will become increasingly painful to bear. In the next five years, your energy levels will be greatly affected by the intensification of cosmic energies soaking into your planet. The higher and more refined the energies, the heavier and denser your old energy signature will become. That is why we have stepped forward in these last ten years with the Circle of Grace clearing meditation, to teach you how to clear your bodies so that you may gracefully, painlessly ascend.

Your priorities must shift, dear one. The intensity of the drama around you is increasing, which will augment the flow of external chaos. If you let it overwhelm you, you will crack and break. If you decide how far and how fast you can move each day, you will retain command of your life. Learn to say no, learn to delegate, and learn to juggle your duties and deadlines. Learn when to keep your mouth shut and simply witness the drama rather than getting energetically involved. Learn to check in regularly with your body and ask it — what do you need? Water? Food? Rest? Exercise? Yes, your body has an awareness separate from that of your mind. The more you treat your body as a beloved friend, the better it will support you!

The Human Energetic Chakra System

In this section, our perspective is focused on how the chakras interact with the physical body. In other words, we are looking at the physical core as we explain the energetic workings of each chakra and which organs are within its governing area of the body. We will begin with a brief description of how the chakra system is linked together.

The root and crown chakras are vertical in orientation, with crown (7) pointing up and root (1) pointing down. The chakras in between (2 — 6) are horizontal in orientation, going from front to back of the body. Each horizontal chakra is shaped like a straw with a flower at each end. These two energy vortexes, one in front and one in back, are linked together by a thin tube running through the body's energetic vertical core. This energetic core is often known as the shushumna, or the pranic tube. The front expression of each chakra is governed by your emotional layer, and are thus emotional vortexes. The back flower of each chakra is governed by your will, which when in balance, is commanded by your mental and spiritual layers together.

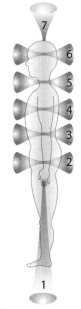

In a balanced system, your will energy flows from the back expression of each chakra to the front, where it is tempered by unconditional love from your emotional layer and processed through the heart chakra before being expressed. Do you see the progress needed here, dear one? First clear and unblock all communications between the seven internal energy centers. Then clear and balance each chakra in order to function in this new, higher harmony of your own internal systems.

Figure 12.1: Seven Core Chakras

Knowing what each chakra is created to do and why is vital to your understanding of what areas you need to work on within yourself. We offer you here an overview of the human (holographic) energetic skeleton with your pranic tube as the spine and each horizontal chakra as a vertebrae rising up through your energetic spinal core. Please imagine, if you will, that your crown chakra (7 — top of head) is the intake end of your pranic tube, whose energetic direction is coming down into you from above your head. Your root chakra (1 — tailbone/perineum) is the other end of your pranic tube, which points down toward Earth from between your legs. The root chakra's energetic expression is also vertical but downward — the exit point for energy incoming from its mate, 7, the crown.

Similar to physical breathing, your entire energetic framework inhales energy through the crown chakra, circulates the energy through its meridian system and releases the spent excess through the root chakra into the earth, which recycles it into positive energy. Then your aura breathes in green Earth energy from the root to balance the intake of divine energy. This is your "as above, so below" connection, dear one. This is how your aura breathes. This is how you connect and harmonize with Earth, you feed her and she feeds you back. This is how you are linked into Earth's energetic grids, as are all living things in the mineral, plant, and animal kingdoms. Of course, did you not wonder about the energetics of how all life on Earth is orchestrated to live, grow, and die with the planet's changing seasons? Did you not wonder how the connectedness of all things truly works? It's invisible. It's energetic. It's as real, if not more real, than your radio waves and satellite transmissions, your TV signals and cordless phones.

We have said this before: all of your wonderful technological inventions mimic some aspect of how the human body functions, relieving you of work by creating machines to do the work for you. Cars run for you, vacuum cleaners sweep for you, washing machines do your laundry, and computers replicate your brain functions and save you time in memorization and calculation functions. Now, in the last five years of this incredible energetic shift encompassing your globe, you have no tangible technology with which to gauge your energetic progress, except by checking into your own body, testing your systems, and weighing what is and is not working in your lives. Once you can see where and why you are stuck, cleaning up those problems becomes easy.

We begin at the base of your system, at the root or first chakra, because your growth at all PEMS levels (physical, emotional, mental, and spiritual) is achieved through balancing the attributes and clearing the lessons held by each energy center in ascending order. That is why your body is designed to clear downward, and that is why your clearing work must start from the bottom up.

First Chakra — Root

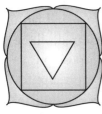

Glands: testes and prostate (adrenals — etheric)

Core Energy: grounding, personal identity, physical survival

Color: red

Note: middle C

Chakra Pair: root and crown (1 and 7)

Figure 12.2

Your root chakra extends from the base of the spine to the perineum, a soft area between the genitals and anus. Its orientation is vertical, pointing downward toward Earth. The body parts and organs in this chakra's sphere of influence are your feet, legs, coccyx, anus, groin, hip joints, and pelvic girdle. Attributes of this chakra hold your survival in the material plane of existence and include your physical needs for air, water, food, shelter, sex, and safety. Root also maintains your grounding to the earth and the 3D reality in which your body resides and functions. Here you house your personal identity that forms who you think you are and how you feel about yourself. Self-worth and self-love are grounded here, and grow into new levels of expression for every chakra above root.

Being well-grounded is essential for materialization of thoughts to ideas to concepts to concrete objects. Also, without proper grounding your body cannot transition from the lower to higher energetic human hologram that is now becoming available in the heightened energy grids of your planet. Issues stored here and lessons to be processed revolve around fears about basic survival, fears of failure, lack, poverty, and needs of the basic sexual drive, which include fear of infertility. (Your drive to procreate is a basic function that is hard-wired into the base of your physical core in the first and second chakras; you call it your "biological clock.")

When your root chakra is functioning well, your body maintains a high level of health and energy. You feel safe and secure in your life, have good relationships with those around you, and reach a masterful comfort zone in your physical domain. When the root chakra is clogged or unbalanced, you feel disconnected from the flow of life, alone and separate from the people around you. You constantly recycle aches and pains because the body cannot release excess pressure from the root and the chakras above. You feel insecure as to safety and survival, as to future, as to purpose. You begin to fear that you cannot manifest your goals, you lose trust and faith in yourself. If these root fears are not faced, assimilated, and cleared, all the chakras above it cannot help but express their negative predispositions as well. Fear travels upward, dear one, distorting the energy of every ascending chakra.

Common physical manifestations of root issues are accident or illness in feet, knees, legs, coccyx, groin and hip joints, varicose veins, and tumors or cancers in the rectum, genitals, prostate, or testes. When illness occurs in these areas, your body is physically mirroring your spirit's energetic inability to move forward (feet, legs, hips), reproduce (genitals), and excrete waste (anus/urethra).

The task we hand you here, should you choose to accept it, is to drain out your fears so that they do not take control over your life. Remember, your fears block your powers. Energetically, your fears prevent a positive expression of your gifts and talents by forming blockages in your energetic meridian system. Physically, fear lodges in the body and blocks your central nervous system from clearing. In other words, your level of physical dysfunction is directly tied to the intensity of the fears you hold in your chakra structure. Do not fear that illness or accident will strike, for that is what you will create. Work on mitigating the strength of your fears by allowing all those blocks to flow down your legs and out your feet. That is your most direct path to walking tall, strong, and healthy with clear eyes, heart, and mind.

Second Chakra — Sacral

Glands:	ovaries
Core Energy:	confidence, creativity, motivation
Core Purpose:	energy storage
Color:	orange
Note:	middle D
Chakra Pair:	sacral and throat (2 and 5)

Figure 12.3

Your sacral chakra is located four finger-widths below your navel. Use your own fingers to measure, please. Since everyone varies in size and shape, we cannot apply an inch or centimeter standard here. The second chakra is horizontal in orientation, aligned from the front to the back of the body. Its practical function is energy storage for the PEMS layers of your body. The body parts and organs within the sacral chakra's field of influence are the pelvis, sacral vertebrae, lower intestine, sexual organs (female), bladder, and chapter 19. We point out here how beautifully your bodies are designed. Your energy storage overlaps the same area as your reproductive space (womb). This is your area of deepest creation and procreation. It is therefore no accident that your core creative drive is also anchored here, which affects your material success in things financial.

When balanced with a solid, clear root chakra below, you will develop a strong self-image that will propel your confidence and motivation to new heights of creative and business endeavors. Yes, circles upon circles, that is how you are built, and that is how we teach. A healthy sacral chakra affords you an optimistic perspective, respect for self and others, and discernment in regards to loving relationships and sexuality. This level of personal intimacy shows a refinement of the root's innate, raw sexual drive.

When your second chakra is blocked, your body becomes physically, chronically low in fuel. Some people cannot hold warmth in their abdomen and always feel chilled. You therefore face energetic lessons revolving around lack: lack of self-worth, lack of material worth, and lack of personal intimacy. This lack translates into an inability to motivate oneself, to function and create in order to earn a living. Chronic lower back pain often mirrors financial lack, as does colitis (or other bowel irritation patterns) in the front of this chakra, in the lower abdomen. Verbal, physical, and sexual abuse also tend to clog this chakra and carry lessons of victimization, manipulation, and power-lessness that can be sexual, financial, or rooted in bigotry (race, creed, gender).

Women traditionally hold lessons in the front of the body, and men in the back. The front is emotionally controlled: the back is mental. Now that more women are facing the task of supporting themselves, there has been a documented rise in female back pain and female heart attack. For women going through abandonment lessons, widowhood, or divorce, a standard pattern of colitis, ileitis, or leaky gut syndrome has arisen that is acknowledged by your medical community to be emotionally sourced. The lower intestine is hampered in its ability to assimilate food and filter out toxins, which is the body's mirroring of the emotional lack of support and safety.

Yes, there is an energetic reason behind every physical symptom. Female dysfunctions include infertility, menstrual difficulties, endometriosis, vaginal infections, cysts, tumors, or cancer of the female reproductive organs. Both men and women can develop pelvic or lower-back pain, lower-intestinal issues, bladder or urinary illnesses, sexual diseases or problems, and low-spine issues.

One vital point we wish to convey here: It is crucial for your self-worth to be rooted [pardon the pun!] in your inner personal identity and not measured by your material wealth. If your self-worth is dependent on how much money and possessions you have, you will never outgrow the "have and have-not" survival lessons of life. Money can be earned, spent, lost, and regained. If you measure your self-worth by your monetary wealth, you will always risk loss. Dear ones, is not love priceless? [Chuckles.]

Third Chakra — Solar Plexus

Figure 12.4

Glands:	gallbladder, liver, pancreas, spleen
Core Energy:	instinct, personal power, social identity, will, self-esteem
Color:	yellow
Note:	E
Chakra Pair:	solar plexus and heart (3 and 4)

Your third chakra is located in the middle of your stomach area, or three finger-widths above the navel. The solar plexus chakra's orientation is horizontal, front to back. The body parts and organs in this chakra's realm are in the front: the abdomen, solar plexus, upper intestine, gallbladder, liver, pancreas, and spleen. In the back they are aligned to the kidneys, adrenal glands, and the lumbar vertebrae. The third chakra maintains balance in physical digestion. Emotional balance is also maintained here, allowing you to trust your own instincts, make your own decisions, and maintain your self-worth intact of ego interference (your ego, or anyone else's). The Solar plexus is your social chakra, whose energy supports your interpersonal relationships and your cooperative ability to work within groups.

A healthy third chakra makes for an emotionally balanced person who can deal honestly and effectively with the outer world in a positive manner. People with a strong third chakra become good social, business, and religious leaders. They have well-defined personal boundaries, and are guided by clear gut instincts that carry intuitive information about day-to-day practical matters. Energetic first impressions occur at six feet apart when your auric fields merge, way before you shake hands! A good portion of success in all things comes from trusting your gut instincts, and a major part of failure comes from not listening to your energetic intuition. (Not to be confused with the third eye chakra, which receives higher intuition, i.e., information coming from your Higher Self.)

When the third chakra is blocked or ailing, a person becomes indecisive, insecure, and feels inadequate to handle their basic responsibilities. They become prey to what others may think or want of them. Solar plexus is the seat of your will or your powerlessness, as measured by your effectiveness in the outer world. When you are locked in fear patterns, you internalize the damage, inflicting self-damage. When you lash out in anger patterns, you externalize your own damage by involving others in the process. Some fall victim to others' control while some feel the need to control others. Some fear criticism and judgment or angrily criticize and judge others. What is the difference? The back vortex of the third chakra is governed by the mental body, expressing logical will devoid of emotion. This blockage results in anger patterns being expressed. The front is governed by the emotional body and when a blockage creates fear-filled victim patterns expressed emotionally, devoid of logic. Again, two sides of the same imbalanced coin, dear reader, anger stems from fear, and fear is what needs to be cleared from your four-layered energetic blueprint. You are so much more than just your physical core.

Illnesses associated with this region include digestive problems such as nausea, chronic indigestion, gastritis, ulcers, food sensitivities, and lactose intolerance; colon and upper intestinal ailments; gallbladder, liver, pancreas, and spleen dysfunctions such as diabetes, pancreatitis, hepatitis, gallbladder/kidney stones, and tumors or cancers. Kidney and adrenal issues also lodge here, along with mid-back spinal problems.

Emotional issues of power and control are intrinsically woven into the third chakra area, including anorexia/bulimia patterns in Western cultures. The solar plexus is also the top of the "lower chakra system" through which your tribal heritage has formed for thousands of years, dominated by fear-based patterns. Is it not amazing, dear heart, how your physical health reflects your overall energetic progress?

Fourth Chakra — Heart

	Gland:	thymus
	Core Energy:	divine flame, compassion, joy and sorrow, centeredness
	Color:	green
	Note:	F
Figure 12.5	Chakra Pair:	heart and solar plexus (4 and 3)

Your heart chakra is the center of your physical chakra system. It is expanding to become the new fulcrum, the new pivot, the new leader of the three chakras above and the three below. When you finally express all thoughts, words, and deeds through your heart chakra, you will have become a fully heart-centered person. This vortex feeds energy to your upper back, ribs, heart, lungs, esophagus, breasts, and to the respiratory, circulatory and immune systems. Energetically, the heart governs how well you love yourself and others, and the quality of your joy, sorrow, and compassion.

When the heart chakra is clear, balanced, and open, you approach life with serenity, peace, and joy. You feel connected to all forms of life without restraint or judgment. Your appreciation for life creates a boundless flow of gratitude, which is the fuel of joy that all beings seek. Your positive attitude is contagious and spreads energetically, as you embody the purity of unconditional love. You will be cool in a crisis, love your enemy into loving you back, and live and let live in peace. You will be harmless, you see? [Chuckles.] Yes, we are describing the mantle of mastery that you will don with your lightbody, the energy of Christ consciousness that is your model to attain. Does it not make sense that your Divine flame is the core energy of your heart chakra?

When the heart chakra is blocked, you attract mostly negative lessons about creating and sharing unconditional love. If all you have experienced is conditional love, you may be afraid to show affection, be afraid of rejection, be unable to forgive, and be jealous of those who can give and receive love. Bitterness and guilt stem from an inability to forgive oneself and others. Your emotional perspective will magnify petty details and be quick to judge, leading to conditional love patterns and more rejection. Childhood abuse and neglect are equally damaging to this area, often resulting in adults who seek love but only know its negative expression. Those who don't know how to love, for whatever reason, are the loneliest people on this planet.

Illnesses that beset this region are heart conditions including heart attack, arrhythmia, enlarged heart, blocked arteries, congestive heart failure; and respiratory issues including allergies, asthma, bronchial/lung problems, pneumonia, cancer, circulatory problems, and upper back issues. Immune disorders can also arise from depression (such as depressed immune response) that can be sourced in chemical toxicity, emotional stress, physical inactivity, or a combination thereof. Energetically, you amass many negative emotions that end up as heart blockage when you refuse to face your problems as you continue to live against your heart. That is the surest path to illness for the heart chakra region. What is the best prevention? Release your emotional heartaches and change your life for the better.

Fifth Chakra — Throat

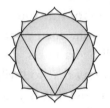

Glands:	thyroid and parathyroid
Core Energy:	personal expression, creativity, social communication
Color:	blue
Note:	G
Chakra Pair:	throat and sacral (5 and 2)

Figure 12.6

The throat chakra's domain includes the thyroid and parathyroid glands (which regulate metabolism and calcium balance), shoulders, neck, throat, and mouth, including jaws, teeth, and gums. The fifth chakra maintains a physical balance between the upper torso and head while its main energy focus is communication. With a healthy throat chakra, all four chakras below have good intercommunication with your upper senses. The front vortex of this chakra is your self-expression conduit to the outer world, allowing you to speak your needs, your love, your will, and your creative ideas. The back vortex of the fifth chakra has been labeled the career chakra, and it supports your outward expression of the reality you wish to create. People with a healthy throat chakra speak sincerely from the heart with no negative intent. Their work is positive, productive, and profitable. They also have a keen intuitive sense, since they are connected to their own inner wisdom and a well-developed sense of the right use of personal will.

People with blocked or damaged throat chakras have experienced life lessons that made them "swallow their words" over and over again. Fears that lodge in this area relate to loss of empowerment, limiting your ability to express your needs, emotions, and dreams. This stifles your creativity and leaves you open to victim patterns. Since you cannot speak your truth, there develops a dichotomy between your words and deeds, plus an inability to blend well in social settings with either inappropriate speech or too much gossiping.

Looking energetically at this area, neck issues reveal an inability to see both sides of a situation (yes, the cliché "stiff-necked" is appropriate here). Shoulder, arm, and hand problems are the body's way of telling you that it cannot reach for that which you desire and require. Regrets also clog this chakra with the inability to express love, sorrow, and forgiveness. Some people with throat blockage cannot shed tears while others cannot laugh. Physical symptoms that arise in this area are stiff neck, shoulder injury, or bursitis/arthritis; throat problems including chronic sore throat, laryngitis, and other vocal issues; teeth, gum, and jaw (TMJ) problems; and tension headaches that occur at the base of the neck below the skull.

The thyroid and parathyroid glands are governed by the throat chakra. These glands work to balance calcium levels in the blood and regulate the body's metabolic functions. When this chakra is blocked, thyroid function is affected. Overactivity (hyperthyroidism) can cause weight and hair loss, fatigue, anxiety, sweating, palpitations, diarrhea, and intolerance of heat. Illnesses include osteoporosis, arthritis, and calcified stones in the urinary tract. Underactive thyroid leads to hypothyroidism, which can impair muscle and nerve function, leading to spasms or seizures. Other organ distortions can occur, such as glandular enlargement due to a mineral deficiency of iodine (goiters), tumors, and cancer. Since the thyroid/parathyroid glands work in a hormonal feedback loop with the pituitary and hypothalamus, imbalance in those glands can also affect thyroid function.

Energetically sourced here are also addiction patterns relating to food, smoking, drugs, and alcohol, all of which are ingested through this area and limit your potential for developing strong will power. Clearing the throat chakra allows you to overcome your self-limitations by exposing and releasing the fears that perpetuate these blockages.

Sixth Chakra — Third Eye

Figure 12.7

Glands:	pituitary and hypothalamus
Core Energy:	higher intuition, intellect, insight, wisdom
Color:	indigo (deep blue)
Note:	A
Chakra Pair:	third eye and soul purpose (6 and 8)

Your sixth chakra is located low on the forehead, centered above the bridge of the nose at the eyebrow ridge. The third eye is a horizontal chakra whose orientation is front to back. It is your source of extrasensory perception, higher sight, insight, and wisdom. Spiritual intuition enters your system here, allowing you to view the "bigger picture" of life with all its levels of energetic interaction. Here resides your clairvoyance, your psychic intuition and personal awareness, your doorway to inspiration from inner and higher knowledge. This chakra works in a unique way with all the other chakras. It has a physical monitoring connection to the root, sacral, solar plexus, heart, throat, and crown.

The body parts governed by the third eye are the eyes, ears, sinuses, nose, and the pituitary and hypothalamus glands. With a clear, well-functioning sixth chakra, you communicate well with both the inner and higher selves; you can accomplish much inner healing and spiritual growth. This chakra allows you to clearly see your energetic issues and lessons, so that you can take responsibility for them. Most hands-on practitioners have a very strong, sensitive third eye because they rely on it for diagnostic input in their holistic work. Just like toning your physical body, the more you exercise your expanding senses, the bigger and stronger they will get. The sixth chakra also connects energetically in a unique way with the entire system, offering the higher meanings of all that occurs in the other chakras.

People with a blocked third eye feel cut off from their intuition, and they often deny the possibility that these higher levels actually exist. Some don't believe in anything other than what they have learned, sensed, or experienced in the physical world. Their ability to cope with life's ups and they downs is severely diminished, so they keep repeating the same lessons without understanding why or how to move beyond them. Fears lodge here about connecting with your inner self and of having to face your spiritual homework. This creates loops of guilt, blame, and shame that block you from taking responsibility for what you have created. Intellectual/creative inadequacy or envy can set in, as others move forward and you do not. This is the lower mind avoiding its growth into a higher framework of reality.

It is crucial to clear the sixth chakra or you will keep getting in your own way.

Emotional issues associated with this region are depression, anxiety, paranoia, psychotic behavior, schizophrenia, and emotional and mental instabilities. Physical imbalances can occur in the eyes, ears, sinuses, nose, and also affect pituitary and hypothalamus function. The pituitary gland regulates your endocrine system (glands that secrete hormones directly into the bloodstream) and thus many of your body's processes. The hypothalamus regulates the pituitary, your body temperature, and your needs for food, sleep, and sex. Migraine headaches can lodge here, either physically sourced by organs in this region or from hormonal issues that imbalance other chakras. Conceptual, or functional, learning disabilities are also governed by the third eye, though they are often sourced in the crown, which regulates the brain and central nervous system functions.

Do you realize now how incredibly intricate the human design is? We are speaking of the holographic, multilayered, energetic being that you are, beyond the physical core that you see in the mirror. When you overlay the energetic picture atop the physical, is it not astounding how perfectly your physical body mirrors your energetic state? Dear one, as you clear your etheric blockages and resolve your emotional, mental, and spiritual issues, your body will rebalance itself into glowing health.

Seventh Chakra — Crown

Figure 12.8

Gland:	pineal
Core Energy:	selflessness, spiritual connection, universal energy source
Color:	violet
Note:	B
Chakra Pair:	crown and root (7 and 1)

Your crown chakra, located at the top of your head, is a vertical chakra whose orientation points up. Crown governs your pineal gland (which produces the hormone melatonin), the brain, and major physical systems; that is, the central nervous system, skin, muscular, and skeletal systems. This chakra is your divine connection to the major source of universal energy that feeds your entire four-layered, bio-body system. When this chakra is strong and healthy it expands along with your spiritual growth by growing larger, like a cap on your head, that eventually covers your crown from ear to ear.

This energy center is your physical and spiritual connection to your Higher Self. A person with a healthy crown chakra has the strength and courage to be comfortable walking in both worlds of Earth and spirit. They have detached from a focus on self, feel compassion for all, and are not afraid of death of the body. Because they have conquered their fears, they hold no conditional expectations of anyone else. They are comfortable with their inner and outer selves, have solid self-worth, and know how to spend their energy with clear intent and focus. They live within the energetic field of higher ethics, morality, attitudes, and values. Thus they have true and clear energy, true and clear purpose, and lead true and clear lives.

When your crown chakra is blocked, your body reflects an all-around lack of energy and stamina. Here is where negative beliefs clog your system and cut off the higher help that so many desperately seek. Crises of faith arise, lack of faith in both oneself and in Spirit to support your life. Denial of your own divinity makes you fearful of change, locks you into the 3D duality-reality, and prevents your spiritual ascension.

Illnesses associated with this chakra region include genetic disorders; brain ailments, such as clots, hemorrhages, comas, seizures, tumors, and cancers; muscular disorders and paralysis; bone/skin ailments and cancers; insomnia and sleep disorders; nervous system malfunctions and related neurological illnesses; nervous system injuries, spinal cord injuries, and strokes.

The most difficult things to heal at this level are your limiting belief systems, especially regarding your body's ability to heal itself. You have been raised knowing that you cannot regenerate organs or limbs, cannot grow new adult teeth, cannot replace lost hair, cannot heal severed spinal cords, and cannot reverse aging. These beliefs are so ingrained within you that the DNA codes that control these functions have shut themselves down. Yes, mind over matter, your beliefs govern your body chemistry. The fear of death keeps the crown chakra closed for many people. Again, the more you believe in life eternal, the more easily you will release the fears that block you from connecting to your Higher Self. And where is that connection? Directly above the crown. So close, dear one, so close. Above all, please believe that Spirit is closer to you than your own skin.

Eighth Chakra — Soul Purpose

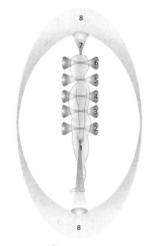

Figure 12.9

Core Energy:	selflessness, spiritual connection, universal energy source
Color:	white/gold
Note:	high C
Chakra Pair:	soul purpose and third eye (8 and 6)

In viewing the eighth chakra, we move beyond the dense etheric body with its linear arrangement of seven physical energy centers. Imagine the soul purpose chakra as a delicate skin or fine membrane that encircles your PEMS layers like a big eggshell. Yes, all around you, above and below too, at a distance of twelve inches from your head and feet. Indeed, your Higher Self is closer than you realize, intimately connected to all that you feel, think, and do. This outer auric layer is similar to the amniotic sac that keeps a baby safe and floating in its nurturing fluids until it is ready to grow beyond, into the air-breathing phase of its physical life.

The function of the eighth chakra is similar in that it maintains your outer spiritual body connection yet steps down the cosmic energies to a denser level so that you can fulfill your role in the blind game of earthly lifetimes. Moving beyond your current 3D duality-reality is the name of the ascension game, is it not? We do not mean to sound frivolous here, but gently remind you that though the stakes may seem very high, though you may be facing difficult challenges and changes, this is not a life-and-death game because nobody ever really dies! The hardest concept to embrace and fully believe is that you existed in energetic form before you entered your current body, and you will continue to exist in energetic form after you wear out and discard that body.

Moving beyond your limited 3D physical life is the doorway offered by the soul purpose chakra, for it is the first of a series of outerdimensional chakras that support your physical existence within the energetic grids of your planet. Beyond your dense etheric body with its interdimensional chakras, this outer chakra layer connects your physical/energetic meridians to the planetary meridians. When you reach the level of eighth chakra awareness, you become the vibratory connection between Spirit above and Earth below. You merge with your own eternal soul, your Higher Self, your God connection (as above). You also merge with the consciousness of the planet and all life on it (so below).

All living things are connected in the energetic soup of life. When we speak of the human consciousness, the global human awareness, the specific human energetic signature that imprints all life with your existence, where is that? In brief, your ninth chakra is the Monad connection, or soul family group. Near the top of the ninth energetic band is a blending into the tenth, which is the global human consciousness. In order to reach those energetic heights, dear one, your chakra core of root through crown must be clear and balanced, solid and stable.

Do you follow? We hope you will!

For now, we ask you to see the eighth chakra as the outer skin of your dense etheric body, encompassing your PEMS levels in all directions. While the eighth chakra encircles the inside seven, it connects directly into your chakra system in two places: above the crown chakra and below the root chakra. Picture this membrane to be twelve inches above your head and the same twelve inches below your feet and also ballooning out around you to as far as your fingertips can reach. We stated earlier that the crown and the root are your two vertical chakras pointing up and down while the horizontal chakras two through six each have an energy vortex front and back, linked by a thin tube through the body. Well, the two vertical chakras each have a second vortex too!

Picture the top aspect of the eighth chakra like a flower pointing down toward your head — it provides the incoming energy for your crown chakra. Now picture your downward-pointing root chakra, and place the bottom flower of the eighth chakra facing up — it feeds you back clean, green earth energy to keep you grounded. There is your full "as above, so below" connection to the cosmos. Is it not exquisite, the human design?

The Veil of Forgetfulness: Location, Form, and Function

At this point, we would like to share with you an aspect of your energetic wiring that has been, up until now, beyond your framework of reference. This has to do with the Veil of Forgetfulness, where it is, and how it functions. We will begin by asking you, dear reader, a question: Have you ever wondered where the Veil of Forgetfulness actually is? This is one of many metaphysical concepts that sounds good and makes sense, but people do not see any logical or physical proof that it exists. Of course, since the veil is what keeps your duality firmly in place and keeps you separate from conscious connection to Spirit, one could argue that you aren't supposed to see it. Yes, all well and good, but it puts the veil back into the conceptual-theoretical arena and removes it from your actual day-to-day existence.

Well, dear one, the Veil of Forgetfulness is not an amorphous concept, nor is it a puffy wall beyond the horizon that you will encounter if you walk far enough. If the veil is supposed to keep 3D duality fixed and keep your sensory level limited, did you ever wonder why people individually attain a heightened vibration in their own time, in their own way? If the veil were the same for everyone (affected each person the same way), wouldn't everyone be making the same progress at the same time? Yes, if the veil were fixed in your dimension outside of your bodies, you would all respond the same way.

Getting clear yet? [Chuckles.] Each person has his or her very own Veil of Forgetfulness built into the chakra system. When we say, "The way up is within" and "the kingdom of God is inside you," we are speaking literally. Your Higher Self connection is the eighth chakra link between the eternal you and the temporarily physical you. Up until now, this connection has been like a one-way mirror, keeping you unaware that you are linked to levels of yourself beyond your physical core.

In some holistic teachings, the eighth chakra has been named your Soul Star/Earth Star connection. Within the neck of each flower pointing down to crown from above and pointing up to feet from below is a little golden filter (see figure 13.10). The filter above your crown controls how much incoming universal energy, and what frequency, your body can handle at any given time. Since your meridian system has a built-in circuit breaker around the head to protect the crown chakra from internal pressure backing up, the crown also needs a way to release pressure. The golden filter

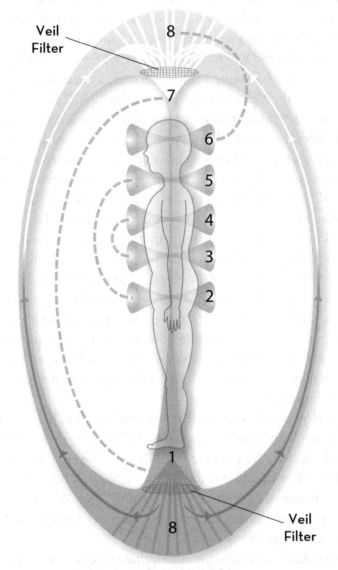

Figure 12.10: Veil of Forgetfulness

above the crown, in addition to feeding universal energy into your energetic system, also reverses to release excess pressure from the crown chakra.

The golden filter below your feet (in the bottom flower of the eighth chakra pointing up to root) acts as a drain for all the excess pressure released from your body, and also determines how much incoming earth energy your body can handle. Yes, each filter has a dual purpose in different directions, acting as pressure valves for the seven-chakra system held within the energetic circle of the eighth chakra.

Now, how do these interactions take place? How does the eighth chakra know the light-density quotient of each of the lower chakras? Ah, the beauty of your design leaves us in awe. Look to the mate of the eighth chakra. In earlier text, we stated that the sixth chakra, your third eye, has a physical monitoring connection to each of the other six chakras. What does that mean? The sixth chakra is constantly reading the energy levels of the other chakras, as well as its own, and relaying that information to its mate, the eighth. Based on these energy readings, the eighth chakra adjusts its internal filters accordingly. Is it not amazingly simple? [Chuckles.]

Yes, where the veil is and what it does are both simple enough to explain, but how the veil filters actually work is beyond the purview of this text. We will add, however, that your eighth chakra intimately knows how the rest of you is doing at the physical, emotional, mental, and spiritual levels. Thus Higher Self constantly knows the specifics of where you are blocked and what still needs to be learned. Even if you are physically healthy, you still need to clear your emotional, mental, and spiritual etheric baggage (dense 3D pressure pockets) from your auras. The lessons you draw to yourselves in life keep recurring because they are magnetizing that specific vibratory level of lesson to them. That vibratory level is controlled by the eighth chakra based on the vibratory health of the internal seven chakras. People in victim mode, for example, keep attracting victim lessons until they heighten their vibration beyond that frequency band and no longer need to attract that level of lesson.

Many of you are probably asking, "How are those vibrations emitted and received?" Higher Self will patiently guide you through your lessons, over and over, until your spiritual homework has been accomplished. All of those lesson vibrations that bounce back and forth between people (to cause drama and stimulate learning) occur because you are unconscious transmitters. You don't realize how much you are energetically broadcasting all the time. Whether it be emotions from the emotional layer or repeating loops in the mental layer, most people are stuck in one or both modes. That is one reason that our teachings include gaining control of your thoughts and emotions. Not only is unconscious broadcasting a huge energy drain, it constantly reinforces the very things you are trying to release, due to the Universal Law of Attraction.

Once you learn how to clear the pockets of the 3D density you all carry in your auras, your vibratory rise will be guaranteed. When you learn how to stop feeding those pockets and start clearing them instead, you will feel better, accomplish more, and improve the quality of your life. The Veil of Forgetfulness lies within you. Each person carries his or her own. That is why ascension is such an individual process. That is how the new generations are coming in with a thinner Veil. That is also why we have stressed throughout our work together that you need to clear your physical core of excess internal pressure in order to be able to resonate with and carry the higher energies.

Do you see now, dear one, why you need a daily practice? Do you see why reading and learning metaphysical concepts only takes you part way to your goal? The clearer your meridian system, the more light you can hold. The higher your light-density quotient, the thinner your veil filters become at the physical level. That is where your etheric layers, your senses, systems, and body parts are all wired together. In order to manifest anything at the material 3D level, you must do it from a higher level — the 5D level, the level of union between all eight chakras.

Once you clear and balance your seven internal chakras enough for their resonance to blend with the vibratory resonance of the eighth chakra, you achieve a unity, or unified chakra field, that becomes all one chakra. You will have total, conscious command of your light-density quotient. You will know exactly what, when, and where you need to clear; you will know when you need to recharge yourself. You will understand and practice care and maintenance of the aura!

To those of you worried about your light-density quotient, what the specific numbers are and what they mean, we say, "Stop worrying about it. Stop wasting energy in that direction." You would have to have a strong working knowledge of sacred geometry to fully understand how this process works and what each gradient means. Ultimately, that knowledge will not serve you unless you know how to apply it. The veil is one of many built-in systems you have that are autonomous. Would you want to be in full conscious charge of your digestion? Of your hormonal levels? Of your bone-marrow production? That level of body awareness would only interfere with your current life. If you just focus on diligently clearing your nervous system of pressure and re-energizing when you feel the need, your PEMS body layers will rebalance themselves.

Once you have cleared enough internal pressure to lift your dense etheric body into a higher energetic band-width, what happens then? You merge with your soul purpose chakra, dear one. Higher Self blends with you by adjusting your golden filters so that all eight energy centers become one vibration. You expand beyond the Veil of Forgetfulness, which you no longer need to keep you blindly focused on the 3D game of earthly life. Yes, you become a truly interdimensional being. Once your chakra system expands into full integration at the eighth level, you won't be reading our channeled words any more, dear precious human, you will be conversing with us directly.

We so look forward to that time, as we cheer and support you along your own individual climb. Remember that your ascension process may be personal but your metaphysical journey is enhanced by like-minded friends along the way. Help each other, work on each other, support each other, and please remember the three Rs: rest, release, and recharge.

(13)

Pre-Ascensionitis

"And the day came when the risk to
remain tight in a bud was more painful
than the risk it took to blossom."
—Anaïs Nin

Greetings, dear ones, from the Brotherhood of Light. We welcome you once again to our energy and our love. More than ever, you need to know that you are all beloved. Each and every one of you, beloved. One day, when we finally meet, you will realize the true meaning of these words. The scope of our divine love for you is colossal beyond your wildest dreams. For, you see, you are all part of us. There is truly no you and us, only All That Is. Since you are part of All That Is, you are Divine Be-ings. Yes, on a marvelous voyage of discovery back to your true selves, back to the source of your eternal I Am essence. Where is it? Why, within you, of course.

You carry the sum total of all the lives you have ever lived within the encoded DNA of your bodies. Those codes are changing, dear ones, be-ing redefined by the planet's increasing frequencies of energy. All of you are changing, each in his or her own time, no need to pay for it. Instead, pay for holistic healing work, pay for massages, use your abundance to see you through the healing aspects of your transition. No matter how much personal clearing you do, one single lightworker doing hands-on or distant healing with you can augment and facilitate your clearing process in a huge way. Dear practitioners, use the new tools coming in. Add to your energetic hands-on work the healing aspects of vibration (sound) and light (color). You will see marvels of release on the table.

Dear reader, we cannot express this strongly enough: Now is the time to be clearing your body and life. Now is the time. Whenever you read these words, no matter the date, is your "now" time too! You who are in the last quarter of the Millennium Shift are beginning to climb the exponential curve of increasing energies — and therefore increasing pressure. Your aura will become more and more palpable. Your energetic body will become a pulsing, sensitive outer skin as real to you as your physical body is now. At first, what will you feel most strongly? Your 3D density. The energetic damage, baggage, and blockages that you carry will become your problem, because doctors won't know what to do for what they can't see or measure.

You will also start to feel the energetic drain from your body required for all activities: You will need to redefine the limits of your time, your energy, and your money. If you work beyond those limits, you will get physically ill. Put another way, imagine the incoming higher energies as a big sieve that you are rising into and trying to push through. All that can get through are the higher-energy parts of you. The lower-energy parts, the PEMS blockages, will get stuck behind and pull you back down. All the layers of your vehicle must be clear enough to pass through the 5D sieve. As the energies rise, you may feel as if gravity is increasing or as if your body is getting heavier. That is why creating a lightbody means making yourself energetically lighter.

How? First, get your PEMS layers cleared and balanced, then work on their integration. That is the ascension process in a nutshell, because full integration opens the door to Higher Self stepping into your life. That is your God connection, your ascent into the higher realms, your union with All That Is. Is that not what you seek? If you are reading this text, you have probably studied different aspects of metaphysics, of religion, of faith. You may have already done much clearing of your emotions and thoughts, and you might be well on your way to defining your own inner truth. We ask you not to ignore the energetic clearing of your physical core, either. If need be, seek help from whatever modalities feel good to your body — massage, acupuncture, or any holistic practice you are drawn to. Explore physical clearing. Since you are changing down to the cellular level, it stands to reason that your body will be affected at all levels of system function. All is coming up to be cleared, and you are feeling it all more clearly.

In this chapter, we would like to address the symptomology that you may be experiencing and explain it to you as an ongoing process. If your medical community had knowledge of the Millennium Shift and were categorizing these symptoms, they would likely label it as "pre—ascensionitis" [chuckles]. And then they would say, rest often, drink plenty of spring water, and find a happy balance in your life, for there's not much you can do but get through it. We say, it is quite logical that as your body changes, so will your sleeping and eating patterns, your health and energy levels. It is essential for you to be very aware of how you treat your body, for it is expending a great deal of energy to shift down to the cellular level in a very short span of time.

Please keep in mind that the following list of symptoms depicts general trends in human response to the internal pressures of these shifting times. Please do not read this chapter and become afraid that you are ill. Remember, you create what you focus on! Conversely, if you are in a great deal of pain or distress, please seek medical help for diagnosis, therapy, and pain management. Then choose holistic support in whatever form suits you. One of the Brotherhood's main goals is to bring science and spirituality together to further the knowledge of healing and well-being for all of humanity. We advise you to use all the tools and technology available, both medical and holistic, to evolve in grace and ease.

Energy Levels: Sleep, Fatigue, and Stress

As the energies expand, so will your senses. You will begin to feel your aura. Your senses are expanding into the realm of what you consider extra-sensory perception, which is actually the full-sensory perception normal in the higher realms. As you grow into this expanded awareness, does it not make sense that you are becoming aware of all the energetic imbalances you are carrying? Hence the onslaught of illness, allergies, phobias, anxieties, old and new, that many of you are experiencing.

Even those of you who are physically and emotionally healthy will still experience symptoms of pre-ascensionitis. Your bodies are shifting and need much rest, quiet, and good nourishment to gracefully weather the process. Below your level of conscious awareness, 25 percent of your physical stamina is used daily for the shifting process, and that percentage is rising along with the energies. Yes, imagine having a part-time job overlaid atop of your current schedules. Why do you think we keep saying that you are doing all of the heavy work? You are in a period of enforced hibernation, as it were, without the ability to rest as much as your bodies require because you still have to function in your everyday lives. That is why we say, rest as much as you can. Allow yourselves that, or the rest you do get will not be restful.

For many people, a good night's sleep is difficult to achieve. Yet when you wake refreshed and energized after that rare six-to-eight-hour stretch of blessed sleep, doesn't the day shine? Don't you have more energy, more patience, and a better frame of mind in which to tackle the day's duties? Yes! Feeling better allows you to function better. When you function better, you get more done, you do it better, and you're happier doing it.

Imagine living a whole week feeling that good, a month, a year. Do you see where we're going? You should feel that good every day. Once you have released enough blockages so that your meridians become free flowing, you will consistently feel better and your entire life will improve at all levels. You say that for every illness humanity suffers, God put a plant on Earth that can cure it. We say, no matter what befalls you in life, God put a clearing process in your body that can help you heal and deal with whatever happens.

Honor all the body signals you get, dear one, to gracefully evolve with the least strain and stress. As the energies thicken, your body will feel heavier, more sluggish, and you may feel tired for no good reason. You will experience changes in your sleeping patterns. It may be increasingly difficult to sleep for as long as you used to; it may get more difficult to fall asleep or stay asleep. Honor whatever your energy level is at any given moment. If you need to lie down for a half-hour in the afternoon, do so; you will feel much refreshed and function better for the rest of the day. If you're wide awake at 4 AM, go do something productive. Or if you're tired, join us in a Circle of Grace session, and we will lull you back to sleep.

Rest is not chatting on the phone or watching three movies in a row. Meditation is a necessary part of the care and maintenance of your aura. Meditation affords you time to release stress and gather universal energy into your energetic body, a time to replenish, rejoin, and re-create a oneness with Spirit. We keep saying this in many different ways; allow your body to guide you. It will tell you of its needs more and more clearly, especially when it comes to rest. If you push beyond your body's reserves, it will become increasingly difficult to keep functioning without getting ill. We do not say this in any way to cause fear. Please understand that is not our intent. But if you ignore your body's needs, it will let you know soon enough.

Remember, your body is expending a good deal of energy to accommodate to the changing tides of the Millennium Shift, which makes you more tired than normal. Then again, your "normal" energetic comfort zone is quickly changing. You can either flow gracefully with these changes and bend them to your will or stand steadfast in your imbalances and feel the increasing stress of going against the tide. Constant stress and strain on something eventually lead to breakage in your physical world, right? That is why we say to listen to your body's needs. Adjust your life to accommodate those needs, or you will fall more and more behind the rising scale of Earth's vibrational tune-up.

Food

Many people are becoming aware of other bodily changes, as well. Is the food you have always eaten changing in taste? Do you get hungry, start to eat, and find yourself unable to finish? Those of you who feel the rising energies, who see a new shimmer in the air, who hear thoughts before they are spoken — you are the ones putting 3-4D food into 4-5D bodies. Are you having trouble digesting food or losing your taste for foods that you once liked? Being sensitive to that dimensional difference is a symptom of pre-ascensionitis.

Remember to bless everything you put into your body. If you are energetically attuned, cup your hands around your food and run a pulse through it for thirty to sixty seconds, both the meal and your glass of water. That will bring the food up to your vibration, and you will assimilate all the nutrition you need from it more easily. Why? By raising the food's vibration, you will feed and enhance who you are becoming; your food will not weigh you down and bring you back to who you were before. If you forget, simply palm your stomach and do the same blessing after you have eaten.

You may be already experiencing changes in your water weight, your physical weight, and your taste for specific foods. Your bodies are truly beginning to reflect the higher vibrations, and many of you are losing your taste for junk foods. To those who are considering vegetarianism only because it may be healthier or spiritually correct, we say that your body is accustomed to meat protein, which is very grounding. Conversely, if eating any type of animal products disagrees with your body, don't apologize. We ask that you compensate with other forms of protein because the higher you rise, the better you need to be grounded so as to stay in balance.

Eating smaller meals — only when you are hungry — will help your emerging lightbody balance at a perfect weight. Yes, the concept of "food as fuel" is your best dieting tool. Listen to your stomach: Eat only when you feel hungry, and stop eating when you feel full. Your body will not digest well if you eat too often, dear one. Nor will you do as well eating large meals that include many food groups. If your body is rejecting food, look to combining less food groups per meal. Mix carbohydrates with dairy or fruit in one meal, then eat protein and vegetable in another. Or put some fruit and ice cream in a blender, and drink your lunch. Also pay attention to the odd food cravings you may have; they are your body's way of telling you that it wants certain ingredients in that food, be it animal, vegetable, or mineral.

Grounding with Food

In regards to food, we would like you to be aware of another energetic rule: eating locally grown food grounds you into the earth. You were originally designed to eat local food to ground you to the plot of earth on which you lived. Local vibration, local food, local grounding, local person. For those of you who suffer from allergies, local honey is a wonderful vaccine against local pollen. Nature has all the remedies within it for anything and everything that ails you.

Granted, you have developed wonderful avenues for providing abundance to all, but here is what is happening: You are eating strawberries from California, bananas from Central America, blueberries from New Jersey, oranges from Florida and Israel, pineapples from Hawaii, mangoes from Mexico, fish from many different oceans, and meat from foreign lands. Food is being transported all over the world, which lessens your proper grounding to your portion of Earth. So plant a garden if you can, or buy produce from a local farm stand. Eat food that comes from the ground around you — food that carries the frequency of where you live — to help ground you better in the ascension process.

Water

Also, you must be aware to constantly drink water now, for the higher frequency naturally burns up more water. Stay hydrated! Why do we keep emphasizing spring water? First and foremost, it comes right out of the ground and is the least processed. Therefore, its molecular structure is healthier and its energetic properties match that of the Earth's shift. Drinking extra water is also vital right now because the rising energies are purifying your body. Toxins, vestigial illness patterns, physical, emotional, and mental blockages, all dense 3D imbalances are rising up to be cleared. Water helps the body to flush out cellular debris from the detoxification process occurring at this crucial time. You will find that the more spring water you drink, the better you will feel.

You will not fare as well by relying on preprocessed foods that are high in preservative content. Manufactured chemicals such as pesticides, preservatives, substitute sweeteners, and synthetic medications linger in your body. Why? Because the human body was not designed to recognize or process these artificially-created, foreign substances. Dear reader, your cleaning products, air fresheners, nail polish, hair dyes, perfumes, all these things can become problematic to have in your environment. The more sensitive you become, the less tolerance your body will have for these poisons. Remember your free will: These are all things within your control to put away in closed cabinets, or if you can, eliminate from your life. Drinking plenty of spring water will greatly help to detoxify your body.

The Ocean and Nature

The biggest storage of Earth's surface energy occurs in the waters of your oceans. You are beginning to recognize the spiritual nature of whales and dolphins. Whales carry the Akashic records of nature within the DNA of their massive bodies. Dolphins are psychic creatures who also anchor the expanded vibrations of 5D in Earth's emotional water layer. Why do you think dolphins are so happy and playful? They embody the direct connection between nature and Spirit and live in a constant state of unconditional joy. Swim with the dolphins, dear one, and be forever changed.

If you have the opportunity to swim in the ocean, take advantage of it. The cleansing power of the ocean is way beyond your current knowledge, for it functions at the energetic level: the constant movement of the waves, the composition of the salted water, and the combination of water energized by the sun all make the ocean a great healing tool. Even the air is energetically enriched by the ocean's momentum. So go play at the beach as much as you can. As time compresses and your to-do list gets longer, remember to spend some time on yourself. Balance your work with a goodly dose of play, so you can keep a more joyous perspective and make that your new comfort zone.

Also, please make time often to sit in the sun and fresh air, for assimilating nature's energies helps to smooth and quicken your transition process. Twenty minutes to a half-hour of sunlight absorption can boost the function of all of your bodily systems! Your sun is called Helios, a huge, magnificent entity who is helping to orchestrate the energetic ascension of your planet. Sit in the sun, call in Helios, and feel the pulses that will begin in your forehead and ripple down your body. Soak in the sunlight to energize yourself, and remember to give thanks when you are done.

If sunlight or the ocean are not easily accessible, we offer some practical advice to shed 3D density in another way. Your bodies are composed of approximately 70 percent water, which is a marvelous carrier for vibration. That is why we recommend long, hot baths at least twice a week. Three times a week or every other day is optimal. Do the Circle of Grace clearing exercise in the tub, and you will be surprised at how much "etheric schmutz" (a Yiddish word for sticky dirt or dust) cascades down your meridians to melt into the water. You will also find much benefit in adding aura-cleansing ingredients into the bath water, like sea salt, lemon juice, baking soda, essential oils, or floral essences. Sometimes just a dose of Rescue Remedy (Bach flower mix) in the water will help calm your transition jitters.

Some people like to float in a cool outdoor pool, others in a steaming hot tub. Whichever you prefer, immersing in water soothes your four-layered PEMS body, and a relaxed body releases much more excess internal pressure. As a general rule, the hotter the water, the larger the clearing. The water will enfold you in the higher energies, for all the water on Earth is humming to a new vibration. Thus you will feel a surcease of the gravity shifts and time fluctuations, which will weigh heavily on you until you are more cleared.

Why do we urge you to soak in water, to sit outside in the sun, and to blend with nature's essence and energies as part of your clearing process? Because nature is in charge of your changes. Earth is dictating those changes by virtue of being the energetic couch that supports your physical presence on her surface. We stated earlier that every life form has similar attributes, first and foremost having a physical core within an energetic housing. Every living thing has an aura, as does your planet, in levels that your body mirrors. Yes, beloved, you are a perfect representation of "as above, so below."

Imagine Earth as a great living creature, energetically housed within the greater body of God by her four PEMS levels: the physical level is the planet, the emotional layer her oceans, her mental layer the atmosphere, and her spiritual layer is Earth's electromagnetic gridwork, from core gravity on out into space. Yet, if this is true, then what is Earth's Circle of Grace clearing process? In your earlier stages of evolution, you called it Mother Nature. You revered her strength and lived by her ever-cleansing life cycles, the seasons. Now, your modern technological societies have reduced it to "weather." You have lost that precious connection to nature that the Native Americans and all other indigenous populations have had. Many of you see their rituals as superfluous superstition. Not so, dear ones, not so.

When you open your senses to the higher energies that nature represents, what are you doing? You are practicing being in the now of God's eternal flowing essence. When we say that the Circle of Grace works at all levels of life expression, we're not kidding. When you relax enough to slip out of your dense 3-4D reality and into nature's climbing 4-5D energies, you are tuning yourself up to the latest incoming shift energies.

Why do we keep asking you to focus on the now? Once you relax enough to reach that expanded meditative state, your enhanced focus allows you to tap into your internal clearing process, to tap into your innate flow of universal energy that cleanses and feeds your body. It is the same flow that fuels all cycles of life in nature. Why do we ask you to be heart-centered? Because that is the interdimensional space within your physical body where your Divine flame resides. By funneling all of your energies and actions through the heart, you create a vibration of joy and happiness that connects you directly to God, or Spirit — or whatever version of universal oneness you believe in. God's energies are eternal, self-replenishing, forever expanding to higher and higher levels of vibrational amplitude. Nature embodies God's energies on this planet, as do you.

Are you beginning to see the connections, dear reader? We hope you do, for they are huge. Nature's energies are in the "joy and bliss" frequency range, since God's essence is the constant give-and-take of unconditional love. Merging with nature and being one with her flows is a direct short-cut to God's energies. You can reach the full physical embodiment of "as above, so below" by merging your inner energy flows (through your favorite form of meditation) to God's outer energy flows in nature. In a nutshell, combining the Circle of Grace patterns with nature's flowing essence creates a full reconnection to Spirit. That is why we urge you to remember to give thanks, to balance the giving and receiving of universal energy.

How do you best give thanks to nature? Through the heart with focused intent and creative visualization. When you are in the physical clearing part of the Circle of Grace, see Earth's physical body being cleared and healed. When you connect with the essence of trees, for example, be aware that they are the lungs of Earth, ingesting carbon dioxide and releasing life-giving oxygen. All plants under water do the same thing for your oceans. Your weather patterns of storms, earthquakes, and volcanic eruptions are all part of Earth's Circle of Grace. That is how the great body of this planet releases pressure at all her levels — physical, emotional, and mental. Her spiritual level (energetic or interdimensional aspect) is also going through a huge overhaul.

As nature's frequency rises to embrace the higher levels of God's essence, you have the unique opportunity to join her on that ride with your full awareness. And remember this: Where the mind goes, universal energy follows. Imagine Earth as pristine clean, a blue-green jewel of life spinning through the cosmos. Imagine all the life forms upon her and within her as healed and happy, for that is the biggest gift you can give back to God.

Clothing

You are also discovering senses that you didn't know you had. Your skin is your largest sensory organ, and how you treat it will change. Certain types of clothing (such as those made from artificial materials) will become stifling to you, simply because your clothes are within your aura and can affect your energy flows. Color will also cause pain or pleasure to your emotional body and influence what you choose to wear. You may gravitate toward solid colors rather than busy patterns or lighter colors rather than dark ones.

The tightness of clothing might become an issue for some people, as they begin to feel their energetic meridians being squeezed or tickled. Some may give up tight belts and high heeled shoes; others may no longer feel comfortable in tops with tight necks. Most of you will find a better comfort zone in loose clothing made of natural fibers. Your clothing needs will change as you grow into awareness of your aura, because your clothing is actually inside your energetic field. Your aura needs the freedom to breathe too.

Heart Palpitations

Do you find your heart sometimes beating erratically, losing pace, fibrillating, and then taking a while to resettle? Yes, that is the body making incremental adjustments at the energetic level, tuning you to Earth's changes. The beat of your heart is the musical conductor for your cellular pulses. Once in a while, the heart must recalibrate to find a truer pace. This will happen most often at night when you are resting, and is no cause for alarm. But if you feel these symptoms occurring frequently, accompanied by nausea, dizziness, and chest or left arm pain, we ask you to please see your doctor immediately. Make sure that these symptoms have not yet reached your physical core. Then you can rest easy [chuckle] and do the Circle of Grace with us when you need recalibration, or re-tuning, to Earth's current energy levels.

Depression

Do you feel as if the whole world is doomed? Do you feel hopeless and helpless, without enough energy to do anything about it? Yes, Earth's frequency is building to clear you at the emotional level. Since 2001, you have been processing a large band of depression held for eons in the global consciousness. We remind you here that each person rises into and through every band of consciousness clearing at his or her own pace. Take heart, dear ones, this phase is but temporary, as the old energy patterns have been replaced with the higher bands of Divine Mother love as of 2004. We use this as one example of many energetic changes that did, do, and will occur for you when you are ready for it to happen. Aware or not matters not, since you are all shifting with the planet. Through the shift process, each rise and swell of energy will be felt more clearly as you fall out of tune and your body strives to catch up.

In the beginning of the shift, each spring and fall brought new frequencies that made the grid signatures swell, then rebalance by winter solstice at the next notch up. Now that Earth is reaching a higher pitch, the frequency is changing more often, and you are becoming more sensitive to every retuning. By the last quarter of the shift (2007 — 2012) Earth's electromagnetic grids will lock into new configurations with no more lows to give you a surcease from the highs. As the Millennium Shift reaches its final years, the exponential changes will curve into a sharper rise that you will feel more keenly.

We would like to point out that many of the pre-ascensionitis symptoms listed here are similar to those of depression, as defined by your medical community:

Feelings of sadness, hopelessness, pessimism, combined with a reduced sense of emotional well-being. More serious cases include loss of appetite, loss of concentration, feelings of tiredness, and a loss of interest and enjoyment in social activities. In extreme cases people may have hallucinations or delusions, and thoughts of death and/or suicide.[1]

If you are struggling with a severity of symptoms, please seek medical help. The standard treatments for depression are psychotherapy and antidepressive drugs. But bear in mind that in this time of climbing energies, the heavier your heart is, the heavier your body will feel. For those of you leading unfulfilling lives, working at jobs you hate, tolerating relationships that no longer fit, you will see much stress and illness arising. We say simply that when you live against your heart, your life will not go well.

The rising energies will force your body to mirror the state of your etheric layers.

The rising energies will also force your lessons home to you with intensified drama, leading you into situations that will necessitate action. In other words, best to clean up now, within and without, while you still have plenty of choices before you. Do not succumb to depression, dear one. Know that the more you clear your physical vehicle and find a joyous balance in your life, the easier it will be to climb out of that pit of despair up into the clean, fresh air of the higher realms.

Sensory Expansion

The good news is, your senses are already expanding. Your intuition has grown enormously and many of you are letting yourselves be guided by a knowing that often overrides logic. What you used to consider extrasensory perception is in truth the full-sensory perception of the higher realms. Some people are having moments of telepathy, clairvoyance, channeling, precognitive dreams, seeing/hearing/feeling different forms of energy, and other strange experiences. What did you think would happen when your senses expanded? You begin to pick up things that used to be beyond your sensory range. No, dear heart, you're not going crazy; you're becoming divine. Since all that lay beyond your 3D senses was invisible, you didn't know it was there. How could you?

That which you see as you is only one part of you, your physical body part. Imagine your body as the inner core of your total Be-ing. Your body anchors your energetic layers, which fan out all around you in ever-widening circles of vibrating energy. So your auras touch each other at six feet apart. Long before you are close enough to shake hands, you are already standing in each other's bodies. Why do you think you get uncomfortable when a stranger stands too close while talking to you? They are standing within the field of your emotional-mental-spiritual layers, which is your dense etheric body (energetically speaking). This discomfort arises from more than just an intrusion into your personal space, for that space is becoming a conscious part of your body that you can feel. As your aura becomes more sensitive, it will become downright painful to you if that close proximity is an unwelcome intrusion.

To give an overview of our work on frequency and physicality, we will say simply that as Earth's energy rises, you will grow into feeling your aura as clearly as you feel your physical body. Your energetic body layers will grow more dense and real to you as you connect with each level of expanding frequencies until you become aware of your total Be-ingness. Once you fully connect with your aura as you are currently connected to your body, watch out, for the world around you will change.

Do you see the beautiful unfoldment here of pattern within pattern and circle within circle? We repeat, you must begin the final stages of your transmutation by healing the energetic imbalances that you carry in your PEMS being, even if you feel healthy. To reach the lightbody stage, you must clear your physical body of low-energy density and damage from this life, and prior lives as well.

Some of you have lost a grip on linear time, and find yourselves confused and dysfunctional in your previously normal 3D routines. Do the Circle of Grace, let us clear your bottom three chakras so we can ground you once again. Do you see how easy it is to think you're losing your grip on sanity? No, dear ones, you are merely finding a new grip on a different reality, that is all. Like a new radio station that fades in and out, you will go through phases of confusing static until the reception becomes clear [chuckles].

As some of you are discovering, your sensory expansion includes new levels of inspiration from the muses that drive you in all fields of thought, from art to science to industry. Prepare for new talents and technologies to emerge in your societies as people follow their hearts and open up their innate gifts and talents to share with others. What happens when you do this? Good, you remembered, you cannot fail!

Long-Term and Short-Term Memory

Are you aware that your memory is being affected by the rising frequencies? For those of you concerned that your memory is slipping, rejoice instead! Specifically, your short-term memory is being affected by now time. Your long-term memory is more fully anchored within you by the emotional state of each experience. Memories with strong emotional content are better anchored in your mind and body than fleeting memories with no emotional attachments. That is why your long-term memory is harder to clear, for the emotional baggage attached to negative memories clog your rise up the frequency scale. Once you clear the physical and etheric damage from those memories — forgive, forgive, forgive! — the memories will still be there, but the pain attached to them will be gone.

Ah, but your short-term memory seems to evaporate, does it not? If you ever witnessed the gradual death of a loved one, you would see a progression similar to what you are slowly experiencing as a vibrational shift. Nearing their physical transition, people lose interest in the outside world and become more focused on their inner world. They quickly forget whether they ate or took their medicine but remember details of the past with great clarity. They are merging into a fog of now time, which is where they are heading, back to the True Reality of Spirit. Along the way, they lose grasp of the daily details of life. So don't worry about forgetting the details. Get used to it, forgive yourself, and keep lists of things you need to do. Just remember where you put those lists. [Chuckles!] Mundane things won't matter as much, dear one, as you expand beyond the matter realm into the spiritual realms.

Changing Focus: Linear to Nonlinear Thought Processes

Your expansion into now time also affects your current sensory confusion by interfering with your linear thought processes. Do you feel as if your thoughts are scattered? Do you often lose your train of thought, sometimes even as you speak? Why? It is becoming more difficult, children, to think only in a logical way. By the same token, it is also becoming more and more difficult to maintain a multitask focus on many things at one time. Therefore, you feel as if you are less mentally capable than you used to be.

Here is what is actually happening: As you awaken and reconnect to your right brain, you will begin to get sensory input from levels you could not tap into before with just your left brain. Even as you continue to function logically, you will begin receiving data from a new source that may interrupt your former left brain way of thinking. Imagine hearing two conversations at once, trying to follow them both, and responding to them at the same time. Not so easy! As you learn to fine-tune your new full-sensory reception and integrate the right and left brain, you will grow beyond this temporary state of interference confusion. Yes, you will eventually become a clear channel for your own Higher Self!

Not to worry, your thought patterns are being restructured as you learn to think more and more out of the box. We guarantee that the shift will not cause you to lose IQ points but instead will expand your thinking at all levels. You will eventually have access to more knowledge than you ever dreamed possible, along with new ways of seeing and understanding the world around you.

Until then, make smaller to-do lists. Take pride in what does get done; the rest will be there tomorrow. Focus on one thing at a time, and do it well. Do not rush, for even your reflexes are in transition and haste will lead to silly accidents. Be patient with yourself and with others. Patience is not only a virtue, it is also a good way to practice being in now time without getting upset.

Sexuality

Not only are your senses becoming sensitive to a broader range of stimuli, your body sensitivity to stimuli (sound, smell, touch, and so on) is becoming more acute as well. Yes, more than just your food preferences are changing. We speak here of the physical aspect of love that you call sex. The most common and intense symptom of the rising energy in your body will be, simply put, a new burning in your lower chakras. Where is your body's energetic storage battery? In your abdomen, second chakra, where you will feel the frequency rising the most.

Your sacral chakra is directly above your root chakra. The root interprets a rise in energy frequency as a signal for the raising of sexual energy. So your sexual urges are being affected. We will again use your language to make a point here. As you mature, you come to the realization that casual sex is unfulfilling. What does that mean? Casual sex does not fill you full of loving energy, feeds your entire Be-ing. That is the main distinction, dear one, that you need to make when you consider physical commitment in a relationship.

Sex is not merely a bodily function. Sexuality is the deepest expression of love that is possible between two human beings. Why? Because it reaches the depths of your physical core. It reaches that place where you build and store energy, and it feeds all of your etheric layers, down into the physical, as well. Do you realize that the energy of orgasm is the closest thing to God's frequency that your body has been able to tolerate (up until now) without burning up?

As you rise through the dimensions, higher, more intense, more brilliant levels of energy will enter your body. Sex is very different in the higher dimensions. Remember, we do not distinguish between male and female as you are forced to do. We merge at many levels simultaneously, directly, to exchange information and to communicate at all different levels. Expressing Self in Spirit is always done through vibrations of love.

Let us look at the word "enlighten." It is a verb that means the adding of light to a state of being. What is that light? It is a physical sine wave of expression, dear one. The ultimate vibration of unconditional love. It is the energy of God. You are beginning to feel that light, that heightening of frequency all around you, and that rising of energy in your very core. Yes, in your place of sexuality, of sensuality, of reproduction. What is reproduction? It is an act of Divine Creation! Look at any baby and you are looking at the face of God's perfect creation. Yes, two people created that tiny new vessel for Spirit while their bodies were enmeshed in a loving explosion of energy that in its expression, created life.

Spirit greatly honors all forms of love. God does not judge which forms are good or bad — all love springs from God, you see, so all love is sanctified — deified. As are you, a marriage of spiritual and physical matter. Do you see, now, how Spirit views sex? As we view everything else: in its purity of expression, sexuality is God experiencing his own creation through the flesh.

As you seek to redefine yourself as an energetic being, your deepest form of energetic expression will, by necessity, also change. Our advice is to honor whatever form of sexual expression is comfortable and honorable for you. Do not ignore those waves of intense need, for their release is healing and helping your body to rise, each time, to a higher vibratory expression. Some people are feeling sensory confusion at the sexual level, either off the mark or not feeling any sexual drive at all. The rising energies are rewiring your electromagnetic blueprint, and this process requires a lot of physical stamina. Do not worry if your sexual responses are different than they used to be. Your entire Be-ing — physical, emotional, mental, and spiritual — is in transition; that is all.

As your sexual needs change, your needs in a satisfying partner will also change. If you rise too much beyond the physical frequency of your current mate, he or she will no longer mesh properly with your energy. Many old, time-worn relationships are ending these days. People no longer fit together the way they used to, if one is studiously advancing while the other remains unaware. Many lesson marriages will also unravel and finally be put out of their misery. We wish you to see you as separate from your lessons so that you may digest them, discard them, and leave them behind.

Lessons only become obstacles if you perceive them to be so.

Sex is difficult for most people to speak about. It is an area of your lives that needs to be cleared of negativity. Dear ones, you will eventually find yourselves gravitating away from sex, seeking instead to make love. Is it not logical and necessary that the physical expression of Divine love should be honest, open, giving, and come from the heart?

Physical love between two people is also an exchange of vital energy. What you do, how you do it, is not just expressed as hands on flesh. You create cords of energy at head, heart, solar plexus, and root. You feed each other universal energy at whatever level of energetic expression you have attained. Did you know that your chakras can merge and blend together in this process, no matter what type of physical communion is achieved? You will become increasingly sensitive to the difference between gut energy (below the belt) and heart energy, (universal energy refined with the divine essence of love from your heart chakra). Once you have elevated your awareness to functioning from the heart level, the lower levels will no longer feed you energetically, especially below-the-belt sex. [Pardon the pun!] To live against your heart will create more and more stress and strain in your physical body, and that accumulation of excess pressure will eventually cause illness. Making love, on the other hand, is a union of two energetic beings that nourishes both with the highest purity of universal energy sustainable in your current electromagnetic structure. Which do you choose, dear one?

Once you fully grasp that every physical action has an energetic component, you will understand why your physical needs are changing. Simply put, sex can be just a biological function while making love from the heart can be expressed just by holding hands. How do you think we express love in the nonphysical realms with no hands to hold? [Chuckles.] With no male or female genders to define or limit us? Ah, the scope of our energetic creations are shared by — you guessed it — a merging of energies. The higher realms have color and sound that is beyond your imagination, a much broader palate of energetic frequencies, if you will.

Since that is where you are headed, we say that your best passport to the higher realms is Be-ing in love with yourself and others all the time! Yes, that is why we emphasize that you must live through your heart, be happy in your life, and surround yourself with people who you truly love and who truly love you. As the energies rise, all of the PEMS experiences you have will increase in intensity. So if you don't have a daily practice, please start clearing your body now. Define and refine your beliefs, gain control over your thoughts, and forgive all. Clearing your PEMS layers will allow you to gracefully resonate to a higher expression of love.

Patience and Perseverance to Clear at All Levels

Patience and perseverance are paramount right now, truly important to consciously practice in order to flow gracefully through the current changes. Patience with all that goes on around you, yes, but also patience with yourself for what is going on within you as well. Patience is a necessary ingredient for self-love. We ask you to take care of yourself through these shifting times, as a loving parent would advise a growing child. Nurture yourself, take the time to do the Circle of Grace with us; allow yourself the time to clear and heal. If we sound like nagging parents, we apologize, but we are trying to guide you toward better self-parenting. If you do not care for your total Be-ing in a way that honors the new energies, you will not be able to care for those around you when they need you.

Perseverance is important because you are finally in the process of consciously clearing at all levels. What does that mean, exactly? You are clearing patterns of imbalance down to the cellular level, from this lifetime and lifetimes before. "Wiping the slate clean" is required so that you can change your energetic blueprint. Where is your energetic blueprint, that which governs the form and functions of your multidimensional body? In your DNA! Your personal akashic records are stored in your interdimensional layers attached by the emotional glue of joyful and pain-filled experiences. The quality of those events and how they continue to affect you depend on how many "good" and "bad" emotions are attached to them. Indeed, this ongoing record of life after life is designed to further soul growth so that your Higher Self can assimilate increasing levels of learning through the diversity of your life experiences.

So when we say you are clearing at all levels, we really mean it. That is why it may seem as if you have an endless stream of stress and strain to release in each Circle of Grace session. Please be patient, dear one, and persevere. It took many cycles to create all of those imbalances, so it makes sense that it will take repeated effort and dedication to clear them. We say gently, do not give up. Take heart, for every little bit of pain you clear makes room for new energy, light and bright, to take its place.

The Breath of Life Exercise

Now, for a specific focus on what you can do to help ease your transition. Once upon a time, long, long ago, before you became fully dense beings of expression, you traveled Earth and feasted on life experiences in a much lighter etheric form. Indeed, you were so light that you breathed in energy through your crown and feet, divine and earth, expressing a true blending of the energies of above and below. Dear ones, you were totally sustained by multidimensional energies. You were fully energetic beings, fully conscious of your divine origins, and fully connected to the Divine Source.

With the advent of these shifting times, you are invited to return to that fullness of connection. You are being bathed in higher and more refined levels of energy. How are you assimilating them? There is no pill to take with your food, no powder to add to your drink. You must learn to absorb the higher energies through the workings of your energetic systems.

Your chakras are intake/output valves that control how much energy resides and flows through each part of your body. You can learn how to clear your nervous system and how to fill up your tank (of energetic reserves) whenever you feel the need.

We speak here of universal energy, the energy that provides the spark and sustenance of your every cell, of every plant and animal, of everything on Earth and beyond. Prana, chi, qi, manna, you have called it many things, so you know it exists. You will need larger and larger doses of that very energy to sustain you as you move into the higher octaves. Your 3-4D food and water will simply not provide enough fuel to your evolving multidimensional Be-ing. We offer below a simple visualization to use when you are tired and need to recharge your body. We call it the Breath of Life Exercise.

[**Note:** Though earth energy and divine energy are both part of universal energy, we separate the two in color and direction to facilitate your visualization in a linear way. This is also a key exercise for those of you who need grounding!]

In alternating breaths, imagine that you are breathing in golden divine energy from above and bright green earth energy from below.

1) Pull in a deep breath of white-gold Divine light through your crown chakra at the top of your head and draw it down through your body to twelve inches below your feet.
2) Pause to blend this golden column of energy inside you and let it fill you up.
3) Then exhale it through all the pores of your skin to feed the energetic layers of your entire Be-ing.
4) Pause again, to allow the golden energy to permeate all your layers.
5) Inhale, pull up green earth energy through your feet and up your body past the crown to a foot above your head.
6) Pause to let it fill your body.
7) Then exhale it through your skin in a cloud of bright-green nourishment all around you.
8) Pause again to circulate and assimilate the green energy, exhale it through your PEMS layers, then start over.

If you have trouble pausing between each inhale and exhale, breathe in and out slowly, and pause just once after each exhalation. Even if you cannot pause between breaths, the visualization will still work. As you do this, be aware that your sacral chakra, the second or abdominal energy center, is filling up with new reserves of universal energy. Repeat this imaging, breathing slowly please, for about ten minutes or until you feel better. This is a new way to eat, children, only with less mess and no dishes.

Do you follow? We hope you will.

Breathing

Since the above exercise entails visualized breathing, we would like to take a moment to discuss one of the most essential of life functions: breathing. The human body gathers energy in various ways, through food, water, air, sunshine, sleep, and exercise. Breathing gathers air into your bloodstream to nurture every cell of your body with essential oxygen, and also releases carbon monoxide, the main waste product of respiration. Focused breathing does even more: It allows the body to assimilate energy and release areas of compacted energy, or energetic blockages. That is why we urge you to relax your jaw and focus on your breathing, to stimulate your meridians to flow freely, to release pain and absorb new, clean universal energy in its place.

In the Breath of Life exercise, we offered you a heightened view of breathing energy in and out of your entire energetic framework to show you how to absorb universal energy into your body and exhale it through your skin and beyond, thus nourishing all of your PEMS layers. Why? Dear one, all the symptoms of pre-ascensionitis involve processes of the body that are affected by internal and external pressure. As you expand into the higher levels of refined energy, your body will become increasingly sensitive to pressure shifts. You must acclimate yourself to different kinds of pressure changes, from osmotic pressure at the cellular level, to gravitational pressure at the muscular level, to emotional and mental pressure at the auric level.

As your senses expand from physical to nonphysical levels, does it not make sense that your body will become more sensitized to foods, to pollen, and to any irritants or allergens that previously went unnoticed? Yes! All of your bodily systems are regulated by pressure, both internal and external. Not only are your internal systems sensitive to pressure, they rely on pressure as a vehicle for function. Since the Millennium Shift is a series of increasing pressures at all levels of planetary function, many people who are feeling sensory expansion while still carrying blockages may have more and more trouble breathing.

Dear one, your patterns of breathing also indicate your emotional state. When asleep or deep in thought, your respiration is slow, even, and measured. When angry, you take in deep gulps of air to fuel all the processes that anger stirs up. When in pain, you breathe in quick, shallow breaths, almost panting, to avoid stirring up that pain. When you cry, you often feel your throat close, your lungs tighten, and your breathing becomes quite erratic. In our work together, the focused breathing we offer has many purposes: to teach you how to best assimilate oxygen, to bring on a state of calm, to teach you how to control a physical system that is well within your reach. Being aware of your breathing leads to controlling your breathing. Soon you will realize that controlled breathing is the path to deepening your meridian release, calming your heart, and learning how to navigate the etheric dimensions of the nonphysical realms.

Here we would like to add one more example: Earth's ascension will make you feel as if you are gradually moving higher and further away from sea level, up into the mountains where the air is thinner and harder to breathe. Do you follow this? Now is the time to release your smoking addictions. Now is the time to learn how to breathe better, for as the energies on the planet rise and thicken, your lungs will be taxed in keeping up. Again, we are discussing invisible forces acting on physical systems. Hard to see, hard to grasp, and hard to overcome if you are unaware and unprepared. But that is no longer the case with you, is it, beloved reader?

Conclusion

We hope you now have a better understanding of what we mean when we speak of the heavy weight of ascension. For those of you cresting the shift, you are feeling the symptoms more keenly now. We ask that you listen to your bodies, for they have awareness separate from mental awareness. The body tells you of its needs through a variety of sensations, and when you don't pay attention, it eventually breaks down. Pain is your best barometer of what's going wrong, where it is, and how bad it is. Analgesics (pain medications) merely block the nerve sensation from the damaged area to the brain that is trying to say, "Damage here, ow!" Without that warning information of pain from your physical body, you can easily re-injure yourself or ignore the problem until it becomes chronic. This is not a good pattern to live by, dear one, for it is literally self-defeating.

Once you get accustomed to doing the Circle of Grace, you will feel moments when pain passes down your arm or leg while you're doing something totally mundane. You may be sitting quietly reading or standing in line at the grocery store. Bless the release, breathe through it, massage that spot downward it if need be, and continue on. These experiences will help you relate to your body's needs better, and show you how much progress you've made.

If you already have a daily health practice, we only ask that you incorporate this information and add in the clearing of stress from your body. If you do yoga, for example, by all means incorporate the Circle of Grace cleansing process into your moving meditation. Start with the healing prayer to give permission, then remember to keep your jaw open so the meridians can release pressure. Whatever healing modality or modalities you use will be enhanced by focusing on clearing the nervous system, since that is how the body naturally clears the residue of all of its layers.

How many of you can slow your hearts down? Do you know that you can? Yes, you are all budding gurus! It may be a novel concept that you can affect and direct an internal physical system in your body, but you can. That is exactly what we are teaching you. Gaining mastery at all levels includes the physical. Clear the body, and you will clear your life. Why? There is an old saying that your body is the temple of your soul, and it should be thus tended with reverence. From an energetic healing point of view, we will modify that statement somewhat. It may surprise you when we say that your body is actually your energetic trash can. All of your PEMS layers deposit their energetic waste products into your nervous system to be released by the body's meridians. Dear one, your temple awaits a thorough cleaning.

Beyond the body's five physical 3-D senses lie many invisible, previously intangible, 4-5D senses. Telepathy will become more common between humans, between humans and animals, and between humans and

Spirit. Thought you heard your dead grandmother speaking to you? She probably was, so pay attention next time it happens. Are your tiny children relating visions and facts way beyond their knowing? Pay attention and absorb the messages; children are much clearer and closer to Spirit than adults. Start writing down your dreams and don't worry about what they mean. They may be precognitive information that hasn't happened yet. Welcome these events, give thanks for each peek through the veil, and don't go into fear because you're not going crazy. The veil is thinning, dear one. As the dimensions meet and mesh, duality will lift and we will finally meet again.

This is the energy of ascension. Simply put, once these frequency shifts take hold in your reality, they will change you and your reality. There are electromagnetic changes occurring from the heights of the planetary grids — and beyond — to the depths of your cellular structure. Your body will respond to this global evolution, changing automatically to a higher expression, to a merging together of your DNA in new ways that will cause your ascent into the energies of the higher dimensions. In this work we seek to explain these changes, to prepare your mental awareness to recognize your accelerating physical changes.

As you heal all of your layers, you will eventually find that you no longer need to seek answers from books or physical teachers, for these will have become old, out-moded ways of spiritual communication. You are, dear ones, the Second Coming of Christ. Yes, though Lord Sananda may choose to appear before you one day, that is not what we mean by the Second Coming of Christ. Remember when He said, "He who believes in Me, the works that I do, he will do also" [John 14:12, NASB]? Well, he was talking directly to you, all of you Shift-babies! And he meant now, right now as the Millennium Shift goes through its final gestation.

You are birthing yourselves, dear ones, into a higher mode of physical expression. We have said that once you reach resonance with 5D, you will have become self-realized and will re-join us whenever you wish. You will do one more thing: You will become walking representations of God on Earth. You will express Christ consciousness and become, yourselves, the Second Coming of Christ energy to this planet. A lovely grand design, is it not?

As the momentum of the frequency acceleration increases, the intensity of everything around you will increase. That is why we say: "Slow down, be kind to yourselves, make smaller goals, and find pleasure in the little things. Find your bliss along the way, for it is truly the journey that counts. We await you, as we line the path to cheer you on. Can you hear us yet? You will soon!"

Until then, we invite you to visit with us often, and allow yourselves to rest and heal. The best way to transform yourselves into lighter beings is to be joyful, hopeful, and grateful, knowing in your hearts that Spirit will always guide and provide.

(14)

Merging Science and Spirituality for Total Healing

Author's note: This channeled session was requested by a doctor faced with an illness. I was urged by Spirit to share this text, for it offers a higher perspective on how the human body heals, along with many relevant issues that most of us are facing in these shifting times.

The Brothers' Introduction

Greetings, dear doctor. We are very honored to be working with you today. What you are doing, indeed, is work on many levels. You are being given a choice to work at more levels than you understand, to have the faith to reach beyond your knowledge and wield your will. And know, dear doctor, that this is a lovely divine setup. You are being guided, supported, and led through this experience with the utmost grace. Though it may not feel like it now, at a future now moment you will look back and say, "Oh my, how perfect was all of that."

So we offer you a change of perspective to balance your fear and make it gone. Simply say to that fear, "All is as it should be." "I Am perfect as I Am." In order for you to move beyond your lesson, you must assimilate

221

it; you must live and breathe it; and you must embrace it, love it, push it through you, and leave it behind. Look at all the tools you have been given, both medical and holistic. In looking at your future potentials, we can say that this is already done, and done well! As a paradigm for the Divine Plan, reaching beyond all that you know at the level that you know it will, indeed, cause a great energetic shift in your body. It will also cause a positive shift toward the true goal of the Brotherhood of Light: merging science and spirituality. For that is the path of full and true knowledge. The more individuals who do this, the wider the path is carved out for others to follow. And now, we will ask for your first question.

That which doctors find as symptomology within the body, is it caused by auric disturbances or is it sourced from within the physical body? Is there pathology present if it is detected by 3D means?

Dear doctor, the problem with the mindset here is that all of these tests and diagnoses are based on looking only at the physical core of a person's body. What medicine sees as a patient represents far less than 50 percent of that total being. Everything that doctors find as symptoms in the body can be explained from an energetic perspective, but they are not looking in the energetic layers.

Every physical symptom begins as pathology — auric pathology — translated into pockets of dense etheric pressure. The more stress accumulates, the less room the aura has to store it. The less pressure released, the more densely layered the pockets become. As they get larger, the pockets sink in through the layers of the aura. By the time they actually sink into the physical layer, that auric damage can be ten, twenty, or thirty years old. By the time it creates physical pathology, that person is in the last stages of auric damage. The human body was created to function in this way: All of the layers function together, physical, emotional, mental, and spiritual (PEMS). All of the body's activities and energetic processes give off a residue. That residue is designed to be released through the physical core through the nervous system. Indeed, the physical body layer is your energetic trash can [chuckles].

Why are small children so alive, so perfect, so healthy, and so joyous? Their auras are new and clear. Why do people age? Why do bodies decay? Because nobody knows about care and maintenance of the aura. Taking care of the physical body is not enough, dear one, for you are not energetically cleaning out the trash can periodically. This is why it is important to work on the nervous system, for is not only a communications network. There circulates within it a flow of energy that absorbs the pain/pressure, that must be released to make room for new energy to replenish the system. Yes, just as oil in a car gets dirty and must be changed periodically so that the engine is not worn away.

Were this clearing process available, known, and practiced from childhood on, you would be living three to four hundred years at this point. The human body was designed to last a thousand years, and you are nowhere near that. As complex as the physical body is, dear doctor, how could its energetic carriage be any less complex, any less incredibly intricate? Your medical community admits that it has only scratched the surface of what goes on within the human body. Once you start looking at the etheric layers, so much of what you did not know will suddenly make sense. The potential here for learning and applying new wisdom is so great.

Going back to your question, when the symptoms are light in the physical body, the auric damage can still be cleared. If the organs have not been squeezed by excess pressure and affected in function, if the cells have not started to distort and grow wild, and if the excess internal pressure can be released, the symptoms will abate. Once the physical body has started to break down from these pressures and true illness becomes diagnosed, the healing becomes more challenging. You have been handed a beautiful lesson with a very light prognosis. You have been given all the tools to say, "I know what the physical path is, and I know what the spiritual path is." The lovely task your soul chose to perform is that leap of faith, to blend the two into one full healing path.

Dear doctor, you would not be sitting there in that space with those questions in hand if your soul had not desired this. So while the human part cries, "I did not choose this, please God, help me," your soul is doing its work and is very pleased. That is why we say the lesson is light. You are surrounded by light. Through will and intent, you can release these patterns and find peace and joy. For amidst your future potentials that we see, your sheer intelligence carries you through. You are wise enough to know that despite all that you do know, there is so much more to learn. Once the energetics of a person are seen and understood, the advances in medical science will affect the balance of everyone's life.

To summarize our answer: By the time the physical body shows symptoms, there is already an upsetting of the balance within the physical core. Emotional, mental, and spiritual dis-ease eventually become physical disease.

When the body gets sick, do you just treat it by 3D means or do you bring energetic tools to that situation?

If you were a carpenter, would you choose hammers and screwdrivers but decide that you didn't want to own a saw? Of course not, you would want a full complement of tools to shape that wood to any and every purpose. In the same way, you cannot separate the needs of the physical body from the needs of its energetic field. The energetic field, the holographic structure of the body, is what animates the physical core. Remember, the electromagnetic system controls to all physical form and function are located in the aura. Indeed, the cellular blueprint and the master pattern controls are in the auric field. To use only tools from 3D, as you say, would simply not address the source of the damage.

Here we are not discussing external trauma or contagious disease, which also create auric damage. In your case, we see auric dis-ease building up excess internal pressure that eventually manifested as illness in the physical layer. Any type of auric damage can linger long after the physical body has visibly healed. Energetic tools alone are appropriate if the body has no physical symptomology yet.

But in order to make a person physically comfortable once bodily symptoms have manifested, we urge you to use all the tools available. Get that body comfortable, get it balanced, get the shock, the trauma, the infection, and the broken bones treated. Your scientific knowledge is still at a level where you must cut out bad things. That is what is known, so that is what works within your belief system. And here we come along and say, "Meditate once a day to keep illness away." All of your scientific and holistic tools must be used to heal the entire person physically, emotionally, mentally, and spiritually.

The second half of your question is about emotional and psychological tools. When you were speaking, you referred to being given this diagnosis, this label, which forces you to focus in a certain way. And yet you know that a label has a sticky back. You can apply it anywhere! Or it is your choice not to apply it at all. Just because you are handed a label does not force you to focus or feel in any specific way, because that is giving away your personal power. In other words, it is always your choice where you put your focus and how you express your emotions.

We will give you this short example, a story from your own Internet: A very powerful, positive, forward-thinking, happy man falls off a roof. As he is being carted away, he sees the looks on the faces of the ambulance people. He knows he is badly injured. The doctors rush him into the operating room, talking in hushed tones, so he says, "Before you put me to sleep, I will ask you only one thing: Operate on me as if I am going to live. Do not touch me and work on me as if I am going to die." He gave the doctors the mindset he required and, of course, he lived.

In terms of emotional and psychological tools to be applied to your healing path, it is an attitude of gratitude, it is a faith that you will live, that you are *not* just your condition. It is a knowing that you are not the label but much more. There is a need to train the emotions to be positive. To break the negative mental loops, to stop yourself from ruminating, we give you the image of a big silver scissor. When doubt and fear rise up, imagine cutting those mental loops and go do something else. Go out for a walk. Pick up a book you enjoy. Change your thought patterns, each time, to more positive ones. You must gain control over your thoughts. Mental and emotional self-control are not taught in a clear, concise way. Children are taught to be polite, to be nice, and to share their toys. But they are not taught how to be in charge of their own minds.

Back to your question. There is nothing wrong with using an antidepressant if it allows you to get past the worst of your fears. It will chemically put you in a place where you have better mental control. That is using a common enough medical tool. Now, once you have this buffer in your system, it will be a much shorter leap to gaining emotional self-control. Then it will be easier to re-pattern your thoughts and emotions so that you are walking in joy and not in fear.

We will say that this question must be qualified now that you are the patient and not the doctor. In regards to healing yourself, it is a question of finding a comfort zone so that you can best apply the medical and holistic tools at your disposal. Your emotions can become self-controlled through training your mind. Once you have formed better thought patterns and emotional habits, you will start to see that you don't need as much medication any more.

In terms of the body being clear or not clear to heal, dear doctor, we recommend daily Circle of Grace sessions with us. We are always willing and available! The more internal pressure you clear from your nervous system, the more quickly your body can rebalance itself and release your need for medication. There is a hand-in-glove effect here: the medications will support the emotional development, and the emotional development will then release the need for the medication. We do feel that your body can definitely clear the antidepressant along with everything else. Yes, we recommend both the medication and the meditation [chuckles].

The beauty of the Circle of Grace process is that you are not examining every little piece, every angle, every nuance of what you are clearing. You can dump lifetimes of baggage in just a few years. It is no longer necessary to sort it all out or relive every memory. Do you follow this? The antidepressant is a medical tool for emotional support, helping to balance the physical body chemistry to a better comfort zone so that the energetic body can then function better to heal itself. Again, the more your clear internal pressures, the more you have to look at your medications and downsize the doses. That is why it is very necessary to keep working with the doctors so that your medications can be monitored, modified, or switched. Again, you must work with tools for all the levels of your PEMS Be-ing! You cannot ignore the physical core and work only on the aura. You cannot ignore the emotional/mental levels and simply work on faith! For indeed, you are housed in an energetic vehicle that is multilayered. All the layers must be tended to in order for you to fully heal.

Due to the Veil of Forgetfulness that creates the 3D duality-reality on your planet, there is a hard-wired aspect to being in body. The soul is wired into the physical body, so it has a built-in fear of leaving the body. If enough people realized they were eternal and could just give up and leave a life when things got tough, there would be suicide and sudden death and accidents everywhere you looked. Yes, the soul is hard-wired at birth into its physical core. It is knitted together because your duality matrix requires that the soul stay in the body. The Veil of Forgetfulness shuts down your conscious awareness of Spirit and the higher realms (which are other dimensions). Only your conscious mind is affected, dear one. Your aura, the 4-5D part of the body, is still fully connected to your Higher Self in the higher dimensions. Even though you don't see or feel your aura, or honor it in any way, it continues to function as best it can.

Your aura animates and maintains your physical core. There is an aura to every life form. If you draw back and look at this beautiful planet from space, the atmosphere is the aura of Earth. It is the same pattern of layer within layer, whether it be a human being, a bumble bee, a tree, or a crystal. You will be surprised at what you find as you create equipment to track the different energies of the nonphysical realms. Earth's life-form patterns are all similar, energetic holograms with physical cores. Then science will focus on what makes a tree as opposed to a flower. [Chuckles.] There will be many exciting discoveries in the next hundred years.

We would also give you another tool to consider: Acupuncture would be very beneficial for you, especially the triple-heater points, to help bring more energy into your physical core. For indeed, your system is very low on energy, and stimulating those points will help to bring in more fuel for you. Universal energy is the etheric food that feeds your cells. The human body needs more than air, food, and water to survive, you see. Maximizing nutrition? Absolutely! The cleaner the food you eat, the cleaner your body becomes. People don't realize how many toxins and poisons they bring home in their grocery bags. Preservatives, colorants, the chemicals sprayed on crops — there is so much chemical garbage in food these days. We advise you to cook with natural ingredients, or better yet, plant a garden. That will also afford you good exercise and time in the sun. Gardening is very healthy for all the PEMS layers of your Be-ing, and it is very grounding too. [Sorry, chuckles, we couldn't resist that one.]

I have always seen myself as a healthy, long-lived person. How do I reconcile that with having a diagnosed illness?

Congratulations, you have just spoken your truest path to total healing. All of your life, you have seen yourself as a healthy, long-lived person. So we say to you, you are a healthy, long-living person with some minor obstacles thrown in your path. Why would you change that wonderful body image you have of yourself, dear doctor, just because someone is coming at you with a label? Why give up that much of your personal power? Only through fear. Fear is the true illness here, do you follow? The more you hold to that beautiful self-image of longevity and the more you hold your beautiful mate, the longer and more beautiful your life will be. If you choose in your mind to give up and succumb to your illness, then that is how your body will go. Do you see the beautiful spiritual setup around you, dear doctor? Bless it, embrace it, take joy from it, and say; Is this all they found? Thank you, Lord. This, I can deal with. This, I can get out of my way.

I find that on days I am working, I am extremely stressed. On days that I don't work I feel much better. I also wonder why I feel that part of me may have manifested this illness in order to change the situation that is causing my stress?

Yes, your feeling, your intuition coming from your own body is correct! It is very, very difficult to be both patient and doctor at the same time. That you already know. You also know that the stressful job you have had all these years has begun to affect your body. Your body is reflecting your need to reduce stress. The dysfunction your body manifested limits that very thing that is causing you stress — your job! Do you see how the mind affects the matter? Your body is a perfect mirror not only of how you feel but also of the condition of your auric distress. So it is important to cut back your schedule as much as you can, even if it is only paring back one hour per day and taking a longer break in between cases. Be aware of how much energy you need to expend for each part of your work. Don't forget that the intensity of focus required for your job also expends energy: Mental attention uses up physical stamina.

When your body is low on energy, dear doctor, where do you pull it from? When the aura has exhausted its etheric sources, it goes to the physical core and pulls energy out of its cellular structure. You can mentally will yourself to work beyond your physical limits. That is how people get weakened and then succumb to illness.

A woman trapped in a position of overnurturing often gives of her energy way beyond what her system can afford, as in cases of children with special needs or ailing relatives. If her life situation requires that she keep tending and tending, she usually ends up with breast or ovarian cancer. Those are the energetic areas of a woman that comprise her nurturing parts. When she goes beyond her stamina limit and must keep giving, it is no surprise that the maternal aspects of her body go into dysfunction, because that is where the needed energy is being pulled from.

Your work now requires more energy output than your body can support, so cutting back your schedule a little will not help much. We urge you to begin investigating other job options. You will be surprised how many teaching jobs are available around you, how many speaking opportunities there will be, and how many hospital training situations you could step into and master so easily. You could be doing three different things, making almost an equivalent amount of money, and truly enjoy yourself. Do you not have faith in your own intellectual abilities? Do you not realize how much scientific and medical knowledge you have amassed that you can share with others?

It is your current belief system that limits you, cornering you into saying, "I must continue this one set path even though it is stressful, because this is all I know." This is just your current comfort zone; that is all it is. When you are required to go beyond your normal routines to do something different, to make a major life shift, fear is the first thing you encounter. Fear is counteracted by self-love, by self-worth, by your loving family network, and by knowing that no matter what happens to you, you can survive. These are all choices; these are all areas on which you can choose to focus your energies. You will find no dead ends in the Divine Plan!

The more you look into related work, the more you will find, dear doctor. We would say that within a year or two, you will be much happier doing different things. You will still be utilizing your knowledge, your training, your experience, and being of excellent service teaching others. If you look at all of life, any one person is expendable in terms of job because there are always four or five others who can easily take another's place. Yet those four or five others need to be trained, dear doctor. It is simply a matter of taking off one hat and saying, "I'm going to do something else. I'm going to wear this other hat for a while and see how it feels. Or I will wear this hat in the morning, that hat in the afternoon, and then take two days off!"

Your wife would like to know how best to support you? Yes, indeed (laugh), we already hold her question. So you would like to know how best to support your husband's path to healing? We already hold this question because we read your heart, dear lady. The best thing to dispel his fear is an hour of cuddling. Part of which may contain tears and fears spoken aloud. You are his sounding board. He must speak his fear to get rid of it, he must cry his tears to get rid of them. Know that all of this passes right through you, and you negate it because you love him. In all, the minor wrinkles you have had on your life path have been wonderful tests. You have stepped over them gracefully and said, "None of this matters; love is more important."

The best path toward helping him is to clear your own vehicle. We see a lovely empathy in you, and we know that you can radiate healing. Once you begin to study and learn, you will find a beautiful balance in this healing experience together. The issues that your husband is processing right now are also contributing to your spiritual growth. Do you see the beauty of this plan? Peoples' biggest misconception is that they must walk the spiritual path alone in order to find God. We say simply that God is in everyone. The more of you who are on the path holding hands and skipping along, the happier will be your journey!

This healing together will create more joy, more clarity, and more peace of mind. In other words, you are the creators of your lives, you just don't know that you have that power. Once you realize that you can affect your own biology with your mind, it will become simpler and simpler to manifest that which you focus on.

What do I need to know for now?

For a smooth healing path, there needs to be support from family, there needs to be support at work, and there needs to be support from your doctors at the physical level. Here again, we are referring to psychological support (emotional and mental) from your family. Working with medical help, that is the physical support. Seeking acupuncture, massage, or simply Reiki to help boost the body's natural healing processes is the holistic support. At the spiritual level, you must decide where to put your focus, and whether in every moment you choose to be in fear or joy. Do you follow this? So those four levels of help can be applied to any healing situation you may be going through.

It may be that through your combined efforts, dear ones, you may end up teaching doctors how to merge science and spirituality, for you will have done so and you will be the living proof. Has this occurred to you? You can, indeed, become that lovely tool for Spirit if you so choose. If you overlay that on your situation as a grander purpose, you will be amazed at the amount of spiritual support that will appear. For every lifetime holds lessons that are much more complex than what is happening to the physical body. And what happens to everybody happens on many more levels than the visible physical one. We honor the soul that has come in with such a great task. We say to you, you already have the tools. And in future potentials, it is already done.

Now you are faced with the task of doing this lesson at the physical level. And if you *know* that you are a long-lived being, then that must be your main focus; that must be your main label. It will cover, obscure, and eradicate any other label that you would try to attach. You have carried that label of living a long, happy, healthy life for so many years. Why would you want to give it up for a label filled with fear? You always have choices, dear doctor, and the power to wield your will.

So there will be ups and downs; there will be joys and sorrows. We are very pleased at how small and thin that little medical label is that you have just been given. It is up to you to decide where you're going to wear it. Are you going to attach it to your forehead and think about it all the time? Attach it to your heart and fear it all the time? We would rather see you attach it to the bottom of your feet and simply walk all over it. [Laughter.] That is your choice, and that is when the mind will determine what happens to the matter.

So we give you our parting blessings, and we say to you, your path is filled with health and happiness and peace of mind. Once you embrace peace of mind, nothing in this world will matter. We are, in all love, the Brotherhood of Light.

The Brothers' Conclusion

There will soon come a time when physical proof of the existence of the higher realms will appear in your tangible reality. You will finally have proof that the essence of God exists — and exists within you. In order for this to happen, your tangible reality must expand to include those very dimensional frequencies that you were blind to before. Yes, science and spirituality must ultimately meet and merge in order to embrace the true scope of sacred science. How your bodies are shaped and hold that shape are still a mystery to you. Why? Because you cannot yet see the energetic components of all life, which will change your knowledge and your perceptions of reality to a huge degree. So much expansion potential resides in your near future, even as that future changes and blends into new paths, driven by the expanding awareness of the human consciousness.

In prior text, we explained that your etheric body is where all your system controls are located. You keep looking in the physical body for ways to fix things that break down. It is the aura that breaks down first, dear ones, long before that dis-ease and excess stress-pressure invade your physical core. Once your scientific and computer-savvy seekers begin creating diagnostic equipment that can scan and evaluate a person's aura, then watch out! There will be a field day of scientific breakthroughs and miraculous cures that will be no more than figuring out how to restructure and balance pressures in your energetic (electromagnetic) fields to prevent illness.

It is you metaphysical seekers who will tip the balance, who will persevere in the quest for better ways to heal the human body, who will create the demand for technology to expand its focus. You must train your focus into the different dimensions, beyond what your current scope of instrumentation can detect. But is that not the way of things? Humanity first masters a talent, then creates a machine to replicate it. That is what you are doing first with your own bodies in this ascension process. Yes, the expansion of the senses, of intuition, of higher connection — that is the seed needed to spark the rise of the human consciousness.

All of your technology mimics a function of the human body. Why? To save you time and money. Each machine you create is designed to lessen your work, to imitate what you can do and save you the physical labor of doing it. The car runs for you, the vacuum cleaner sweeps for you, the stove saves you from hunching over an open fire, and the blender whips faster than your wrist. Look back in your own history: Each time you got tired of a task or saw a way to make it happen more cheaply, you created a machine to replace yourself. Even tollbooths are often now unmanned [chuckles]. Your recent technology has gone beyond normal human capacity, creating calculators and computers that now think faster and hold more data than you can. So where there is a proven need, you create a machine.

Dear lightworkers, it is time to create a need for auric medical technology. Sounds great, but how? The key to global success of holistic healing is in its blending with medical knowledge. First, the holistic practitioners must learn to work together and see their respective modalities as tools to apply to the rebalancing that needs done. Each person has different needs at different times. Imagine teams of healers scanning a person, deciding which modalities are required, and working around the table as a group. Yes, it is in the merging of your tools and talents that real progress will be made and notice taken by your larger collective community. Once you blend your holistic knowledge and experience with the copious medical information already gathered, it will all begin to make sense. Once science and spirituality meet and merge, the gaps will be filled in, dear ones, answers and shortcuts will abound. Your human lifespan and the quality of that life will greatly increase. True, total healing will be within your reach.

If we could speak directly to doctors, we would say, learn about how the etheric body functions and then work within those rules on the physical core. Please, never put surgical damage on the nondominant arm of a heart patient. Yes, even put the IV needle in the hand that writes. If you take a replacement vein from that left (nondominant) arm, the patient may have complications or simply not recover well. The heart cannot clear through its normal path down the nondominant arm if there is surgical trauma to that limb. Take the replacement part from the right side or the patient's dominant thigh, for example, and watch them recover much better.

Also, please pay attention to the chakra pairs, and you will see why cancer metastasizes from one area of the body to another. Patterns that you only partially understand will become fully explained. If you consider how the body energetically releases internal pressure and follow the rules by which the nervous system truly works, your effectiveness in healing will more than double in dramatic ways.

There is so much work to be done! So many glorious discoveries awaiting your seeking minds as you incorporate the higher energies into your physical existence. You will find new sources of clean energy, new directions for math, physics, art, science, music, and medicine. There is so much potential waiting to be created. In order to tap into these higher levels of inspiration, information, and creativity, you need to clear your physical vehicles to better receive the new frequencies and merge with them. How is this blending achieved? At every level! The physical body must be cleared and balanced, the emotional body must be healed, the mental body must be redirected to share time equally between body and aura, the spiritual body must be prepared to guide and lead.

Do you now understand why all energetic imbalances are rising up to be cleared? Earth's shift to a higher level of expression necessitates the clearing of all old patterns, which is why you are developing many symptoms at the physical, emotional, mental, and spiritual levels. These symptoms will often elude medical diagnosis or seem to spring from unknown origin or are resurgences of old illnesses you thought long gone. Achieving a "lightness of Be-ing" means clearing out all the heavy, dense energy damage that was normal for you to carry in the 3D energy signature. In energetic terms, health represents a balance in the total body of all PEMS layers, achieved by clearing the energetic meridians of your nervous system of pain and stress. Relieve that internal pressure and the body will regain proper function at all levels by itself.

Yes, we teach with repetition, for that is how you learn best [chuckles]. Circles upon circles and patterns within patterns — that is what you will find when you explore the intricacies of the total human Be-ing. Go beyond the range of frequency scales that you normally use. Whole worlds of exploration wait to be opened as you tap into different dimensions. That is what your planet is doing now, expanding her vibratory range into a broader band of existing dimensions. From there, your reality will change and grow in remarkable ways. The more you expand your learning, the better you will function in harmony with the rising tides of the Millennium Shift. You will learn along the way that you are dearly loved. We await your reconnection to Spirit and your entry into the higher dimensions with great anticipation.

Dear readers, we close this chapter of Frequency and Physicality with many blessings for your health, wealth, and peace of mind. If you only knew how many Be-ings are gathered in the higher realms, cheering you on through good times and bad, yet never giving up hope for you. You see, we know the truth: You are eternal, you will never die, and you will increase the Divine light on this planet through your efforts, which enriches us all. We bless you and give thanks for your enormous contributions to the Divine Plan.

(15)

The Completion: Healing Your Life

All of Life Is a Circle

That which you now pretend,
You will Be in the end.
The end is a new beginning,
That is the way of Eternal Beings.
Come do the Circle of Grace with us,
And find your way back to Godliness.

Through this text and our work together in the Circle of Grace process, we hope to help you evolve beyond the limited existence you have experienced up until now in human form. A new form of human is rising up, and the rising up creates the new form. [Chuckles.] We await impatiently for you to call us in so we may begin to walk up that road together. We commend you for having read this far. Each step is honored, dear one, no matter the size.

Have you learned what your God-given gifts are? The power of intent, plus will, plus universal energy moving through your body in the Circle of Grace will bring you through healing into spiritual harmony. What is that?

Why, all of your layers blended and singing together to form the unique chord of your spiritual essence.

The eternal you will soon walk within the human you on Earth.

Once enough of the population has evolved, the dynamics of the human consciousness will be forever changed. But know that your work had to come first in order to raise human awareness enough so that the needs of the many become most important. You will then outgrow the need for war and fighting. Why? Because you will have outgrown the need to continue feeding the karmic engine of your 3D duality. Then the tides will turn, and you lightworkers will be much needed. We are here for you, for those who seek to know and learn and grow, for those who know that there must be more to life than what is apparent to make it all meaningful and worthwhile.

Have you ever wondered why people are born, only to grow old and die? Those of you who said, "This is a colossal waste of energy with no point," were called crazy by everyone else. But if you overlay the grander plan of Spirit on these endlessly repeating lives (as some of your oldest religions do) then it all begins to make sense. If you realize that each life earns you love and wisdom, each life brings you a step or two closer to remerging with God, would that not be worthwhile? Would it not make more sense?

We are not trying to convert you from your mode of beliefs [chuckles], but we are merely pointing out that being part of a glorious Divine Plan makes a lot of the bad stuff more bearable. It allows you the clarity to see the true shape of your lessons. What once were huge obstacles in your life will become temporary delays. Simply put, once you identify a lesson, you can complete it and move beyond it, up the path toward Home.

Life is much harder for those who are fixed in duality, who have given up believing that there is a God. Why? Because you and God are one. To deny the existence of God is to deny your own self-worth. You are so much more powerful than you know! If you resonate with these words, this information, and this exercise, it is no coincidence that you are reading this book. It will be no accident when you lie down to do the Circle of Grace and feel our presence.

Are you aware by now that there is no such thing as coincidence? That accidents don't just happen? That luck is being prepared when opportunity presents itself? Your journey can be as simple or as complex as you make it. The choice is always yours. Though certain aspects of your life were predetermined, those things were also chosen by you at the soul contract level before you came in to this current life. When you take responsibility for all parts of your life, the good and the bad, you will realize that your future is yours to create.

Once you know that you are in full charge of your life, you will have the power to command and manifest your destiny. You will have the power to create anything that you desire or require. That is the meaning and the power behind the phrase, "You are god."

We wish to clearly state here: God is All. You are God. We are God. We are all One. Therefore, you have the power of Infinite Creation.

Taking on God's mantle and being one with God is your goal in the ascension process. For some, it happens in a split second; they step into the reality that "all is as it should be." They know beyond a shadow of a doubt that God exists everywhere, in everything, including within them. Others need to absorb these metaphysical concepts, expand their mental frame of reference, and incorporate this into their daily lives, then live through the lessons of becoming One with God. There are always lessons within lessons within lessons. Nothing is as simple as it appears to be, and yet simplicity is what you should strive for. If this sounds paradoxical, we say that paradoxes are also lessons!

Your body is always fighting off germs and occasionally gets sick; this cycle serves to strengthen your immune system. Next time you catch a cold, think of how it is helping your health. A paradox? Yes, but that is how the body works. It needs to be challenged and taxed, within reason, to stay balanced and healthy. How? By being put off balance and having to regain balance. Had you not developed resistance to germs in your environment, the human race would have quickly died out. Similarly, your body — at all levels — needs clearing and balancing to stay whole and healthy.

In the same way, life serves you up lessons to strengthen you physically, emotionally, mentally, and spiritually. Do you recognize these layers by now? They are the layers of your true, total Be-ing. In the same way that your body represents the microcosm of the macrocosm, so do you, each and every human being, represent God in physical embodiment. Does it not make you smile, the complex simplicity of God's consciousness?

In our healing sessions together, one of the things we remind you to do is to bring us your conceptual problems so that we may help you assimilate this new information at all levels. Your main goal is to become Godlike, and to embark each day in that mental state of waking meditation that is a merging, a blending of all of the dimensions into which you are growing. In order to become a fully blended Be-ing, one that walks in conscious connection with Higher Self, you must fully understand, digest, and function in the new incoming energies.

In the healing of your body and the assimilation of your divine birthright, you are creating a new, evolved paradigm of the human being. God is very pleased, children, to see you thus learn and grow. We, the Brothers, are humbled to be a part of this process, and we are delighted to be working with you magnificent Be-ings! Some of us have shared incarnations with you, some of us have never served time on Earth. It matters not, as long as we all contribute our talents and devotion to the Divine Plan, as you are doing in your everyday lives.

Though you may not be consciously aware that you made this choice, if you are present in body at this time in human history, then you signed up for this last and first life as evolving Be-ings. That was your goal back in Spirit, when you chose this life and then piled on top of it all the lessons you had left to learn. Yes, you still have some clearing to do, but in retrospect, you are clearing more in this current life than in the last hundred lifetimes put together. Your work with us in the Circle of Grace will serve to move you forward quickly on the path back to self-realization, back to Higher Self awareness, back to the Divine Source of All That Is.

There will soon come a time when the refined frequencies of the higher dimensions will lock in all over the planet. Remember, you are helping to fuel Earth's ascension, as all levels of life must rise together. What will that bring? Heaven is a state of consciousness that you can achieve while still in body. Be-ing in 5D is like being in heaven from a 3D perspective. But from that 3D perspective also came the separation of humanity from its own divinity. You believed that your body had to die before your soul would be released and returned to God. As you think, so it is, and so it has been for thousands of your Earth years' history.

The good news is all of that no longer applies! There are new rules in 5D, new ideas, new strength, new support, and new love from Spirit that you will all feel directly. Then you will know, beyond any question, that you are a part of God. You have always been and will always be a part of God.

We offer you an image to help you see your divinity, to see yourself as having moved through and beyond your lessons. Take all of your experiences learned from and stack them as a broad foundation that you stand squarely upon. See your legs as towers of strength, your torso as one big heart representing your truest wish, arms held up to the skies to direct the flight of your prayer, head held proud and tall to be the crowning glory of God in humankind, and eyes closed to the minor outside reality as you focus on the magnificent inner reality of Spirit that you carry within.

We strive to paint a picture in words of you standing huge and tall, connecting Mother Earth to Father Sky. Connect the precious dirt beneath your feet to your glorious ascent into the heavenly skies. You are the "as above, so below" connection between earth and God. Through your physical transmutation from dense 3D human to lightbody 5D human, you will connect Spirit's ascension to the planet's earthly ascension. You are the catalysts, brave volunteers who took on the task of being the glue between Spirit and matter by coming in as living creatures that represent both. As you progress in your spiritual transformation of matter — for that is what you are doing — the frequency changes you create will affect all levels, all dimensions, and all of life everywhere. Why?

We are all One. We are all Brothers in the Divine Plan, working for the expansion and edification of All That Is. This time in human history, brief as it is, is a huge window of opportunity for each and every soul now on Earth. If you are here for the millennium shift, your soul wanted to be here. We await you with celebration in our hearts, for no matter what happens you will return to the higher realms. You are eternal, remember?

Death is a transition back to the True Reality of Spirit and is no more than that. Fear of death comes from ignorance (as all fear does) and comes from not knowing what lies beyond. Due to the Veil of Forgetfulness, people have built up much negativity around death. Many have distanced themselves from that part of the life process so that growing old and dying has become a shameful, ugly thing, not to be watched or felt too closely.

This, we find sad. Yet it is just a mindset; mindsets can be changed, improved, and refined.

Dear ones, we ask that you care for your dying relatives and help them through the door back to Spirit with lighter hearts. Look toward the reunion, not the separation. Again, it is a question of perspective. When you cannot change a situation, you can change your perspective of it. In so doing, you change the energy of that situation and how it plays out. Can you see the need to honor those souls who are leaving as much as you honor those coming in?

You will all be together soon enough, for nobody really dies!

Be heartened, for there is no hell except for in your expectations. You create what you focus on, remember? [Chuckles.] We hope this material will facilitate your progress on the path to self-mastery. Many of you are further along than you think, and many more are awakening at an earlier age. Time as you know it grows short. Time as we know it is endless. This too you will soon come to understand.

How do you know when you have reached Selfhood? When it no longer matters! When you no longer feel ego attachment, you will have developed spiritual detachment. You will find yourself standing witness to other peoples' lessons, seeing their maya, or drama, for what it truly is: the acting out of lessons in the physical Earth reality of 3D. In your current now of 4-5D, you are learning to identify and move beyond those lessons. When you can see this happening all around you, identify it for what it is, and not react to it except with love, you will be perceiving life from 5D. You will know when that happens, dear one; you will most certainly know.

Of all of the steps needed for the Divine Plan to unfold, this willful evolution of mind over matter is one of the hardest steps to achieve. We honor humanity greatly for the burdens you have shouldered, time after time, to move the karmic wheel forward. It is now time to step off it and stride back into the True Reality of Spirit with no more need for karma or for the Veil of Forgetfulness. This is such a monumental achievement!

Once you have fully blended with your Higher Self, what will you do? We hope that you will stay in body and shine your ascended light on all who draw near. We will guide and support you in a concrete way because you will have concrete communication with the higher realms. Once you are fully in the flow of the new energies, your shining light will be that of unconditional love, God love. God loves all things, great and small.

Once you are cleared and balanced to the new frequencies, you will find room in you heart to love all of creation. Your senses, talents, and gifts will unfurl. Time will become merely a staircase that you will use to get where you want to go. Your life will become healed and balanced as you become the healed and balanced master of your cocreative reality. Start now, please, start wielding those universal laws. Each time you lie down and reach up for our help through the Circle of Grace, pretend that you are already self-realized. Pretend that you are already healed, already tuned in, already joined to Spirit, for indeed, you already are One with us. Can you not see our words before you? [Chuckles, and a big hug from Spirit!]

We end our Circle of Grace teachings with one simple question, one that is already in your present-day frame of reference. Overlay this question on your future creations and shape them with the loving support of Spirit. Our question for you is simply this:

If you knew that you could not fail, what would you do with your life?

Do you follow? We hope you will!

We await you, in All love, your Brotherhood of Light.

Practitioner's Manual
Advanced Teachings

(16)

A Message to All Lightworkers

Author's Note: This introduction is for all lightworkers. The text is a combination of two live channels before audiences of holistic practitioners in Pennsylvania, U.S.A., in 2003 and 2004. The Brothers hold a special loving space for all hands-on healers. You are bravely cresting the wave of human transformation and are much needed in the shifting times to come!

Greetings, dear ones, we are so delighted to be here among you lightworkers (and readers) today! The press of Spirit is quite strong as many, many beings gather to watch the unfolding perfection of your lives. For no matter how sad it seems, no matter how difficult it feels, each day brings a new solution, a new answer, a new direction. Each problem facing you is an opportunity to learn and resolve the lesson within. Yes, changing your perspective is the easiest way to get out of your own way.

Here we will gently remind you that no matter what you have accomplished at the spiritual, mental, and emotional levels, your bodies still need to be cleared. In order to attain and maintain a positive perspective with which to create a joyful future, your PEMS layers must be cleared and balanced. It is that simple and that difficult. Indeed, the weight of the new energies through which you are rising may make you feel as if gravity has actually gotten heavier. What you are sensing is the push-pull between the rising energies, which are clearer and cleaner, and the lower energies that hold you down in density. Why? Those dense 3D etheric blocks contain the debris of everything in your electromagnetic field rising to be cleared, even issues and illnesses you thought long healed. All old patterns leave etheric debris chronologically layered in your PEMS field, which must be flushed out. That is why some of you are suffering relapses of illnesses back through your childhood years. That is why we have come forward at this time with the Circle of Grace exercise, to help you gain mastery over your health, your energy, and your lives.

Dear practitioners, the more you work on each other, the more all will benefit. Yes, the cleaner the vessel (that's you!), the clearer energetic and intuitive channels you become. It is now time for the lightworkers to focus on their own healing. When the masses become aware that they are shifting, well, you will not have enough hands or time in the day, and money will never be an issue again. Your talents will be sorely needed. From that need will come a new understanding and a new appreciation for your holistic modalities. So, dear lightworkers present or reading our words, be patient and persevere. Your holistic work will get easier, it will get stronger, and the need for it will grow.

The need for you lightworkers to work on each other now is vital, to share your information is vital, to share your love and support is vital. Vitality is essence. Essence is light. All is light. We ask that you seek a lightness of Be-ing. We hope that you find humor in every moment, and we hope that you choose love and laughter at every turn. When you see people in drama, forgive them for being in that unconscious pattern, wait until they are done and then very gently say, "Dear one, isn't it exhausting to keep doing that? Wouldn't you like to take a break and just sit with me for a while?"

You will find that listening is one of your best healing tools. That means allowing others to express where they are at all PEMS levels without making the conversation about you. Allowing the person to talk is very, very important. But keep in mind that fine line between allowing and enabling. If you see no forward progress, no resolution of the issues and illnesses that person is carrying, and no positive changes made in lifestyle to reduce stress, either that person is not doing his or her homework or the modalities you are using do not resonate for him or her. Always strive for that higher perspective; let your actions be guided by what is best for both you and the patient's highest good, in divine timing, under grace.

Please, dear practitioners, set your egos aside. Pride is a very low-density vibration and perspective. It is time to form a more consistent energetic view of the four-layered PEMS beings that you truly are. Learn how the body is designed to function at all four levels, and your work will become important preventative health care. This is no small task we are handing you. In order to do this, you must put aside the little egos that say, "My way is best." Do not judge one another, for all of your varied skills are equally important. As for those who say, "I have the strongest energy," well, walk around them, dear ones. They will wind down soon enough [chuckles].

Being an effective holistic practitioner is not a question of strength, it is a question of combining knowledge and insight, experience and ingenuity, but most of all, it is a question of working through your heart. Work from compassion, not pity. Work with a smile on your face and allow the rest to unfold. Detach from the outcome, dear facilitators, for that is not your responsibility.

As you progress in your holistic careers, you will find that each patient's needs are as unique as their past and current history; what works for one may not work for another. That is why we urge you to see each modality as a healing tool. Pick and choose the ones that feel right for you and create a toolbox for your holistic work. Make the Circle of Grace your foundation, and build on it. Yes, all modalities are compatible with the Circle of Grace release patterns. All of the work you do will be more efficient and effective if the person's meridians are cleared first.

One of the most valuable things you can do for your clients is to teach them the Circle of Grace. We urge you to do so, for it will help each individual to quicken their pace up the metaphysical path. This miracle of internal clearing is within all of you, and the knowledge of it belongs to all of you.

We know that not all of you are active practitioners, but you can still be of service to the Divine Plan. Whether you are working or retired, there are always ways to share your energy and your love. For example, you can practice radiating joy wherever you go. Even a joke that makes the person at the cash register smile is a moment of healing, you see. So many of you are empaths. You do not realize that you have an uplifting impact on others. Your very presence is healing, and your positive attitude helps to open shuttered minds.

Through all of your work, we ask that you develop compassionate detachment. In some cases, a person may have too many blockages or be too ill to recover. Dear lightworkers, you can still facilitate their energetic transition in a big way. We greatly honor those who do hospice work; it is the most difficult level of healing work for humans to handle. In facing death comes your biggest tests of faith, alongside the greatest of learning and healing.

There will be many transitions around you in the upcoming years, and many trials and tribulations. But the more you see them as lessons, the more quickly the pain will evaporate and leave you the joy of learning. You will get to a point where none of it will hurt any more and none of it will matter, because the mind indeed is stronger than the matter. You will learn that what's the matter with most people is that they don't understand the workings of their own minds.

Some of you are angels, yes, walking angels spreading sweetness and light. There are some who are on a mission, yet others who are here to finish lessons left undone in prior incarnations. Everyone in this space (and reading this text) is in transition, for the Earth plane itself is in transition. We remind you here that you are eternal, that you existed before your birth and will not cease to exist after your death. Indeed, your death is the finest out-of-body experience you will ever have [chuckles].

On a more serious note, know that many deaths are specifically planned as part of a soul contract, karmic balancing, or the culmination of lessons. Once these experiences are assimilated, the soul is done with that lifetime. This is especially true for children who die young — they took on that contract before they came in. They are very much honored by Spirit for embracing a short life in order to be the object of the lesson for those around them. In linear terms, they earned twelve lifetimes for volunteering for such a difficult task. Take heart and be at ease, for their pain is done and their spirits are free.

In the years leading up to the Millennium Shift and beyond, there will be many choices before you. Remember that your decisions must come from the heart, not from the mind, for the mind will keep you trapped in duality. For those of you seeking to move beyond duality, beyond linearity, we say, dear ones, you will still wake up in the morning and see that same face in the mirror. The fact that you are in body will not change. Yet as your senses expand and your wisdom grows, your understanding of nonphysical energetics will increase. Your face will shine more and more with unconditional love, and you will attract back to you that new higher resonance you are projecting. Have patience and faith in yourself, despite any setbacks or criticism from others — setbacks are part of your lesson — negative judgements of others are part of their lesson, not yours.

It is truly vital to work from the heart, which often seems illogical to those around you. Have faith in yourself and your own potential, and others will soon reflect back to you these positive changes. That is the Law of Attraction. Once you understand and assimilate how to use the universal laws, you will naturally start to process the final stages of your rebirth. The manifestation of all these concepts is taking them into your bones and cells and believing them to the depths of your being. We speak here of having full faith in all that you feel, think, say, and do. No doubting! Be-ing totally in your beliefs will propel you into a joyous state of Godhood.

So speak your intent and know that you will get what you ask for. You are the material creators. You can consciously create new opportunities and avenues for your future to emerge. Look for a moment at your past accomplishments; they have created your current reality and the current person you are today. Look at what you are doing currently, for in your daily efforts you are creating your future reality. And if you don't like what you see, change it. That is why you are here, not to accumulate cars, houses, and other possessions. Those things stay behind and others inherit them, so nothing material is ever totally yours. What do you take back to Spirit? The lessons you learned, the love you created and shared, and the wisdom and compassion you gained in the process.

The soul's true treasure is its progress toward re-immersing into God's energy. Again, our definition of God is much broader than most of you have been taught to believe. We are a totality of energy that is differentiated at the soul level, at the monad level, at the master level, and beyond in ever-expanding dimensions of reality. In truth, all life is a flowing totality of essence that is All That Is. All That Is, is truly God. It is not a separate image or entity. It is not one force or another. It is All.

God is all science, all sacred geometry, all philosophy, all that which you have ever discovered, and much more. Divine guidance causes the universes to dance next to each other, which you have not figured out yet. The higher knowledge is here for all of you, waiting to be discovered when you tap into the right frequency in order to receive.

Above all, as practitioners you must always keep in mind the parameters of your freewill zone. Do not tell anyone how they should think. Do not let anyone tell you how to think. Do not allow anyone to force you to worship in one way or act in another. Always remember free will. Free will governs all action at all levels. Expect the highest from everyone, see their potential, and then allow them to reach it. Sometimes the lessons you witness will not be pleasant; understand that all people choose their own way. No matter what you do or do not do while in body, you always return to the totality of essence of All That Is.

So, in truth, you are much more free than you realize. You are much more powerful than you realize. You are already complete, whole Be-ings, and by being in the now, you can easily connect with your future selves. Did you ever think to ask for help and information from your own future self to create your new foundation? See yourselves as already having achieved what you wish and that imagining will bring it into your now. Intent is all. We say you are so powerful because you are already masters of deliberate creation. The only limit you have is your own imagination.

Yes, you can go beyond the bounds of linear time. That is the most difficult thing for you to do, for you are creatures of linear time and that is all you know. The past is behind you, the present is around you, and the future is further on ahead. Within your duality, the past and future are each compartmentalized so that you cannot reach them. Cosmic humor here, dear ones, even in your habitual linearity all that you can access is your current now moment. [Chuckles.] We are merely teaching you how to expand and augment that which you already have.

Those of you who study Reiki know that the symbol for distant healing transverses time. You can send healing into the past or future for loved ones alive or gone, for situations unresolved or poorly done, to forgive those that have harmed you, and to ask forgiveness of those you have harmed. You can access and affect your future by intending what you want and pulling it in with your will. We say, "Here's the rope and here are the instructions. Go hand-over-hand. That is the best way to manifest." The more of you that line up and pull on that rope, the faster the goal comes in. You are all singular, yet equal in your potential for effectiveness within the Divine Plan. One of the reasons this planet has been shrouded is because of your enormous power, though you are not aware of it yet, which has many other species quite relieved.

Once you are fully opened to the flow of now time,
the past and future open up to you!

We speak to all lightworkers who truly desire to evolve, both here tonight and reading these words. It is a solitary march first to survive, then to be part of a tribe, then to become an individual, and from then to find your way back to Source. Now you are at the stage where you are leaving the material path and embarking on the spiritual path, and you begin to see what is truly important — merging them and living in balance with both. This higher perspective will also give you a better understanding of others as you see them struggle, trip, and fall over unresolved issues, again and again and again.

This is the last life for many on the karmic wheel. You may look at someone and think, oh, poor soul, what was he thinking bringing all of that in at once? All of their lessons ignored or undone, thrown in a heap to try and finish. We honor those as well: Those who are on track, those who are catching up, those who are unaware — it matters not. We honor anyone and everyone at their level of awareness. If you carry this approach into your holistic work — honor rather than judge, allow rather than resist, while embracing all of it — you will see miracles abound.

If you can lend a hand to those who cannot see why things are going wrong, that is a blessing. Every time you reach out and help someone from the heart just for the love of doing it, that is a blessing. The more we do this (we use the collective "we" now, for many Brothers have incarnated and sit right next to you), the more we all help each other, the faster we will all ascend. As 3D rises into 4D, and 4D into 5D, where do you think 5D is going? Yes, 5D goes to 6D! This is not just your personal human ascension, dear lightworkers. You are the fulcrum of a much larger shift. The

---

All is changing and yet All is One, so we all rise together.

---

changes occurring around you are much more than global, much more than galactic, they are universal. [Universe — All, chuckles.]

We would like to take this opportunity to say thank you. We thank you for being here tonight and for reading this work, for honoring our energy, and for allowing us the opportunity to fulfill our role in the Divine Plan. We are the spiritual caretakers of humanity. It has been and always will be our greatest joy to help you to evolve. So as we guide you, hopefully gently up the path, we say thank you, for we are striding along right beside you. Your doing holistic work allows us to do our spiritual work, and for that we hold great love in our hearts for you. We are, in All love, the Brotherhood of Light

Practitioner Information

Greetings, dear ones, from the Brotherhood of Light. We are waiting to work with you, in your own space and time, to help you gracefully weather these shifting years. In this practitioner's section (level two) of the Circle of Grace material, we offer you a higher perspective of your true energetic nature. The more you understand how your invisible parts work, the better you will be able to heal yourselves. Yes, it is by blending your knowledge, tools, and talents that the bigger healing picture will become clear.

Energetic View of the Human Form

We begin this section by offering you a multidimensional perspective of the human form. From our expanded view, you are each a vibrant, pulsating "egg" of light: all one chakra, all one in form, from the most refined to the most dense of energies. Drawing closer, we see your form individuate into bands of color, under which are areas of varying lightness and density. These colors to us represent the rainbow of your chakras — red, orange, yellow, green, blue, indigo, violet — the ascending colors of your vibratory being. You are "as above and so below" at the same time. Your etheric parts are the spiritual matter, and your physical parts are the earth matter. The marriage of the two is the resultant human. Cosmic humor here: You have not yet the eyes to see your true selves!

This above/below reflection is mirrored between aura and body, for each physical system and organ has a nonphysical counterpart. Your nervous system runs along the same pathways as your energetic meridians, one in the body and the other in the aura. Every organ has a governing chakra. There are many layers of chakras, down to a teeny-tiny chakra for every cell. Every living component of the physical body has an energetic counterpart. In order to maintain the health of the inner body, one must keep the etheric body clear of pressure. The system controls for the body's physical workings are held in the aura. Their functioning is calibrated to internal pressure, as is their dysfunction.

The core of your body is made of matter, houses your vital organs and systems, and is the physical pump for feeding and clearing your total PEMS Be-ing. The body filters and distributes universal energy through invisible energy centers called chakras. Each major chakra maintains balance for the organs and systems in its region. The chakras are all interconnected by energetic meridians, which are reflected in physical form as the body's nervous system. Your nervous system carries a constant intake-outtake flow of universal energy that feeds your entire electromagnetic Be-ing and also clears the debris (or excreta) from all the body's layers.

The energizing and cleansing functions of the nervous system are similar to that of the blood flow system and its heart pump. If not properly maintained, both can build up plaque, or blockages, within their circulation. While you have many preventative tools to insure heart health such as diet, exercise, and cholesterol testing, little attention is paid in modern societies to the care and maintenance of your nervous system. Dear ones, we gently point out that this is a big gap in the spiritual training market that you can fill by teaching your family, friends, and clients the Circle of Grace.

Pain and Energetic Blockages

What is pain, dear ones? Why can you feel it but not see it? Pain is internal pressure, yes, but it has mass, density, and weight in your body, like a golf ball. Imagine an injured shoulder that becomes chronically stiff. There is a mass of etheric damage stuck in that shoulder akin to a solid ball. You can't see it or measure it by 3D means, but it is etheric damage that causes the chronic condition to linger long after the physical body has visibly healed. Clear the pain-pressure blockage out of that aching joint and the surrounding meridians, and that body will function much better. This also applies to excess pressure throughout your nervous system, which makes you tired, grumpy, confused, and causes all manner of sensory, emotional, and mental dysfunctions. Given enough time and buildup of pressure, those symptoms can worsen into chronic fatigue syndrome, high blood pressure, fibromyalgia, depression, arthritis, migraines, and other pressure-related disease patterns.

Etheric blockages are pressure pockets held within a person's electro-magnetic (or auric) field. Painful emotions that people stuff away, physical illness or accident, worries and fears, regrets and revenge, all form blockages that layer together in a chronological pattern containing their past history. These pockets of pressure find room where there is none, wedging them-selves into the aura like so many layered lumps of lead. When an issue be-comes chronic, those pockets can't go anywhere except spill out beyond the meridians and seep into the tissues, causing a density of flesh that constantly expresses pain. These areas may show no bruising yet be tender to the touch.

Dear practitioners, we have tried to give you sturdy guidance in your work. Most of all, what you will see and come to understand is that heal-ing the body does not heal the person. Help them face, process, and release their emotional issues. Teach them to let go of their mental worry and anger loops, for those bad mental habits cause more density and attract to them what they fear most. Show them that their bodies are truly the temples of their souls, and then show them how to keep them clean. To quote an old Zen proverb: "Before enlightenment, chop wood and carry water. After enlightenment, chop wood and carry water." [Chuckles.]

Clearing Old Damage

All trauma to the physical body causes auric damage, which remains as auric blockage after the body has visibly healed. This includes accidents, illnesses, and surgery. Dear ones, since you don't often look beyond the physical core, you are simply not aware that your entire Be-ing suffers damage — at all levels — when you are ill. Visible healing of the physical body is only one level of the total healing picture. To help you plan your holistic work for each case, we will review some of the common factors involved, so you can better understand the different patterns that people exhibit.

To interpret the energetic meaning of an injury, look to the physical function of the damaged area. For example, foot and leg injuries indicate an inability to move forward. Hip and lower back damage speak to foundational fear, money, and survival issues. Hand, arm, and shoulder injuries prevent a person from reaching for what they desire or grasp that which they need to work on. Neck injuries prevent a person from seeing both sides of a situation. Trauma to the head, face, ears, and eyes keep a person from expanding their senses and broadening their mental frame of reference. Do you see the patterns here? That is why we urge you to slow down and be aware of everything you do, so as to avoid injury. Since all of your PEMS layers are shifting, even your reflexes are in a state of flux. Yes, your old adage, "Haste makes waste" truly applies in now time.

We have stated before that there is no such thing as coincidence, and that everything happens for a reason. In the case of fatal accidents that seem to make no sense, there may be karmic balancing at work from past lives that you are not aware of, for the person involved and for those around them. The death of a loved one also tests the survivors to the height and breadth of their own life lessons.

The same rule of "no coincidence" applies to illness, though the cause may seem to be coming from a different direction. Whether the illness comes from an internal source or an external contagion, your physical body always mirrors what is going on in your other layers. Diabetes, the inability to process sugars, speaks to third chakra blockage. The overworked and overburdened person holding too much responsibility becomes unable to enjoy the sweetness of life. Depression, categorized as a mental condition depresses all of your systems and can often lead to suppression of immune function. This leaves a person open to developing or catching an illness that affects that weakened system. In other words, all physical damage includes etheric damage, whether it occurs before or during the illness event. Just healing the body does not make a person healthy. The person's mental attitude must also improve, or the illness will return.

Here we will emphasize stress to any body layer results in damage to all layers. Which comes first? Your scientists are looking at how long-term, unrelenting stress affects DNA.[1] Their studies have found that stress damages immune system cells in a way that may speed up the aging process. As we have been saying all along, your energetic well-being governs your physical health.

That is why a happy person can carry many genetic illness patterns that will never manifest. Unhappy people who are not in charge of their lives will find stress inflicted upon them by external events. The level of health or dis-ease in your auric layers is what stimulates your genetic weaknesses to flare up. Sudden heart attack? Yes, after years and years of accumulated fourth chakra blockage. To those whose heart suddenly malfunctions, this is a new illness. But if they were cognizant of their auric health, that illness would not be sudden and indeed could be circumvented.

Regular care and maintenance of your aura would prevent many maladies from materializing in your physical core. Yes, that is what we are here to teach. If you have an illness you thought healed yet it comes back, that means the etheric damage or source of stress from the original illness is still there. What you call remission is truly your window of opportunity to make the changes in your life that will release those sources of stress. For example, staying in an unhealthy relationship is energetically toxic, for it means·that you are living against your heart. People who cannot move beyond obligation and duty often opt out of an unhappy marriage through illness. Then it is simply a matter of where their physical make-up is weak (we are looking at all PEMS levels here) or genetically predisposed to cancer, immune failure, hormonal system malfunction, specific organ failure, and so on.

So please remember that all blockages must be cleared, no matter how old the injury or illness. A childhood ankle injury can be causing adult hip or back pain by blocking the foot chakra's ability to clear pressure from that leg. Injury to the knees can also cause a backup of excess pressure, resulting in chronic cramping in the abdomen or stomach region for women, and lower-back problems for men.

Post-surgical patients can develop severe pain in their nondominant hips, the hip being the largest joint on the meridian path clearing down the nondominant leg. Even when surgery is done elsewhere on the body, the sudden physical trauma of surgery can overload the surrounding meridians and pile up as blockages behind a large joint such as the nondominant

---

1   *Time Magazine*, December 13, 2004

hip. This can cause severe pain that often confuses doctors, who then pre-scribe pain medication as a temporary solution since they don't connect the source of the pain to the surgical procedure just done.

Jaw joint damage (or TMJ, as you call it) blocks meridian release at a very crucial point in the human energetic system. It causes tremendous pressure to build in the head, ears, eyes, face, neck, and even the upper back. This excess pressure can lead to chronic ear pain, eye issues, or sinus condi-tions that flare up when the person is overstressed. Migraines can also result from jaw joint damage, if a person's biology is predisposed to headaches.

So heat and pull, dear practitioners, or clear and balance. We use Reiki as a common example of hot energies, for there are too many holistic tech-niques to name here. Axiatonal alignment energy is an example of cold ener-gies. By combining the two, you will be able to release stress and pressure beyond a person's aura so that it cannot be magnetized back. Yes, learn to cleanse the meridians and body layers first. Then you will have a clear field to apply more refined techniques to fix the electromagnetic grid work that sup-ports and defines those PEMS layers. Thus you can work effectively and ef-ficiently to help uplift your clients all the way back to their original blueprint of Adamic perfection. If you are doubting that you can do this, we gently remind you that when the student is ready, the teacher will come.

To practitioners who are only open to one technique of healing and tout that to be the best and only, we say, you are limiting yourselves. Un-less, of course, you are performing wonderful healings, then by all means, keep on! But many of you go from seminar to seminar, modality to modal-ity, learning this from here and that from there, only to find that nothing really does it all. Why not? Because all of these wonderful teachings and methods are tools, tools to be applied to clearing the body of blockages at all levels. Tools that trigger the nervous system to release excess pressure. All modalities are tools that work in tandem with the Circle of Grace clear-ing process. And remember, dear practitioners, you are your own best tool. Keep yourselves clear, sharp, and bright.

Heart Clearing

Please keep in mind that each individual is a unique composite of biology, experience, injury, and level of awareness. Due to the Venus eclipse of June

8, 2004, a huge influx of Divine Mother energy caused people to begin clearing the heart chakra. Many experienced symptoms of heart disease, yet the doctors could find nothing wrong. Some may have even experienced their symptoms of pressure above the skin, the etheric portion of the heart chakra swelling with a need to release. Your heart clears down your left arm and out the left hand, which is the closest exit point for pressure from that fourth chakra. Hence the symptom of left arm pain in heart issues, for both right- and left-dominant people. Also, the nausea listed as another heart symptom is actually a response from the mate to heart, solar plexus, ailing and rising up in need of balance. Do you see how the chakras' paired energetic interactions lead to the physical symptoms?

Again, we caution you: If a client is exhibiting symptoms of heart illness (or any severe illness) and if those symptoms are intense and they are in pain, ask them to seek medical help. Dear practitioners, if the doctors find a physical anomaly that needs to be dealt with, it is the patient's responsibility to follow their doctor's advice. They must decide what medical treatment to choose, and then find holistic support for the process. Many practitioners require their clients to sign a waiver of responsibility for legal protection. In your modern societies, this is not only logical but also legally and spiritually correct. It is all lesson, you see, lessons in discernment, lessons in honoring and honesty, lessons in taking responsibility for one's own life and body.

Your role is to help, guide, and support, not to make life choices for others.

If the doctors can find nothing wrong but conclude that the symptoms point to this or that, then you will know that the damage is still auric. The aura can sustain much pressure blockage before the physical core is truly affected. The holistic practitioner can be of most benefit before that happens. Yes, follow the pain down to the nearest exit. Pain management is vital for the patient to find a better PEMS balance from which to clear and heal. Healing requires energy, and in some cases, people are too sick to pull themselves out of their wounded state up into a healing groove.

Reiki is proving very effective in pre- and post-operative settings, and also before and after chemotherapy. These are all times when a person most needs added energy and a release of internal pressure. We hope that you will teach every person you treat how to do the Circle of Grace on their own in between treatments. This will greatly augment their healing process and facilitate your work too. Depending on the situation, mixing holistic with conventional physical therapy and pain medications may be the best path to follow until you feel well enough and have enough energy to begin your own self-healing.

Your most effective modalities (or tools) to apply first in each case will be those who channel universal energy to strengthen the body and tools that clear and balance the PEMS layers of the body. Once the meridians are free-flowing and the chakras in balance, your other modalities will work better. All forms of holistic therapy will increase in potency and effectiveness as the energies rise. You don't have to take our word for it. You will see little miracles happen more and more over the next few years. Does it not make energetic sense?

The Circle of Grace as a Practitioner Tool

Allopathic (medical) doctors undergo years of intense training in order to learn how to read symptomology within the body from which to draw a diagnosis and recommend treatment. They have the advantage of thousands of different tests with which to look within the body at organs, bone, muscle, blood, and hormonal levels. Doctors who deal with emotional and mental issues are also trained to look for patterns of behavior that indicate chemical imbalances or physical illnesses after they manifest in the body. Great strides have been made in discovering cures, synthesizing medicines, and creating therapies to aid all kinds of diseases.

By contrast, holistic practitioners have very different tools available, sacred geometry tools of sound, color, and energy. Most practitioners have intuitive sensations in their hands or inner sight to guide them. Yes, and outer multidimensional sight will also develop, as will other psychic abilities. The more you seek to know, the more you grow. There are many modalities that teach different movements around the table, for example, with similar yet different purposes. Some teach at the purely energetic level so that the practitioner needs only sit in a chair, lie face up, or work by phone with the client. We honor all modalities, for they are all needed or they wouldn't be here. What we are teaching you here is not a modality at all but rather a bodily process vital to keeping you healthy. The Circle of Grace shows how the human body was designed to maintain its inner balance. Working with and within that sacred design will bring you tremendous results.

Working with the Chakra Pairs

Now, for those of you actively seeking higher levels of hands-on practitioner information, we would like to discuss the pairs of chakras and why it is essential to honor these pairings for effective clearing and balancing. In a prior chapter, we explained the following pairs of the main chakras at the level of physical function:

1 and 7 — root and crown

2 and 5 — sacral and throat

3 and 4 — solar plexus and heart

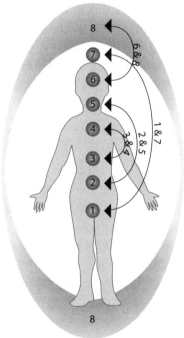

We stated that the sixth chakra, the third eye, works in conjunction with all the rest. That is quite correct, but we wish to add here the fourth pair, which will add complexity to this work and your tablework as well: 6 and 8 — third eye and soul purpose:

What a marvelous combination: intuition and Higher Self! Inner sight and higher sight! Many of your modalities are expanding in scope to include the eighth chakra, which has already attracted many labels — soul star, transpersonal chakra, higher self chakra, and soul purpose chakra, to name a few. Well, you are on the right

Figure 17.1: Chakra Pairs

track, for the eighth chakra encompasses all of these functions. Seen energetically, each chakra is actually two spinning disks, one in front and the other in back, linked by a hollow tube through your body. Each of these energy centers is linked to all the other energy centers in your energetic framework via the meridian pathways. In this work, we have focused on simplifying our explanations so as to allow you full focus in the Circle of Grace clearing process. By clearing and balancing the internal seven-chakra system, you will reach a high enough internal vibration to safely mesh with the higher energies that comprise your total energetic Be-ing.

If you draw back and look at the human energetic carriage as a whole, you will see circles on circles and circles within circles, like a beautiful multidimensional Flower of Life [chuckles]. That eighth chakra connection is what expands you beyond your dense PEMS form into a 5D light-bodied human. Again, we are not dealing with the specific details of how this occurs, for that would fill many tomes and take years of keen study to understand. When we took you through the twelve steps to ask for in healing sessions, we kept to the seven chakras for the sake of simplicity. Here, we offer you this knowledge: the donning of your lightbody requires the eighth chakra level to mesh with the inner seven. This relates to a linear view of increasing energy levels, dear reader, for we remind you that the eighth chakra is paired to the sixth.

All the pairs we have covered — one and seven, two and five, three and four, and six and eight — relate to basic physical functions calibrated to harmony or disharmony by the level of internal pressure held within the body's dense (PEMS) body layers. Chakras are also paired in other ways that are not germane to this body of work. One of the biggest challenges that we, the Brotherhood, face is to keep things simple. Many of you have learned different styles of holistic healing presented with similar yet varying information. Once you have standardized equipment that can read the energetic layers of a body, much of this confusion will be erased. The eighth chakra not only connects you to the divine energies coming in from above the head but also connects you to the earth energies coming up through the feet. In this view, we would say that the Soul Star/Earth Star name is the most accurate, yet for our purpose in working together we ask you to see this link as reaching up into and uniting you with your soul purpose. Or see it as your soul purpose from above guiding your sole purpose down below. [Chuckles, forgive the pun; we could not resist!]

Once your eighth chakra is fully assimilated and aligned with your expanded energetic body, then your Higher Self will be in command. Then your lightbody will become fully activated and you will become consciously interdimensional. When you work on clearing and balancing the eighth chakra on others, dear practitioners, make sure you clear out that portion of the eighth chakra below the feet, for it also acts as a drain to release pent-up pressure from the entire system down into the earth to be recycled as positive energy.

Another point we would like to clarify is how the chakra pairs rebalance into a new configuration when heart becomes the fulcrum for the three chakras below it and the three chakras above. When we spoke in earlier text about living below the belt, we meant that in the old fear-based paradigm, the lower chakras ruled over the upper ones. Thus, root was in charge of crown (1 & 7), sacral controlled throat (2 & 5), and solar plexus ruled over heart (3 & 4). In other words, your survival (root) dictated what the mind did (crown). Your personal relationships and sexuality (sacral chakra) controlled your means of expression (throat). How well you functioned in the tribe (solar plexus) ruled over your emotional health (heart).

As you grow into the fullness of your energetic system and learn to funnel all of your thoughts, emotions, and actions through your heart, that old balance of power flips into a new configuration. The heart chakra provides the tone of unconditional love to all of your PEMS energetic processes. Therefore, crown becomes master of root (7 & 1), higher expression guides your personal relationships (5 & 2), and heart becomes the true leader of how you interact with the world at large (4 & 3). Do you see the pattern here, how lovely the shift that you are expressing?

We are explaining this, dear practitioners, to give you more intellectual tools with which to work. Once you fully understand this expansion process, you will begin to see clearly where people are making progress and where they are stuck. Their behavior, issues, and illnesses will indicate which chakras are blocked and which are in charge. Just listening to a person express what is going on in his or her heart, mind, and life will give you a clear picture of the holistic work that needs done. And please remember to always work on the mate to the ailing chakra(s).

No matter how you label each chakra or what attributes you grant it, these energy centers are woven together in more ways than we can describe here. In striving for simplicity, we say that each chakra of a pair supports its mate in form, function, and vibration through all the layers of your dense etheric being down through the physical core. When one chakra is damaged or distorted by illness, accident, or pressure blockage, its mate works doubly hard to compensate. If the situation is not energetically addressed, the mate chakra eventually follows into illness. Or sometime in that person's future an accident may strike, causing damage to that other chakra region because it is a weak point in the system.

We point out here that it takes many, many years of layered blockages before a pair of chakras fail. When the affected chakra's mate can no longer compensate for the imbalance, the source chakra begins to present physical symptoms. Know that symptoms arising from too much internal pressure can be reversed before damage occurs to the body proper. If balance is not achieved, both areas eventually succumb to illness.

The physical symptoms can fit into a discernible pattern, yet when doctors look for the illness they expect, they may not find it. When physical symptoms first appear, there is a window of time in which clearing the excess internal pressure will allow the body to rebalance toward health. In other words, people can demonstrate symptoms before the full illness sets in. Once the compromised organ, area, or system loses function from being overpressurized, then the physical body part/organ/system will begin to distort at the visible (testable) level. When we say "overpressurized," we literally mean squeezed out of shape or squeezed out of space. That is what is happening to the human body at the untested etheric level. Now that the Millennium Shift is requiring your PEMS layers to accept a higher form of energy, it will collide with the old, dense pockets that still need to be cleared. So, dear practitioners, no matter where illness symptoms may present themselves, please spend some table time working on the mate to the ailing chakra region.

In regards to tablework, the more blockage a person carries, the less he or she will feel — at first. By the third session, they will usually feel pressure changes occur in their bodies, and be able to express them aloud. If awake, verbal feedback from the patient is priceless, for they can guide you as to where the pressure is rising next. During the clearing process, you may find that after you have cleared a good bit of pressure out of a chakra, its mate will rise up and become the more critical of the two. When there is substantial blockage, you will see a seesaw pattern arise; as the pressure changes in one chakra, its mate will respond rather quickly. Remember that the nervous system and the aura are self-pressurizing and constantly self-adjusting. In severe cases, you will need to devote half a session to each of the pair. If the damage is not quite so advanced, work on the ailing area for 45 minutes, then its mate for 15 minutes.

These instructions may conflict with your linear concepts of cause and effect, but you must keep in mind that illness symptoms can often be sourced from imbalance elsewhere. Yes, with abdominal issues, the throat needs clearing. Lower back pain? Don't forget to work on the shoulders! These are examples of imbalances in chakra pair 2 and 5, throat and abdomen. Why do heart attack symptoms include nausea? Because heart (4) and stomach (3) are paired chakras.

A fall on the coccyx bone (1, root) in childhood can affect a person's mental processes (7, crown) years later. They may develop insomnia or excess worry. Excess pressure in the head can also result in a migraine condition, or sometimes ear, eye, or sinus problems. Some forms of brain cancer also exhibit this 7-1 pattern, metastasizing to the rectal area. Doctors have recognized this pattern, though they do not know why crown and root are linked. They do know to test for many of these interrelationships, which eventually show abnormalities in laboratory analysis or physical examinations.

But what if the test numbers are high (or low) in range, but fall within normal or acceptable limits? Going by those test results, most doctors can do nothing. That person is left hovering at the edge, not knowing which way the body will go. Not knowing causes such fear, dear ones, and fear forces you to focus on the negative, inviting it to manifest. Even with conscious clearing of the pairs, accident or illness can still recur in one or both areas. Sometimes an energetic weakness persists, since the meridians in those areas have been so sorely taxed. Teaching your clients the Circle of Grace, and encouraging them to do at least three sessions per week in between visits, will greatly help both practitioner and patient. Care and maintenance of the aura is the ultimate prescription for health and vitality. Dear practitioner, your role is to help them get clear; it is their responsibility to stay clear.

Identifying Other Energetic Blockage Patterns

The other main chakra blockage pattern you will find is sourced from the chakra above or below the area of illness. Finding the true source of illness can be tricky, especially if one is only looking in the physical body layer.

Sometimes a blocked chakra or ailing region can cause symptoms to arise in the chakra area above or below it.

This is a different cause-effect function of internal pressure when over-pressurized areas impinge on (or flow into) areas of less pressure nearby. If you take an air-filled balloon and squeeze it in the middle, what happens? The air within the balloon bulges above and below your hand. If you squeeze the top and bottom of the balloon, the air moves into the middle and creates a bulge there. So the throat (5) can affect the heart (4) region below and the third eye (6) above. The sacral (2) can affect the root (1) below and the solar plexus (3) above. Root (1) blockage can cause pressure in the sacral (2) up to solar plexus (3). Blockage around the crown (7) can cause symptoms to manifest in the third eye (6) directly below, which eventually puts excess pressure on the throat (5).

For example, some chronic sinus irritations (apart from allergy issues) can arise from a blocked throat chakra or from injuries to the neck or shoulders, which will block the throat from adequately clearing excess pressure down the arm meridians. These cases often cause a person to feel run down, with a chronic cold coming on that does not fully materialize. When the meridian system is thus blocked at the neck, pressure in the head region cannot release through the open jaw joints and down the arms. Chronic sinus trouble can also be triggered by sixth chakra blockage at the forehead, since the sinus area is between chakras five and six. Finding which chakra is blocked, or tending to a series of blocked chakras, is far more effective to relieve sinus pressure than taking medication to temporarily breathe better. Treating the symptoms is vital for patient comfort, yes, but clearing the source of internal pressures alleviates the need for palliative measures.

---

*Just taking pills to relieve pain without addressing
the source of pain allows illness to truly form.*

Grinding the teeth, or damage to the jaw joints (TMJ), can trap excess pressure above the jaw in the head. This can cause ear, eye, or sinus issues for some people, or headaches for others. TMJ blockage can also cause pressure downward in the neck, shoulder, and upper-back region. This is a crucial point in the meridian system. The jaw joints must be open for your nervous system to release excess pressure. When those joints are closed, nothing flows. *For any type of meridian-clearing modality or meditation to succeed, the jaw must be fully relaxed.*

We have been discussing blockages in the chakras, or energy centers of the body, that use both the nervous system and etheric meridians of the body to clear pressure and re-energize. Another form of blockage that can affect the entire energetic system is meridian blockage that clogs the pathways by which the chakras are designed to clear. The aura carries etheric damage from trauma to the body (illness, accidents, and surgical intervention) long after the physical body has visibly healed. Until the meridians are cleared of blockages, the chakras cannot release from the head on down as they were intended to do. Meridian blockage can be localized to a specific body part, area, or system and still affect a chakra region or eventually impinge on the entire system.

In brief, your meridian system is designed to expel pressure in different ways, as explained in the Circle of Grace release patterns. We have advised you to begin with the fully blocked pattern for new clients, and open their hand and foot chakras to drain pressure. Then observe how their bodies are releasing and where the flows get stuck. Make sure that the upper chakras are clearing down the arms before energizing the crown chakra. Adding new energy at the crown to a system that is already over-pressurized will give the person an instant headache. Think of a balloon blown up so much that the rubber is stretched taut, adding any more air would cause it to explode. Here is where our balloon image breaks down [chuckles], but we will remind you about the circuit breaker meridian that protects the crown chakra. In cases of extreme pressure in the head, you will find a band of deep blockage around their heads at ear level as if they were wearing hats. They may not feel it, but you will! Clearing that band will help with migraines, eye, ear, and sinus issues. Mental confusion, insomnia, fogginess complaints, poor memory, excess worry, and other mental faculties can also be dampened by excess pressure in the head.

So you will find cases where people feel pain or tenderness in an area that shows no evidence or history of damage. Test results will come back negative, nothing will be found. We say here that every twinge, every pain, every dysfunction in the body arises for a reason. The human body never stops functioning "just because." If there is no physical evidence or history of trauma, then the blockage is still etheric. For example, a backup of pressure can form in the thigh/hip/lower-back area that has sustained no discernible injury, yet knee surgery twenty years prior has left meridian blockage that eventually prevents the thigh meridians from releasing downward past the knee. Hence the thigh tissue may be sore to touch, sometimes feel hot, yet not show any diagnosable or treatable cause, and the knee appears symptom-free yet is the true culprit here. Years after the incident, the person may have hip problems, lower-back pain, or pain piling up all the way to the shoulder on bad days.

Similarly, a person who fell on both knees as a child and recovered, developed intestinal or gastric issues as an adult. In such cases, unreleased etheric blockage from the knees will back up past the hip joints and into the body. Cumulative blockage will squeeze the organs in each chakra region until it meets a blocked chakra. Then the pressure will spread across the body, often creating ileitis (1), colitis (2), or gastritis (3) symptomology. Again, a person's detailed history will expose old blockages as well as current issues, which must both be addressed.

Let us look at another example of old blockage that can truly affect a growing adult. A girl breaks both of her wrists, is treated, and recovers. As she grows, that etheric damage will prevent her upper body from properly clearing down both arms. The accumulated stress and strain will eventually clog her arms, shoulders, throat, and either clog up or down from the throat (5), either heart (4) or third eye (6). Let's choose 5. Heart blockage can affect the entire upper torso; combined with throat blockage, it will cause the child to be unable to express emotions and will cause phobic reactions to be linked to ongoing drama. Phobias attach along the sternum, from heart (4) down to stomach (3), hence the nausea associated with phobic reactions. The fresher the event, the easier it is to pull off and release back into the earth. In this type of blockage pattern, you will find depression, poor self-image, fear of responsibility, delayed maturity, victim patterns, even suicidal tendencies. Now, you fill in for us what happens if that throat blockage travels upward.

In our last example, let us look at a right-handed boy who breaks his left ankle, is treated, and recovers. With a blocked nondominant foot, his body has trouble releasing pressure from the armpit down the nondominant side. By full adulthood (around age 30, chuckles) he finds his body aching more on the left side than the right. His left leg feels "heavier" than his right, and by age 40, it feels like he is walking on a wooden leg that drags behind the right one and causes him to limp. The hip becomes involved, then the blockage eventually spreads to chronic lower-back pain by age 50. Degenerative arthritis is the doctor's diagnosis and recommends the eventual need for a knee or hip replacement. All this from a broken ankle in childhood!

There are many cases in which the chakra pair information does not suffice to explain the symptomology. One must observe carefully the COG meridian release patterns your client displays to understand what blockages are causing which symptoms.

In some cases, a person may feel better after you have cleared the source of the imbalance and choose not to continue having you work on another area that is asymptomatic. Be flexible in your approach to clearing, since each person has individual needs. Feel your way through as to how much energetics you can explain to a client, and at all times honor their free will. Dear ones, knowing about these interconnections will enable you to see the bigger "healing picture," so that you can help each client find a better level of health and a better quality of life.

List of Illnesses

The most prevalent medical symptomology in the upcoming years will circle around pressure-related issues. Common diagnoses will be:

High blood pressure: overpressurized circulatory system; upper torso needs clearing, 3-4-5, and arms

Fibromyalgia: overall skin tenderness from excess internal pressure; check all chakra pairs for blockage, starting with the 7-1 pair.

Depression: inability to release emotional-mental body density; check chakra pair 2 and 5, then 4-5-6.

Phobias: usually centered in chest; clear chakra pair 3 and 4, heart and solar plexus. In long standing cases, also clear 2 and 5.

Migraines: often caused by food intolerances (nuts, dairy, and so on) or environmental allergies; pressure headaches can indicate back-up of the nervous system to the circuit-breaker meridian around the head at ear level, which protects the crown chakra. It is also the reason for occurrence of strokes around the head. Clear 7 (and 1) plus 6 and ears. Also check 5 (and 2) and arms.

Sinus, ear, and allergy flare-ups: overpressurized cranium and face, usually from throat blockage below; clear 5 and 2, plus 6. Clear ears separately to balance pressure within inner ear to match new internal head pressure.

Arthritis: crystallized anger in the joints, creating joint blockages that impinge on meridian flows; work on the joints! Check chakra pair 5 and 2. Anger issues clog the throat area, which is also responsible for calcium balance. Heart issues, palpitations: body's rhythmic adjustments to the increasing frequencies. Clear 3 and 4, front and back.

Gastritis-colitis: pressure blockages affecting the gastrointestinal tract; clear 2 and 5, then 3 and 4. Check root for blockage, hip to foot on both sides.

Sugar imbalances: too much unhappiness in life can result in an inability to process the sweet. Clear left side at base of ribs and 3rd chakra, solar plexus. Clear spleen-pancreas-liver-gallbladder connections to 3rd chakra. Work on mate, 4, heart.

Lower back: foundation and money issues; clear 1 and 7, 2 and 5. This is also reflected in the shoulders, the other horizontal axis of the body. Do you see how clearing 1 and 2 for lower back necessitates clearing of the mates 5 and 7 for shoulders and head? God's plan in balanced perfection!

Water retention: fluctuating pressures can affect osmotic fluid balance in tissues; check electrolyte balance. Can be regulated with individual tissue salts or all twelve in Scheussler's Bioplasma or any brand combination cell salts. For severe electrolyte imbalances, replacement electrolytes are available over the counter in liquid form for children and as tablets for adults. If fluid retention is in an isolated part of the body, clear directly from that area and out the nearest hand or foot exit. For generalized (systemic) fluid retention, clear 1-2-3 (adrenals, bladder, and kidneys). Also recommended is lymphatic drainage massage to help the body process fluids.

Before addressing any pattern of illness, whether for yourself or others, please make sure to consult a physician.

Holistic Tools

The Millennium Shift is causing energetic frequency changes both around you and within you. As you approach 2012, these rising energies are being grounded in more and more people whose bodies can assimilate the full change, people dedicated to Spirit who agreed in their spiritual contracts to spread the higher energies. Look to the new energetic healing tools they are creating. Some are made of metal alloys like copper or brass, others with plastic, crystals, or glass. They may contain crushed herbs, crystal dust, or gemstones, or they may be designed with sacred geometry to house the new frequencies. Look for the tools that pulse when you touch them; they will be empty of mechanism! They all vibrate with increasing levels of divine healing, anchoring the energy and making it available for you to take home and use.

You will recognize this energy when you feel it, for it is the same range of 4-5-6D frequencies that we surround you with in our healing sessions together. Explore different colors of light in your work, and match those colors to the ailing chakras presented to you. Play background music with healing tones during your tablework sessions, and see if that speeds up the patient's process. Use all the tools that resonate in your hands and heart, for those will suit you best.

Make no mistake, we greatly honor energetic healing when done bare-handed. That is, indeed, how it all began! But know that the process is enhanced if you hold a vial of herbs or essential oils appropriate to the healing and pulse your energy through it. No need to open that vial any more, its essence blends with your channeled energy and goes to where it is needed. As your senses expand, many new vibrational modalities will call to you in new ways. To the purists who scream that it must be done the old way, we say, the cases you face have gotten more complex; don't you want to keep up with new and most efficient techniques?

Your surgeons train for many years to learn what to do in surgical procedures. Then they suit up in sterile gowns, arm themselves with sharp knives and bright lights and then surround themselves with life support equipment and a trained staff to help. Would you want any less if you were the patient about to be cut open? So we ask you gently, why should the holistic patient deserve any less than the newest and best in alternative treatments? Allow the awareness of new information to filter through and decide if the vibration of it suits you. Decide for yourself if you wish to use it, learn it, or move on. Be open to all of it, and make up your own mind.

The Circle of Grace is your simplest and least invasive way to attain mastery in self-healing. Learn what it feels like to release pain and stress. Learn how you are energetically wired. Heal and blend your layers together. Let us teach you and lead you to wholeness. Then you will be ready to wield those tools and apply your healing knowledge to the Circle of Grace in others.

Working in Groups

We have explained why your body is your own best tool or vehicle for the ascension process. We have also discussed the concept of seeing each holistic modality as a tool you bring to your tablework practice. Now we would like to expand that concept even more and ask that you see yourselves, dear practitioners, as holistic tools that you gather around a table, according to the needs of the person on that table. Yes, learn to work in groups. As the masses truly begin to shift, you will have to adjust your techniques to accommodate the numbers that come seeking help. Can you picture many holistic healers gathered around one patient? Feel the energy, the power, the range of possibilities that form when you pool your talents.

We ask you to share your knowledge, experience, and energies as you work toward the highest good of each person, devoid of pride or ego attachments. Support each other, consult with one another, and refer patients to each other. Build a morally correct network of practitioners that the public can regard with trust rather than one riddled with lessons in discernment. The level of spiritual integrity that you each bring to your work will pile up, you see, and expand rapidly with much benefit for all. Work at our level, dear ones, and you will be the first to reach us. Wield your tools together, support each other in your works, and you will create a beautiful symphony of healing energies that will enfold and heal your globe.

Never Give Up

When God created this beautiful corner of universal reality and planted on it every life form that He cherished, His question was simply this: If I were part of this creation, would I recognize my own Divinity? Would I find My way back to My own identity? And so came the great test. And so came the great angels who volunteered to go down into density and forget who they were, and in that blind state, rediscover their own divinity. Dear angels, you volunteered for this a long, long time ago.

It has been a lovely experiment, and it is unfolding beautifully; we are almost up to the final celebrations. This last decade of the Millennium Shift will go by very, very quickly. Your spiritual momentum will greatly increase. As the energy rises exponentially, so will the awakenings. There will be much need for healing as people begin to hear dead relatives, see lights in the sky, or feel inexplicable waves of energy coming from their hands. There will be factions that cry, "The devil is returning!" There will be others who cry, "Fear the Armageddon; it is coming." That is all the old, fear-filled 3D energy. It is being phased out and will not touch 4-5D energy. It will not matter. It is simply people holding on to outdated lessons that they have not completed.

Anyone who tries to peddle fear in your vicinity, disallow it! Take a step back, cross your arms over your chest, wait until they have finished, ask them if they are done and then walk away. The path of least resistance, least argument, and total denial is how to reach these people, for they are very loud and will keep screaming until nobody listens anymore. Just as there still will be screamers, there will be those who rise very far, very fast. There will always be extremes in a range of what is normal, but now the range of human normal is changing.

Those of you with expanding awareness, expanding senses and expanding thoughts will function at different levels simultaneously. You will draw many people who will play out their lessons in front of you. Time and time again you will wonder, "Why me? I was just standing here and they all showed up!" At the soul level, many of you active lightworkers agreed to be catalysts (for the benefit of others) as you were planning this life. You are the dimensional bridges for others to follow. We say again: 3D, 4D, 5D, and so on and so forth, all reside in the same place. Earth's energetic rise is actually an expansion of her range of vibratory expression. This same expansion process is happening to you too.

Many people have asked us, "Well, when the dimensions finish changing, will we have two Earths, a 3D Earth and a 5D Earth? How will we know which way to go? Who will be put on one, who will be put on the other, and how scientifically could it possibly work?" It is actually a much simpler process; its very simplicity escapes people. All the dimensions exist in the same space, separated by different bands of frequency. We have been saying that you are in 4D, but that is already changing, you see. As soon as you reach one dimension, you are already halfway up to the next. Yes, that is why we refer to 3-4D, and 4-5D. A student of 4D that reaches 5 is automatically a student of 5-6D. You will eventually remerge with the Divine Source and have no more need for lessons at all.

As the energies expand, your senses will follow. You will start feeling the pulse, the heat, and the new weight of your planet. You will feel the presence of unseen guides, have vivid dreams that then come true, and begin to see miracles abound in your life. Start to expect synchronicity. What you seek, demand it! Come cocreate with us. It is a new time.

We have spoken about two-way communication, about communing with your Higher Self all the time, and about the waking meditation that your life can be. Here we offer to work with you, dear practitioners. Call us in, speak aloud the case, and expect to get intuitive input during the session. We can work with you, alongside you, and guide you. If the client feels extra hands on them, thank us. If you feel a line drawn on you, know that it is where we are working on them. If you have inner sight, you will see our energy in a field of white-gold, purple, and cobalt blue. Count on us, dear children, expect our help, for we will never disappoint you.

Indeed, we are the ones honored to be in your presence, for it is we who continue to learn from you, we who are shown time and again that our teachings are of value to you. For that, we are very grateful. It is thanks to your efforts that we perform our service to the Divine Plan. There are no words to convey how grateful we are, except to say, dear ones, never give up!

Never give up hope, for you are all so vital to the work we do together. Do you follow? We hope you will!

(18)

Practitioner's Manual: The Circle of Grace Hands-On

Level One: Personal Clearing

The Circle of Grace is a simple exercise that heals you at all PEMS levels — physical, emotional, mental, and spiritual. At the same time that it releases pain and stress, it replenishes your body with new energy. It is a process that occurs naturally in your aura and body while you sleep. It is how the human body clears itself of excess internal pressure and then refuels. This process clears the meridians of the aura through the meridians of the body. Both come into play when you do the work of releasing excess pressure from your PEMS layers. In learning to master this internal system, you will gain mastery over your own healing and health.

We are so proud of the progress you have made. We cheer every time you tap into the Circle of Grace for needed energy or to release pain so that it does not accumulate, clog your meridians, and make you sick. Next, in level two, the practitioner level, we focus on how to use the Circle of Grace clearing process to help others clear their bodies of pain and pressure. As you do this blessed work, don't forget to teach your clients the Circle of Grace! The Mission Statement of the Brotherhood of Light:

When science and spirituality finally meet and merge,
healing will become a simple process.

Overview

Successful healing for a person must occur on three levels: physical (medical), emotional/mental (psychological), and spiritual (auric or energetic). The biggest obstacle to healing in the 3D world is the presumption that the physical body comprises the entire human being. Energetic practitioners know that the physical core is only the visible part of a person. Third-dimensional medicine does not yet honor the parts of each patient that are invisible, because they are intangible. Once humanity begins to flower into the 4-5D sensory range, all of that will change.

Many hands-on modalities have been developed and fine-tuned to release stress from the aura before it causes a physical illness. Reiki is the most well known as a foundational modality that uses universal energy to clear and balance the aura, so we chose it as our prime example. There are many other wonderful energetic modalities coming into your awareness now. Plus, there are traditional modalities like acupuncture, shiatsu, and reflexology, which work directly on the physical meridians to clear blockages. These are all tools, dear ones, to apply to the Circle of Grace clearing process.

In essence, the Circle of Grace process is your energetic plumbing. Your work is to find and release the etheric clogs in people's systems so that they can ingest new, clean energy and excrete old, tainted energy. You are also training their auras to remember how to do this. That is why we urge you to teach your clients the level one personal information, so they can get used to clearing and re-energizing on their own. Once an illness has manifested in the body, it is more difficult to clear. Heal the damaged aura, and the person will not get sick.

Author's note: In preparation for the level two practitioner's seminar, I ask that students study chapter one and section four of the book.

Identifying Illness Patterns

In order to plan your holistic work for each case, we will review the different factors involved so you can better understand the patterns that people exhibit. We have stated before that there is no such thing as coincidence. Everything happens for a reason, whether you see it or not. To interpret the energetic meaning of an injury or illness, look to the physical function of the damaged area: Leg and foot injuries speak to an inability to move forward. Hip and lower-back damage speaks to foundational fear: money and survival issues. Hip problems can be attributed to root or sacral issues. Hand, arm, and shoulder injuries prevent people from reaching for what they desire, or grasping that which they need to work on. Neck injuries prevent people from seeing both sides of a situation. Trauma to the head, face, ears, and eyes keep people from expanding their senses and seeing and hearing what they need to face. Do you see the patterns?

The same rule of no coincidence applies to illness, though the cause may seem to be coming from a different direction. Whether the illness comes from an internal source or from an external contagion, the physical body always mirrors what is going on in its other layers. Diabetes, the inability to process sugars, speaks to third chakra blockage. The overworked and overburdened person holding too much responsibility becomes unable to enjoy the sweetness of life. Depression, categorized as a mental condition, depresses all of your systems and can often lead to suppression of immune functions. This leaves a person open to developing or catching an illness that affects that weakened system. In other words, all physical damage includes etheric damage, whether it occurs before or during the illness event. Even surgery leaves etheric damage that can linger in the aura long after the body seems healed. Just healing the physical body layer does not make a person healthy.

Defining Etheric Blockages

Stress is also low-grade pain. While the conscious mind may dismiss stress as part of everyday life, the body accumulates this type of pressure like all other types of incoming damage. To the aura, etheric blockages are as real and dense as a broken leg is to the body. If people grind their teeth at night, their bodies cannot release current, chronic, or genetic damage normally. If they wake up with chronic spots that hurt, those areas are holding pressure pockets that prevent natural clearing during sleep. Those are your target areas, dear practitioners, that tell you where those blockages are that need work.

As holistic practitioners, you know that the emotional, mental, and spiritual state of a person directly affects physical health. While your goal is to clear the body of excess pressure, you will see a direct link between people's symptoms and their physical states. Help your clients face their sources of stress (bad marriage, lousy job, and so on) and change their situations for the better. Their mental and anger loops — their negative thought patterns — must be identified and released. Then the clearing work will truly take hold, and they will show great improvement at all PEMS levels.

When an issue becomes chronic, these pressure pockets can't go anywhere except spill out beyond the meridians and seep into the tissues, causing a density of flesh that constantly expresses pain. These areas may show no bruising yet be tender to the touch. Those PEMS issues cause more density and attract to the person what he or she fears most.

That is how blockages are formed, dear ones, and these blockages bring the Circle of Grace flow to a complete stop. Once the flow is cut off, there is no way for the body to clear itself in that area. The body switches to alternate meridians in order to release pressure in the entire system. The more alternate routes it is forced to take, the weaker the flow becomes. The weaker the flow becomes, the less life force people have to get through each day. People can carry etheric damage for a long, long time before it invades the physical core of their Be-ings. Teach them the Circle of Grace, and it can have a positive impact on their lives forever.

The Healing Room

Taking a Client's History: *Important:* Have a glass of water ready for your client, and ask the client to drink it as you take the client's history. It is vital for the body to be fully hydrated before the tablework begins. It is also important to write down a history of each client's illnesses and injuries, all that can be remembered back through childhood (see sample form on pages 303 and 304.) That will be your truest blueprint for clearing out the layered accumulation of blockages each person carries.

Take note if the client is right-handed or left-handed. Write it down, so you don't have to ask the person before each session. This is vital to know and remember, since your work will be guided by the client's dominant/nondominant wiring. You may have to adjust your table placement accordingly, so you can target the longest area to "pull" in, depending on where the client's blockages are. After the session, take a few moments to write down a summary of what happened (see sample form on page 305.)

Clothing: For both practitioners and clients, it is important to wear loose, comfortable clothing. Before he or she climbs on to the table, ask the client to remove his or her shoes. Also ask the client to loosen everything possible: ties, belts, or bras. Any constriction of the physical body causes restriction of the energetic meridians, just as any injury, illness, or surgery to the physical body also causes damage to the etheric body's energetic structures. Since there are many temperature changes during a session, you may want to ask the clients not to wear any perfume, makeup, or hair spray. Scents will intensify, makeup will smear or run, and hair spray will stick to the practitioner's hands. Better to avoid a mess rather than deal with one.

Jaw Position: A note for people who have physical damage in and around the jaw: The jaw joints, or temporal-mandibular joints (TMJ), are the only joints in the body that work in tandem, as a pair. All of your other joints, both fixed and moving, are single joints that work alone. The lower jaw is suspended like a seesaw. If one jaw joint is damaged, the other joint eventually suffers damage by force of misaligned pressure.

Dear practitioners, even if your client insists that only one side hurts, always clear both sides. For TMJ sufferers, use a high pillow beneath the head so that the jaw naturally points down, which makes it easier for the client to keep the jaw open to let the pain flow through. If the client lies too flat and the lower jaw slides back instead of forward, this position will cause more pain rather than relieving what is there.

Keep reminding your client to let the jaw sag open. Explain that the jaw is the on-off switch that starts and stops the Circle of Grace. As you progress through the pulling out of blockages, some clients will get tense when they feel their pain moving. Once the jaw tightens, the whole body gets tense. Keep an eye on facial expressions as a quiet guide to know how the client is feeling. If the flows shut down, simply ask the client to open the jaw again and resume the clearing.

Breathing: Ask your clients to focus on breathing in and out slowly and evenly. If the client is able to follow the details of yogic breathing as we explained in the main text, that's even better but not necessary for the tablework. Listen as you work. If the client holds his or her breath, the client is usually tensing up. Tell the client that the pressure or pain being felt is the client's own. You're not adding to it; you're just moving it out. When people feel pain; they have a tendency to hold their breath, which means the jaw tenses and the flows abruptly stop. That is why, in the beginning, you may have to keep reminding your clients to relax and loosen the jaw. Breathing in and out through the nose is preferable in order to reduce dry mouth. Always have a glass of water available for your clients in case their mouths get too dry.

Opening and Closing Healing Sessions for Your Clients: If your client is uncomfortable with New Age spirituality and you don't feel that it is appropriate to ask the client to say the healing prayer aloud, do so before the client arrives as you are preparing your workspace. Yes, speak aloud to the empty room! Call in all four levels, explain to us briefly the client's issues, speak your intent to clear blockages, clear and balance meridians and chakras, and repolarize the energy fields. (These are the first three questions on the List of Questions to Ask the Brothers in Healing Sessions.)

If your client is open and willing, hold the client's hands and say the healing prayer aloud together. Please include this in whatever opening ritual you hold dear. By giving us verbal permission to work with you, the entire session will be greatly heightened for you and your client.

Finally, we will explain why we do not ask you to close a healing session. We bring you into 4-5D when we work together, which is where Earth is now vibrating. Closing a session in the old, fear-based thinking locks the client's body back down to where you started. Your leaving the session open at your end allows the client's body to gently oscillate back down to the current vibration of the moment. You can close the clients aura with clockwise sweeps above, below, and along both sides, leaving the crown open. Sweep upward if it's early in the day, and sweep downward if your client is going home to rest. Dear ones, do not be afraid of having the client's energy drain away if you leave a session open. Have we not shown that you are a self-contained, self-maintaining, electromagnetic life form? [Chuckles.]

Tablework Techniques

Practitioner Table Position: The most effective clearing occurs four to twelve feet beyond the table. The strongest pull occurs at eight to ten feet. Set up your work area with a wide space all around the table, so you can walk away without bumping into furniture. The dense etheric body (PEMS layers) extends as far as a person can reach, so get at least four feet away from the table as you begin draining old energy. Since you are working with an electromagnetic field, you must go beyond that field to fully release etheric pressure. Otherwise, those pockets will stay magnetized within the client's field.

Client Position on Table: When beginning a session of the Circle of Grace, have your client lie down face-up with the spine straight and arms at the side. Place pillows beneath the head and knees (to prevent lower back strain). Ask the client not to cross the arms or legs, since physical pressure short-circuits the meridians and the flows may momentarily cease. If the client cannot lie comfortably on the back, have him or her curl up on the dominant side, or less-injured side. Use three pillows: one beneath the head, one between the knees, and one to hug to the chest (this last pillow reduces upper-back strain from the weight of the arm).

Explain the COG process, where the meridians are and what the flow patterns are. Keep asking for feedback if your client is awake. Ask the client to report any sensations, from pressure to pain to moving lines anywhere in the body as you are working. The client will tell you if and when the next blockage is moving up to be removed, even as you begin to feel it happen.

Practitioner Hand Positions: For right-handed practitioners, your dominant hand is usually the right, or positive, hand. Your left, nondominant hand is the negative, or pulling hand. Once enough pressure has built to require a pull, do so with the left hand, using a counterclockwise turning motion. Fan the "thread" you are pulling with the right hand also in a counterclockwise motion to move the energy beyond the person's aura.

If you find it difficult to remember which direction to use, imagine a clock placed on the person's body, facing you. Look at the clock face and you'll instantly see which way is counterclockwise. For left-handed practitioners, you will pull with the right hand and fan with the left. If it is a large pull, you can drain it double-handed — still counterclockwise — but with both hands moving together in parallel motion.

As you drain down the pocket, the thread you are pulling will begin to drop down toward the floor; follow it if possible, as low as you can reach. When you are done with each pull, simply shake your hands to clear the energy before going back to the table. Some practitioners prefer to have a bowl of saltwater and a towel handy. Whatever works for you is fine.

Always keep the fingers of your pulling hand pointing down toward the floor. If you keep your hand horizontal to your arm, you may feel the negative energy you are draining spread along your arm to your elbow or shoulder. This is easy to clear by doing Reiki above the elbow or shoulder after the session to trigger the reverse pattern. You can also soak in a hot tub, keeping your arms submerged, and feel the pressure drain away.

Always keep your feet away from beneath your pulling hand, or you may feel the draining energy go through your feet. Though not harmful, it can be an uncomfortable feeling until you clear it as explained above.

When working with a new client, expect to find the nervous system to be in the fully blocked pattern. Keep in mind that you are also training the aura to open the main exit points counterclockwise — hands and feet — and stay open for the whole session. At first, those chakras will tend to return to their normal clockwise spin, and the clearing flows will stop. As a result, the client might say, "My left hand feels tight or full or heavy." Go back to that chakra, and reopen it. Drain that pressure for a while, until the client remarks on another area that feels dense. That will be the next blockage popping up to be released.

What to Expect in Energetic Feedback: Practitioners have learned in their own, unique ways how to do hands-on work. We speak here in generalities, and we honor all differences in style. Most practitioners already pick up sensations of hot or cold. After the class attunements, what may be new are sensations of pressure in the hands, increasing as you move away from the table. Intuitive information also comes in to be shared. It may not make sense to you, but it will have meaning for the client. Some lightworkers may feel little electric shocks, or "sparkler," sensations as their hand chakras interact with a client's aura. As each pull dwindles, go back to the table and apply universal energy (Reiki) to the area you just cleared. That will fill the space with hot, healing energy, and at the same time, it will bring up the next layer of blockage to be released. The heat will turn to cold just moments before the pressure builds for the next pull.

Remember: When doing clearing work, you are clearing from the outside in. You will encounter three major levels of blockage pressure to clear.

The topmost layer you encounter will be the most recently added. Beneath recent or current stress and strain, you will find chronic layers of etheric damage that have accumulated in this current life. Beneath that is the genetic level, including past-life damage, unresolved issues, and faulty belief systems the person has carried forward to clear. How fast people clear depends entirely on how much accumulation they carry, what types of blocks, and their conscious mindsets. The more they feel happening at each session, the more they will believe they can improve. The energy of this work builds, gaining in intensity by the third or fourth session. Some people feel the pull gradually increase until they start to tense up and stop breathing in anticipation of your next pull. It is important to be aware of their facial expressions and to keep reminding them to relax, breathe, and keep the jaw loose.

There is an anesthetic quality to this energy as well, so many people fall asleep quickly. While robbing you of verbal feedback, this sleep state allows the client to be fully relaxed and open to your work. If your client does fall asleep, continue through the session and gently wake the client up at the end.

Do not allow others to remain in the room while you work. These energies go well beyond twelve feet, and you will find the observer falling asleep and getting worked on too. This type of situation will divert energy from your client and result in much weaker sessions with minimal improvement. As a practitioner, you can explain this point beforehand. If need be, allow extra people to watch from a distance of twenty feet. It is preferable to ask them to wait in another room or come back when the session is over.

Triggering the Circle of Grace in Others: Where do you begin to help activate and drain the meridian systems? First, attune each foot. Begin with the nondominant one. A Reiki attunement opens the chakra counterclockwise to release or absorb energy. If you are not trained in energetic attunements, do six to nine counterclockwise circles over and below each foot, then cup for a moment to run energy through the chakra. Intent is all! Once you have the feet chakras open and flowing, the legs will begin to clear. Move to the hands, opening each to trigger the upper body to output etheric pressure.

If the person is in an acute state of pain, open the door closest to the damaged area first, and start to release pressure. Then focus on treating the illness area, pulling directly out from the body and walking away. As you reduce the size of that pocket, the client's aura will self-trigger once the meridians can handle the reduced load. Also, pull directly from the body, not over it. For example, the heart must be cleared from the client's left side or other blockages will seek the pulling, and you end up with congestion instead of clearing.

If your client has no acute symptoms, open the nondominant hand and foot first, then the dominant hand and foot. Why do we instruct you to open the system from the hand and foot exits? Imagine the blockages all lined up from the head on down and facing their exits: the hands and feet. It's one lane only, and no blockage can jump ahead of another one. So the blockages must be released from the feet on up the body. Let's say that the client has head issues, such as migraines, vision, or jaw problems. If you attune and open the crown chakra first without having the system open and draining, it will cause excess pressure to flood into the head. The new energy will have no room to enter fully, but it will try, causing more pain. The client may even complain of a sudden headache. Never pull from the crown unless you see the need; it will make your client instantly nauseous. When you honor the body's natural direction of energetic flows, you are working with the body to clear it.

Once the arms and legs are clear-flowing, you can focus on the torso and start clearing individual chakras. Working from the root on up, attune each chakra to open it. If you are working on an illness or injured spot, attune that too. Or do a series of counterclockwise circles, then add energy to open up the pressure pocket. This will greatly enhance whatever clearing process you use. Chakra tuning forks are a wonderful tool to use at this point in the process. You can locate and break up blockages with their notes of perfect health.

We add a note here to traditional Reiki teachers and teachers of all energetic modalities that only attune the students' hands: Why are you not attuning their feet as well? Please, at least think about it. "As above, so below" must be honored in every attunement process, and the feet chakras are equal in size and strength to the hand chakras. Being attuned from head to toe creates a much stronger energetic connection, as well as a better foundation of grounded energy. Attuning the feet also facilitates the drawing of green earth energy up through the body, which is vital to balance the intense divine energies coming in from above. It also helps to keep you in tune with Earth's rise.

Establishing Energetic Dominance

Dominant and Nondominant, Right and Left: Most practitioners know which side of their bodies is dominant and which side is nondominant. An energetic healer or Reiki practitioner can also determine the natural polarity of the body. This dominance aspect of the body also defines which hand is positive in hands-on healing and which hand is negative. For most practitioners, your dominant hand is the positive flow of energy and your nondominant hand is the negative flow. Together, they form a closed circuit by which energy is channeled through the body of the receiver. When working with a left-handed person, please remember that your approach is simply the opposite, or mirror image, of the standard (right-sided) flow patterns.

For example, in the balanced Circle of Grace pattern, the receiving foot is the left, and you will feel energy rise up the client's left side. Their releasing foot is the right, and you will feel more clearing occur down the right side. If you are unsure, you can sense (and see!) during the session which foot is receiving (it will look like it is being pushed back and upright) and which foot is releasing (it will look pulled forward and down). You can also tell which side is dominant by tracking the path of the release, for it will flow strongly down the nondominant side, and that will be the side in which you may feel more of the energetic movement.

It is rare to find a person who is clear enough to demonstrate the balanced pattern at the beginning. Most people present with the fully blocked pattern, which requires you to first open the hand and foot chakras, then start to clear the arms and legs. Expect that the person's aura will switch patterns when it is able to with no added work required on your part. Remember, you are just guiding the releases, then refilling that space with new universal energy. This work becomes a beautiful dance in which the practitioner moves back and forth, to and away from the table. No matter what combination of biology and biography each client presents, you will discover that the releasing patterns work the same way in person after person. You are now working with sentient energy, or auric information, that knows what the body needs. This is why we say that you are not responsible for a person's healing; you are there to guide and support the process. The more we watch you master this dance of healing energies, the more we cheer you on, for we are so very, very proud of your accomplishments.

Let the Circle of Grace show you the dance steps, and let us take care of the details. The joy of doing this work and being of service to others will lead to your biggest rewards in energetic advancement.

Do you follow? We so hope you will!

Working with Energetic Blockages

Please remember that the Circle of Grace can run in any direction you choose during a session. No one pattern is better or healthier than another. The human body needs them all, at different times.

Fully Blocked Pattern: For people who are totally blocked, the direction of the Circle release will begin from the top down, using both sides of the body to flush out pain and stress. If your clients require visualization, offer them the golden cloud exercise (see page 299). Tell them to imagine a golden cloud or shower of universal energy above their heads, descending down and around their bodies, inside and out. It may take a few sessions to clear the arms and legs, depending on the client's history. Just make note of the various patterns the client is exhibiting in your work history. The only pattern you should need to trigger is the reverse blockage when you are releasing an acute pocket.

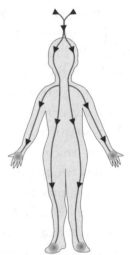

Fully Blocked Pattern

Simply open and pull on the closest exit chakra until it starts to release, then go back to pulling directly from the traumatized area. The aura will do the rest.

Alternating Blocked Pattern: While the alternating pattern is a great marker of personal progress, it applies more to the individual level than to the practitioner level. Your table-work is focused on clearing all of the twelve major clearing pathways, as explained in chapter one.

Balanced Pattern: Once the client has reached this stage, he or she may ask if you tilted the table. The client's dominant side will feel hot and puffy while the nondominant side will feel cold and flat. Hence, the tilt effect! Other sensations will arise, such as pressure on the chest while you are doing

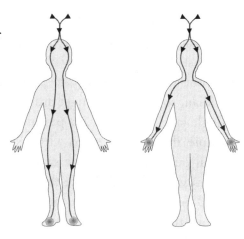

Alternating Blocked Pattern

heart clearing and the feeling of a tight belt around the waist when clearing the solar plexus. New sensations await your discovery as the energies rise to

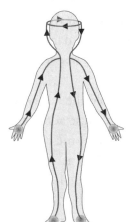

Balanced Pattern

climax. The client may feel a ball of pressure release from a chakra and bounce around the body as it seeks an arm or leg exit. Yes, this may sound far-fetched, but the miracles awaiting you in your daily holistic practice will literally re-form [chuckles - what a pun!] current medical perspectives on illness and healing.

Reverse Blockages: For energetic practitioners, know that you can attune the exit chakra and the site of blockage to open them energetically. Then you can add energy above the blockage and move it down and out (the hand or foot) with a gentle stroking motion. If you do not know how to do energetic attunements, simply make six to nine counterclockwise circles with your dominant hand above the exit chakra and then repeat above the area of blockage. Your intent to open and clear that pressure pocket will work just as well.

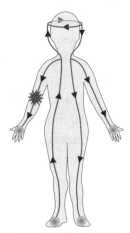

Reverse Blockage Pattern

Multiple Blockages: When clearing multiple blockages, please know that the one nearest the exit must clear first. The very nature of a blockage does not allow any energy to pass through that meridian, so nothing can get around it. Yes, like a single-lane road with no passing allowed! For example, if a client presents with a sprained wrist and an ear infection on the same side, the wrist pain must be released first or the ear pain will stay lodged behind it, unable to move down the arm and out the hand. Practitioners, you can "pull" directly from a pressure pocket to reduce its size, and what is left will flow down and out the meridians much more easily.

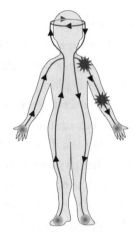

Multiple Blockage Pattern

Old Damage: All trauma to the physical body causes auric damage, which remains as auric blockages after the body has visibly healed. This includes accidents, illnesses, and surgery. In your tablework, you will have many experiences proving that the entire human Be-ing suffers damage at all levels when ill. Visible healing of the physical body is only one level of the total healing picture.

So please remember that all blockages, no matter how old the injury or illness, must be cleared. Yes, a childhood ankle injury can cause adult hip pain. Injury to the knees can cause backup of pressure and chronic cramping in the abdomen or stomach region. Jaw damage — TMJ, as you call it — causes tremendous pressure in the head, ears, eyes, face, and neck, leading sometimes to chronic ear pain or sinus conditions that flare up when the person is overstressed. Migraines can also result from jaw-joint damage, since it blocks the major path of pressure release from the head on down. Similarly, a twenty-year-old skiing injury to your left ankle can still be causing blockage to your meridian system at another crucial point: the nondominant exit (foot chakra) of pressure for the lower body in right-handed people.

Regarding cases of injury, surgical damage, or arthritis in the hands or feet, your client may tell you that the Circle of Grace is making the condition worse! Yes, any damage, old, new, or chronic, must be cleared from the exit sites in order for the aching limbs to express the accumulated pressure. Since arthritis truly distorts the physical body, it is much more difficult for people with this type of condition to do the clearing meditation by themselves without holistic help.

When scanning the body for pressure pockets, observe carefully the head, neck, shoulders, elbows/wrists, hips, knees/ankles. Make sure all COG exits — hands and feet chakras — are open and cleared to drain. Work in reverse blockage pattern to release all major blocks via the nearest exit, or pull directly from the blockage area until the meridians can assume part of the clearing load. If a client is sensitive to the process, he or she can usually tell you when the arms/legs are clearing as well as when they clog up and where. If you scan the body slowly, your hands will detect hot/cold areas, also areas of packed-in pressure that may not correspond to the client's conscious awareness of pain. For example, an old injury can still be blocking the meridians even though the person assumes it is long healed and does not feel pain in that area.

The Circle of Grace Flow Around the Head

No matter which pattern flow the body requires, there is a separate circular meridian that goes around the head, above ear level, like wearing a hat. This is described in chapter three. In the balanced pattern, new energy enters the dominant side at the hand and foot, rises up to circle around the head, then descends down the nondominant side, pushing old, spent energy down and out the system. The separate circle around the crown has a dual purpose. It acts as a circuit breaker for the entire system. Most blockages cannot back up beyond this circle to affect the crown chakra, no matter how blocked the system. This is why many people suffer strokes around the head at ear level. In our Circle of Grace healing sessions, this separate circle also helps to awaken the right brain, and align the right and left brains to work together as they were originally meant to do. When you scan a new patient, always check the pressure levels around the forehead, temples, and the sides and back of the head. Make sure that you clear each ear separately to balance internal pressure to the new pressure level of the head. Each ear is a small pocket that contains its own pressure level. If you do head work and you don't balance the ears, the client may complain of ear pain upon rising.

Note: Heart clearing must be done every day or every other day. Otherwise, the client may start exhibiting heart attack symptomology.

Why Stress Leads to Illness

Your living environment dictates the stress you are under, unless you are in charge of your life! The level of health or dis-ease in your auric layers is what stimulates your genetic weaknesses to flare up. Sudden heart attack? Yes, after years and years of accumulated fourth chakra blockage. To those whose hearts suddenly malfunction, it is a new illness. But if they were cognizant of their auric health, that illness would not be sudden and, indeed, could be circumvented.

Regular care and maintenance of the aura would prevent many maladies from materializing in the physical core. Yes, that is what we are here to teach. So if your client had an illness that he or she thought seemed healed yet it came back, that means that the etheric damage or source of stress from the original illness is still there. What you call remission is truly a window of opportunity that you have to make the changes in your life that will release those sources of stress. Staying in an unhealthy relationship is living against the heart. People who cannot move beyond obligation and duty often opt out of unhappy marriages through illness. Then it is simply a matter of where the physical makeup is weak (we are looking at all PEMS levels here) or genetically predisposed to cancer, immune failure, hormone malfunction, specific organ failure, or other terminal conditions.

Modalities as Tools

The Circle of Grace is not a modality. It is a body process already built in to your human form. In our teachings, any type of energy channeling (we use Reiki as a common example) is combined with techniques that pull out blockages. There are Reiki pulling techniques, integrated energy therapy (IET) techniques, and other modalities that pull, brush, or swipe at the aura to release etheric blocks. Whatever modalities you are trained in will blend with the Circle of Grace work, as long as they apply the empty/refill cycle on the client's four-layered PEMS body. Some modalities will vary in focus and technique yet still be compatible with the COG to clear blockages as needed.

Massage of all types can be applied to the COG release patterns. Working on muscle knots and dense tissue pockets toward the hand/foot exits helps to flush out and clear meridian blockages. Jin shin jyutsu is excellent to combine with the COG, because it works on acupressure release points that trigger meridian release. Once you understand how the body naturally clears itself, you can work within that knowledge and apply all of your tools more efficiently and effectively.

COG techniques can be applied directly to the body to clear a specific area of illness, injury, or imbalance. You can directly drain down a pressure pocket until it is small enough to start releasing down the nearest meridians. Then you can clear the rest of it down the arm/leg paths and out the hand/foot exits. Physical tools can also be applied: tuning forks to break up chakra blocks, or crystals, herbs and oils; or light and sound tools. All energetic tools are gaining in strength as the planet rises in frequency.

We use Reiki as a common example, for there are too many holistic techniques to name here. Learn modalities that channel energy to a body and those who train you to release pain and pressure. Many of you go from seminar to seminar, modality to modality, learning this from here and that from there, only to find that nothing really does it all. Why not? Because we see all of these wonderful teachings and methods as tools, tools to be applied to clearing the body of blockages at all levels, tools that trigger the nervous system to release, tools that help relieve pain and stress, tools that help re-energize the body, and tools that all work in tandem with the Circle of Grace. And remember, dear practitioner, you are your own best tool! Keep yourself clear, sharp, and bright.

The Future of Healing

Your most efficient modalities (or tools) will prove to be those that channel universal energy, clear and balance the PEMS layers of the body, and stimulate the nervous system to release excess pressure. All energetic modalities are gaining in potency as the energies rise. You don't have to take our word for it, you will watch it happen over the next few years. Does it not make energetic sense?

The Millennium Shift is causing changes all around you, within and without. This same healing energy is now being grounded in people whose bodies can assimilate the full change, people dedicated to Spirit who have agreed in their spiritual contracts to spread the higher energies. Look to the new energetic healing tools they are creating. Some are made of metals like copper or brass, others with plastic, crystals, or glass. They may contain crushed herbs or gemstones, or they might be designed with sacred geometry to house the new frequencies. Look for the tools that pulse when you touch them; they will be empty of mechanism.

You will recognize this energy when you feel it, for it is the same range of 5-6D frequencies that we surround you with in our healing sessions together. Look to the tuning forks, crystals, and chimes. They all vibrate with increasing levels of divine healing, anchoring the energy, and making it available for you to take home and use. Explore different colors of light in your work, and match those colors to the ailing chakras presented to you. Include music with healing tones in your tablework sessions, use all the tools that resonate in your hands and heart.

Make no mistake, we greatly honor energetic healing when done barehanded. That is, indeed, how it all began! But know that the process is enhanced if you hold a vial of herbs or essential oils appropriate to the healing and pulse your energy through it. No need to open that vial any more; its essence blends with your channeled energy and goes to where it is needed. Healing is enhanced by sound, color, and many other vibrational modalities rising up into the human consciousness. To the purists who scream that it must be done the old way, we say, your needs have gotten more complicated. Don't you want to keep up with new and more efficient techniques? We are not adding complexity to this work but rather specificity. There will come a day when your only tools will be your intent and a beaming smile! [Chuckles and a big hug.]

*　　*　　*

Through the Circle of Grace healing process, you will truly, consciously become a multidimensional Be-ing. Why do we spell it thus? As a trigger word for your higher consciousness: We use the verb "to be" to indicate the full blend of all your aspects, physical and nonphysical layers, with a capital letter as homage to your divinity in the same way we pay homage to God and His works. The "-ing" part of the word "Be-ing" indicates the now aspect of your ascension in the present tense to remind you to keep hold of that higher perspective in every moment. We say to you, simply:

Let us help you to evolve
To the higher levels of love.
Let us teach you how to heal,
And in healing, Be-come real.

Healing your body will heal all of your lifetimes. Heal all the layers of your total Be-ing, and rejoin us in the True Reality of Spirit. It is time to remember who you are!

Appendix

The Circle of Grace is your body's natural cleansing and refueling mechanism. While you sleep, your nervous system releases internal pressure and intakes universal energy, the body's etheric food. Your dense etheric body is designed in four layers: physical, emotional, mental and spiritual, which we call the PEMS layers. In concert with your energetic meridians, your nervous system flushes pressure from all four layers and rebalances your internal pressure with an equal amount of new energy. There is never a drain without a gain!

The COG exercise teaches you conscious participation to activate this natural clearing whenever you feel the need to rid yourself of pain and stress or feel low in energy. The Circle of Grace is a healing exercise that can be performed personally as a self-guided meditation. It can also be triggered to flow by trained practitioners.

Steps of the Circle of Grace Exercise

1) Say the healing prayer aloud, plus your list of requests for the session. It is important that you speak aloud, as the vibration of your voice gives permission for Spirit to work with you in your physical space.
2) Lie face up with pillows beneath your head and knees. Keep your feet uncrossed, hands at your sides, and align your spine and head. You may also lie on your side with one pillow beneath head, one to hug, and one between knees.
3) Open your jaw, tip your head to either side, then back to center. Keep your jaw joints open!
4) Relax your body and focus on slow, even breathing with pauses.
5) Report aloud what you are feeling if you are awake.
6) Give thanks to Spirit when you are done!

You may feel the energy flowing through your body in waves of pressure, tingling in your hands or feet, or changes in temperature as your aura repressurizes. Most people develop a greater awareness of their bodies through this exercise and learn the nerve pathways to effectively clear and recharge themselves. An hour of the Circle of Grace exercise provides an abundance of energy for the entire day. Even a half-hour session with the Brotherhood of Light helps release 3D density from your body. If you don't have time during the day for a full session, start the Circle of Grace as you are falling asleep at night.

The Brotherhood Healing Prayer

If you wish, light a candle or incense to help focus your senses. Adapt the first two lines of this generic prayer to reflect your personal belief system. Please use the eternal divinity of your beliefs in place of Father/Mother God. Add any religious figures you hold dear, along with (or in place of) the ascended masters, guides, and angels. Speak aloud your desire to have a healing session with us in this four-part prayer:

Dear Father/Mother God, Creator of all that is, was, and ever will be, please join me in this healing session.

Dear ascended masters, guides, and angels, please join me in this healing session.

Dear Brothers, the Brotherhood of Light, please join me in this healing session.

Dear Higher Self, please join me to guide and lead this healing session.

Say this prayer aloud. Say the words, say how you feel, and say what you choose to manifest and what you desire to release. (A simple example: I choose total health in my joints; I release my arthritis.) The vibration of your voice brings your ideas, sentiments, and desires into the fruition of your third and fourth dimensions — the dimensions of material and materialization. Due to the parameters of your freewill zone, we await your spoken intent before we can begin. Why? Saying the Healing Prayer aloud creates a vibrational bridge between dimensions, giving us your energetic permission to join with you, to merge our 5-6D energies with your 4D space, in order to work with you at your physical level.

The Breath of Life Exercise

In alternating breaths, imagine that you are breathing in golden divine energy from above and bright green earth energy from below.

1) Pull in a deep breath of white-gold Divine light through your crown chakra at the top of your head and draw it down through your body to twelve inches below your feet.
2) Pause to blend this golden column of energy inside you and let it fill you up.
3) Then exhale it through all the pores of your skin to feed the energetic layers of your entire Be-ing.
4) Pause again to allow the golden energy to permeate all your layers.
5) Inhale, pulling up green earth energy through your feet and up your body past the crown to a foot above your head.
6) Pause to let it fill your body.
7) Then exhale it through your skin in a cloud of bright-green nourishment all around you.
8) Pause again to circulate and assimilate the green energy, exhale it through your PEMS layers, then start over.

If you have trouble pausing between each inhale and exhale, breathe in and out slowly and pause just once after each exhalation. Even if you cannot pause between breaths, the visualization will still work. As you do this, be aware that your sacral chakra, the second or abdominal energy center, is filling up with new reserves of universal energy. Repeat this imaging, breathing slowly please, for about ten minutes or until you feel better. This is a new way to eat, children, only with less mess and no dishes!

Do you follow? We hope you will.

The Golden Cloud Visualization

Some of you are protesting here: "I don't meditate. I don't care to." Know that if you are opposed to the very idea of meditation, then don't do it. Call it visualization if you prefer. We ask that you lie down anyway, and imagine a golden cloud of energy entering the top of your head and flowing down your body like a shower. In the beginning, don't try to choose which pattern to do. Allow your body to do what it needs to do. Allow your group of Brothers to choose what you need at each session. If you feel the blocked pattern begin, track your golden cloud visualization straight down both sides. If you feel energy enter your dominant side, go up and around your head, and then down the nondominant side, visualize your golden cloud following that path. Then see this golden energy surrounding you like a cocoon, permeating every level of your total Be-ing with healing energy.

For those of you who have no time to meditate, you can activate the Circle of Grace as you're falling asleep. That simple act will augment and intensify the work that your body naturally does at night to clear itself. This can be a very active process or not, depending on your views and needs. Eventually, you will find that every time you lie down to watch television, read a book, or rest, your body will automatically begin clearing. Once the Circle of Grace becomes part of your life, you will make great strides toward full mastery.

If you are still protesting, then we gently ask, "Do you enjoy getting in your own way?" If you are reading this text, you are a seeker of spirituality, of faith, of Oneness. We offer this information to you as an aid "up the ladder" to the next level of human evolution. We hope that you will incorporate this exercise into your life, for your own healing and to help others. This clearing process is in each and every one of you. Seek it, find it, and use it. You will soon shine brighter and brighter as you discover and explore your inner world, your God-self, your portion of the I Am All That Is. Our gift to you is one of natural healing through the Circle of Grace.

Twelve Steps to a Lighter Body

Please note: These stages of healing are meant to be done in the order that they are presented here. Also, when asking anything from Spirit, include the words "gently and gracefully," for the power of Spirit can be much greater than the expectations of the physical body.

1) Repolarization: ask to be repolarized, at all levels, in every session
2) Clear and balance the energetic meridians
3) Clear and balance the energy centers (chakras)
4) Clear and balance the lower three chakras to the upper three with the heart as the new fulcrum
5) Clear and balance the physical heart chakra to spiritual heart chakra
6) Awaken, clear, and balance the right brain
7) Clear and balance the left brain
8) Align left and right brain together
9) Physical reconnection of the body to the aura
10) Flower gently into 5D senses
11) Don your lightbody
12) Care and maintenance of the aura

Ask for *only* one thing at a time! Each level can take months to clear and balance. You are clearing lifetimes of auric pressure. You can't do it all at once. Consider it like peeling an onion; each layer must be removed before the next one can be reached. In every session with the Brothers, make sure to ask for repolarization. To maintain clarity and balance, repeat steps 1 through 5 at least once a month.

Intent and Healing

You only need to give verbal intent to do the Circle of Grace and call in the higher help as described in the healing prayer. Then lie down and speak to us aloud. Tell us what you wish to focus on, either from the list of questions we have provided or specific personal issues (physical or conceptual). Tell us aloud if you feel a blockage, and we will work on releasing it for you. Some of you will feel us working, some not. If you fall asleep, know that we tended to the needs of your PEMS layers while your conscious mind rested.

You may find yourself weeping (clearing emotional stress) or bathed in waves of tickling energy (energizing the body) or notice your arms or legs filling with pressure seeking to release though your hands or feet. The Circle of Grace clears the meridians of the aura via the nerve pathways of the body. Both come into play when you do the work of clearing your energetic system. Once you get accustomed to doing this clearing exercise, you will gain mastery over your own healing. You will learn to tap into the Circle of Grace whenever you need energy. You will learn to release stress and pain as it comes in so that it does not accumulate, clog your meridians, and make you sick.

Problem-Solving Checklist

1) Not saying the Healing Prayer aloud
2) Not keeping your jaw loose or open
3) Not focused on breathing and/or inner movement
4) Not speaking aloud what you are feeling
5) Not feeling well enough to do a session
6) Room is too hot/cold/noisy/distracted by pets: alone is best
7) Clothes may be too tight
8) Too wound up or distracted to relax, can't silence left brain, may need exercise or a hot bath to relax
9) Trying to do the balanced pattern when your body needs to clear via the blocked patterns
10) Visualizing the right-hand meridian paths as dominant when you are actually left-handed

Circle of Grace
Client Health History

NAME	TODAY'S DATE	HOME PHONE
ADDRESS	WORK PHONE	CELL PHONE
CITY, ST ZIP	OCCUPATION	BIRTH DATE AGE
EMERGENCY CONTACT NAME	RELATION	PHONE

Referred by: _____

1. Primary Complaint:_____

2. How did this condition develop?_____

3. Does your condition interfere with: ☐ Work?   ☐ Sleep?   ☐ Recreation?

4. What makes it worse?_____

5. What makes it better?_____

6. Have you seen a physician? _____ Whom?_____

7. What did your doctor say?_____

8. Have you had any recent injuries?_____

9. Have you seen a chiropractor? _____ Whom? _____

10. Have you had energetic therapy before?_____ Where? ____

11. Medications you are currently taking and their purpose:_____
_____
_____
_____

12. Surgeries and When: _____
_____

13. Have you broken any bones and when?_____
_____

14. Please list any accidents or major illnesses: _____
_____

15 Circle (Right Handed) (Left Handed) _____

16 Please check any of the following conditions if you've had them recently:

_____ Abdominal Hernia	_____ Fainting Spells	_____ PMS
_____ Allergies	_____ Fatigue	_____ Ringing in Ears
_____ Arthritis	_____ Headaches	_____ Sciatica
_____ Back Pain	_____ Heart Condition	_____ Severe Depression
_____ Blood Clots	_____ Hepatitis	_____ Shortness of Breath
_____ Bursitis	_____ Herniated Disc	_____ Shoulder Pain
_____ Cancer	_____ HIV	_____ Sinusitus
_____ Chest Pain	_____ Insomnia	_____ Skin Disorders
_____ Cold Feet	_____ Loss of Balance	_____ Spina Bifida
_____ Cold Hands	_____ Low Back Pain	_____ Stomach Disorders
_____ Constipation	_____ Low or High Blood Pressure	_____ TMJ Dysfunction
_____ Diabetes	_____ Neck Pain	_____ Varicose Veins
_____ Diarrhea	_____ Numb Feet	_____ Warts
_____ Dizziness	_____ Numb Hands	_____ Other
_____ Edema		

17. On the following diagram, please indicate areas of discomfort:

18. Do you have any other medical conditions (both major and minor) not already covered herein that you think the practitioner should be aware of? If so, please explain:_____

_____

IMPORTANT: PLEASE READ!

Because a practitioner must be aware of any existing physical conditions that I may have, I have listed all my known medical conditions and physical limitations, and I will inform my practitioner of any changes in my physical health. This therapy does not replace any medical care or therapy for any condition, nor am I using this modality to treat any medical condition without a physician's consent. I understand and agree that: 1) the therapy that I am given is for the purpose of stress reduction and energetic balancing; 2) that a practitioner neither diagnoses illness, disease or any other medical, physical or mental disorder; 3) that I am responsible for consulting a qualified physician for any physical ailments that I may have; 4) This therapy is strictly therapeutic and completely non-sexual.

I AGREE THAT ALL SERVICES RENDERED ME ARE CHARGED DIRECTLY TO ME AND I AM RESPONSIBLE FOR PAYMENT. I AGREE TO PAY FOR ALL SCHEDULED APPOINTMENTS THAT I AM UNABLE TO KEEP UNLESS I NOTIFY THE PRACTITIONER AT LEAST 24 HOURS IN ADVANCE.

_____   _____

Patient Signature   Date

Circle of Grace

Session Notes

Practitioner Name _____   Date _____

Client Name _____   Dominate Side: **R**   **L**

Primary Complaints: _____

_____

_____

_____

_____

Blockage Patterns Found: _____

_____

_____

_____

Notes: _____

_____

_____

_____

_____

_____

_____

<u>Tools:</u>

	<u>Chakra Blockages</u>	Tuning <u>Forks Used</u>
	Crown _____	_____
	3rd Eye _____	_____
	Throat _____	_____
	Heart _____	_____
<u>Crystals Used</u>	Solar Plexus _____	_____
Hematite _____	Sacral _____	_____
Citrine _____	Root_____	_____
Clear Quartz _____		
Amethyst _____		

"Eternity is very long, especially near the end."
—*Woody Allen*

NOTES

NOTES

NOTES

About the Author

Edna Frankel was born in Cairo, Egypt, to a middle-class Jewish family. Her father was Romanian and her mother was Greek-Turkish. Edna's family was evicted from Egypt in the Suez Crisis of 1956, escaped in 1958, and arrived in America in 1960. Edna was raised in New York City.

While in high school, Edna suddenly found God in a way that made more sense to her than any religion after reading *Seth Speaks*. She began reading every metaphysical book she could find, not realizing that she was already in training for her soul's intended path. Both her parents worked for the United Nations, and she attended the U.N. International School in New York. Graduating high school one year early, Edna moved on to college at Washington University in St. Louis. She graduated at the age of twenty with two degrees, French and psychology.

After ten years as wife and mother, Edna began Reiki training in 1985, becoming a teaching master by 1994. She also studied freelance editing and the art of writing. In 2000, she began channeling in spoken and written forms. Her first article appeared in the *Sedona Journal of Emergence!* in 2001. In 2005, *Le Cercle de Grâce* was published (French), and the French audiobook was released in 2008. Edna participated in two French anthologies for Ariane Éditions, 2007 *Le Retour de la Lumière* and 2008 *Au-delà du voile*. This final expanded version (English) of *The Circle of Grace: Frequency and Physicality* brings together all her knowledge and experience about holistic healing, including the seminar materials she brings to her teachings. Her dearest wish is to follow the Brothers around the world, traveling and teaching the Circle of Grace.

Learn more about Edna and the Circle of Grace at www.BeyondReiki.com.

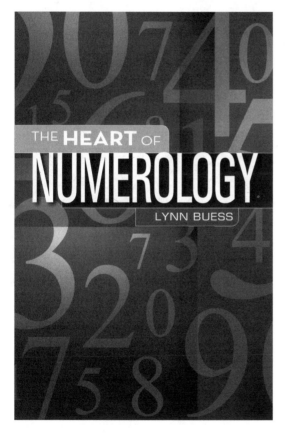

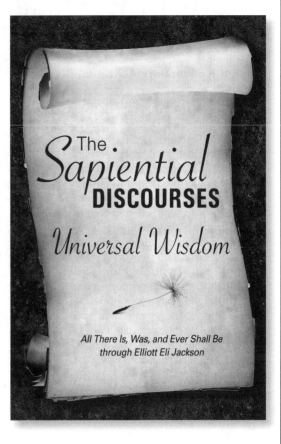

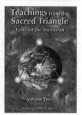

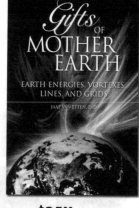

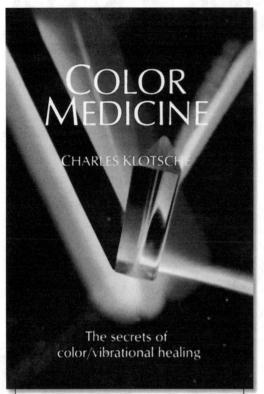

⚜ *Light Technology* PUBLISHING

The Books of Jasmuheen

Ambassadors of Light

In this book, Jasmuheen offers practical solutions to world health and world hunger challenges through her Luscious Lifestyles Program and also effective ways to redirect global resources. This entails an in-depth look at global disarmament, the dissolution of prohibition, the forgiveness of Third World debt, holistic education programs, and the elimination of the need for personal pharmaceutical use through the elimination of all disease.

$16.95 | ISBN 13: 978-3-929512-70-0 | Softcover: 253 pp

Harmonious Healing and the Immortal's Way

This book details Jasmuheen's personal healing journey and includes information on the magic of meditation, plus pragmatic tools to reenergize and find the perfect program for healing. Today one in four adults dies unnecessarily from one of the seven deadly diseases. Perhaps this is due to a lack of holistic education, or perhaps it is just that person's time to die. But how do we know if what we are facing is our checkout time or just a life challenge?

$16.95 | ISBN 13: 978-1-891824-59-3 | Softcover: 194 pp

In Resonance

This book is a manual for personal self-empowerment and self-mastery. It is filled with inspirational information of experiential research and channeled guidance from Jasmuheen and the Ascended Ones. *In Resonance* offers practical tools utilizing specific programming techniques and tuning, and mind mastery for reality creation and creating a purposeful and passionate existence. It addresses issues from meditation to telepathy and the universal laws.

$24.95 | ISBN 13: 978-3-929512-36-6 | Hardcover: 312 pp

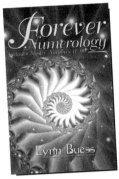

TOOLS FOR TRANSFORMATION

VYWAMUS channeled by Janet McClure

PRELUDE TO ASCENSION
Tools for Transformation
Janet McClure channeling Djwhal Khul, Vywamus & others
Your four bodies, the Tibetan Lessons series, the Twelve Rays, the Cosmic Walk-in and others. All previously unpublished channelings by Janet McClure.

$29.95, SOFTCOVER 850 P. • ISBN 0-929385-54-3

THE SOURCE ADVENTURE

Life is discovery, and this book is a journey of discovery "to learn, to grow, to recognize the opportunities—to be aware." It asks the big question, "Why are you here?" and leads the reader to examine the most significant questions of a lifetime.

$11.95, SOFTCOVER 157 P. • ISBN 0-929385-06-3

SCOPES OF DIMENSIONS

Vywamus explains the process of exploring and experiencing the dimensions. He teaches an integrated way to utilize the combined strengths of each dimension. It is a how-to guidebook for living in the multidimensional reality that is our true evolutionary path.

$11.95, SOFTCOVER 176 P. • ISBN 0-929385-09-8

AHA! THE REALIZATION BOOK
(with Lillian Harben)

If you are mirroring your life in a way that is not desirable, this book can help you locate murky areas and make them "suddenly . . . crystal clear." Readers will discover an exciting step-by-step path to changing and evolving their lives.

$11.95, SOFTCOVER 120 P. • ISBN 0-929385-14-4

SANAT KUMARA
Training a Planetary Logos

How was the beauty of this world created? The answer is in the story of Earth's Logos, the great being Sanat Kumara. It is a journey through his eyes as he learns the real-life lessons of training along the path of mastery.

$11.95, SOFTCOVER 179 P. • ISBN 0-929385-17-9

LIGHT TECHNIQUES
That Trigger Transformation

Expanding the heart center, launching your light, releasing the destructive focus, weaving a garment of light, light alignment and more, this book is a wonderfully effective tool for using light to transcend. Beautiful guidance!

$11.95, SOFTCOVER 145 P. • ISBN 0-929385-00-4

Shamanic Secrets Mastery Series

Speaks of Many Truths and Reveals the Mysteries through Robert Shapiro

This book explores the heart and soul connection between humans and Mother Earth. Through that intimacy, miracles of healing and expanded awareness can flourish. To heal the planet and be healed as well, we can lovingly extend our energy selves out to the mountains and rivers and intimately bond with the Earth. Gestures and vision can activate our hearts to return us to a healthy, caring relationship with the land we live on. The character of some of Earth's most powerful features is explored and understood, with exercises given to connect us with those places. As we project our love and healing energy there, we help the Earth to heal from human destruction of the planet and its atmosphere. Dozens of photographs, maps and drawings assist the process in twenty-five chapters, which cover the Earth's more critical locations.

498 p. $19.95 ISBN 1-891824-12-0

Learn to understand the sacred nature of your own physical body and some of the magnificent gifts it offers you. When you work with your physical body in these new ways, you will discover not only its sacredness, but how it is compatible with Mother Earth, the animals, the plants, even the nearby planets, all of which you now recognize as being sacred in nature. It is important to feel the value of oneself physically before one can have any lasting physical impact on the world. If a physical energy does not feel good about itself, it will usually be resolved; other physical or spiritual energies will dissolve it because it is unnatural. The better you feel about your physical self when you do the work in the previous book as well as this one and the one to follow, the greater and more lasting will be the benevolent effect on your life, on the lives of those around you and ultimately on your planet and universe.

576 p. $25.00 ISBN 1-891824-29-5

Spiritual mastery encompasses many different means to assimilate and be assimilated by the wisdom, feelings, flow, warmth, function and application of all beings in your world that you will actually contact in some way. A lot of spiritual mastery has been covered in different bits and pieces throughout all the books we've done. My approach to spiritual mastery, though, will be as grounded as possible in things that people on Earth can use— but it won't include the broad spectrum of spiritual mastery, like levitation and invisibility. I'm trying to teach you things that you can actually use and benefit from. My life is basically going to represent your needs, and it gets out the secrets that have been held back in a storylike fashion, so that it is more interesting."

—Speaks of Many Truths through Robert Shapiro

768 p. $29.95 ISBN 1-891824-58-9

Light Technology PUBLISHING

BOOKS BY TOM T. MOORE

THE GENTLE WAY

A SELF-HELP GUIDE FOR THOSE WHO BELIEVE IN ANGELS

This book is for all faiths and beliefs with the only requirement being a basic belief in angels. It will put you back in touch with your guardian angel or strengthen and expand the connection that you may already have. How can I promise these benefits? Because I have been using these concepts for over ten years, and I can report these successes from direct knowledge and experience. But this is a self-help guide, so that means it requires your active participation.

$14.⁹⁵

140 PP. SOFTCOVER
ISBN 978-1-891824-60-9

CHAPTER TITLES

- Angels
- How I began
- Easy Steps
- Home Life
- Politics

- Travel
- The Radiant Effect
- Living Prayers
- "I Hope" Requests

THE GENTLE WAY II

BENEVOLENT OUTCOMES: THE STORY CONTINUES

You'll be amazed at how easy it is to be in touch with guardian angels and how much assistance you can receive simply by asking. This inspirational self-help book, written for all faiths and beliefs, will explain how there is a more benevolent world that we can access, and how we can achieve this.

These very unique and incredibly simple techniques assist you in manifesting your goals easily and effortlessly for the first time. It works quickly, sometimes with immediate results—no affirmations, written intentions, or changes in behavior are needed. You don't even have to believe in it for it to work!

TOPICS INCLUDE:

- Safe Travel
- Your Home
- Your Work
- Medical Issues

- Home Finances
- Your Pets
- Work Relationships
- Personal Relationships

$16.⁹⁵

303 PP. SOFTCOVER
ISBN 978-1-891824-80-7